G000071264

Since before he knew how to write, Nicholas has always enjoyed telling stories, his entire life, all he has ever wanted to achieve was to become a screenwriter. As the years passed, he began to realise, living the life you wish to lead is much harder than living the life you find yourself leading. After years of bullying, epilepsy and dealing with political bullshit, he decided to take his life back and in doing so, he ended up writing his first book.

This book is dedicated to every unique individual who has taken the time to read through my journey, I am forever grateful. I only hope that by sharing my life, I can help make yours easier, this book is dedicated to you.

Nicholas Napoli

POLITICS, BULLIES AND YOU

ONE SMALL COUNTRY, ONE WORLDLY PROBLEM

AUSTIN MACAULEY PUBLISHERS™

LONDON • CAMBRIDGE • NEW YORK • SHARJAH

A CIP catalogue record for this title is available from the British Library.

ISBN 9781528907514 (Paperback)
ISBN 9781528907521 (Hardback)
ISBN 9781528958622 (ePub e-book)

www.austinmacauley.com

First Published (2019)
Austin Macauley Publishers Ltd
25 Canada Square
Canary Wharf
London
E14 5LQ

Eileen

Mom, if anyone deserves a part in this story from beginning to end, it's you. Thank you for always being there for me, helping me deal with my problems, even when I didn't have the strength to deal with them myself. Had it not been for your support, this book would not have had an ending, thank you for always believing in me, especially back in 2011, when I first told someone I planned on writing this book.

Stanley

Dad, joining you on our Sunday taxi tours, driving tourists up the Rock of Gibraltar are one of my fondest memories as a child. These tours helped start my career, by inspiring me to always work alongside people from abroad, in our case tourists. You helped me begin my journey, I'm glad we can now read about it together. Thank you for always being there for me, I hope this book makes you proud.

Stacey

Thank you for watching my shows when we were little, even when you weren't interested. Thank you for listening to my stories as we grew older, even when you weren't interested. A special thank you for putting up with me all these years, especially taking out a loan for me when I had stayed penniless, thank you for being my sister.

Kaylie

Thank you for laughing at my dark sense of humour when we were little. Thank you for reading my stories as we grew older, I'll never forget how for the longest time, you were the only person willing to read my screenplays. A special thank you for giving me Aiden, someone who has admired me when no one else would, thank you for being my sister.

Dear Nephew Aiden

You are the most important person in the world to me; when I was at my worst, you were born and helped me find my strength, you appreciated me for who I am. As you grow older, I realise how intelligent you are; this is how I know you'll be able to read this whole book very soon. And I promise you, one day I'll take you on holiday to Hollywood, it's full of many silly creatures.

June

Mama, I know how excited you've been to read my book, I'm just as excited to know what you think of it. Thank you for always making sure I maintained a healthy diet, making me feel special and providing me with my first chance to visit America. We both miss Grandpa Alberto very much, I hope that with this book, I'm able to help keep his memory alive.

Arthur

Uncle, when I was trying to get my life together, when I tried returning into a working society, you gave me a chance when no one else would. Working at the pet shop helped me find my confidence again, I hope that with this book, I'm able to help you find the confidence to finish writing your own story. Grandpa Arturo and Mama Angela must be very proud of you.

Jensen

We don't get to choose our family, but we do get to choose our friends. I'm glad I chose you, it's been a fun ride, which only keeps on getting more interesting along the way, as exampled at the end of my story. Thank you for your friendship and knowledge, good luck with your future, I'm always rooting for you.

Germaine

Everywhere we go, no matter how far we travel the globe, we always end up beside each other. Gibraltar might be a small country, but we prove it's a small world after all; when two people are meant to be in each other's lives, the universe always finds a way. Thank you for always being there for me, I wish you nothing but the best with your future.

Cristina

When I was at my worst, when I wanted my journey to end, I turned to strangers, hoping to find my strength, I found you. Thank you for replying to my email when I was only but a stranger in your life, it is my honour to now be your friend. Your positivity and kindness know no boundaries, the world needs more people like you.

Bill

When we first met, I could not speak, I was not ill, I was not shy, I was simply experiencing being starstruck for the first time. Thank you for being so patient with me, teaching me how to format a screenplay and even helping me with my grammar and wording. I will always admire you, not necessarily for what you do, but rather for who you are.

Heidi

I remember travelling to London, attending a meet and greet with my favourite characters and whilst waiting in line, I met you. When we said goodbye that day, I had no idea what an important part you would play in my life. On my next visit to London, you cured me, you gave me my life back again, I am forever grateful.

Brian

When nobody would publish me, when I felt like writing was a waste of time, you gave me a chance. You allowed me to share my articles on your blog, you will always be my first publisher and a great friend. Thank you for always allowing me the chance to keep on writing.

Steve

We've only ever met a few times, but in my mind, I feel I have known you a lifetime. When I was six years old, I witnessed your performance on the big screen and have admired you since. Throughout my life, I've found my confidence through you, every time I wanted to give up on myself, I would turn on my TV, watch all your many performances and I'd remember who I hoped to be in life.

Jim

I've only ever had one idol my entire life, a man I have never met yet has inspired me, throughout my life. You left this world, having made it a better place, for having been here. Thank you for the lessons and continuous inspiration you provide me with, as you do with many others. Although you might be gone, your work, your characters, your messages, all continue to live on, I am forever thankful for this, without meeting you, you've helped change my life.

The Team at Austin Macauley

All my life, I've ever only wanted to achieve one main goal, to become a published author. Thank you Austin Macaulay Publishers for believing in me and giving me a chance to finally accomplish my goal.

Chapter One
Third Rock from the Sun

The universe is home to everyone, everything and every-matter, a world for all to exist, consisting of galaxies scattered throughout a vast ocean of darkness, locally known as space. Each galaxy, a country of its own, each solar system, its own state and finally every planet, one's hometown, we have much to continue exploring. Space separates life, loopholes bring us together, it's all a mystery, one that can never be solved but to an extent understood. We all make up the universe, energy flows through everyone and although our bodies might deteriorate, the energy within will always remain alive, for all eternity, the soul never dies.

The sun, our brightest star, located at the centre of our solar system, bringing life to all around it, luckily for us, this hot ball of plasma is visible from where we stand. If you take a sharp turn and travel 92.44 million miles away from the heat, you'll find yourself at the out-of-control party known as earth, my hometown. Earthlings of many species, race, nationalities and beliefs roam the blue planet, grateful for their existence yet unaware of the reason behind it.

At the beginning of time, those who inhabited earth worshipped the sun; it was their king, their saviour, God looking down on them from above. When God graced the sky, the earth became visible; light, warmth and life graced their home. When God went to bed, the moon would rise, guarding the darkness left behind, life would sleep and spirituality awoken. It was a simple time, an easier spell, a happier life, humans, animals, plants, energy thrived throughout the world, one untouched by war.

As earth evolved, so did its inhabitants; the fastest of all creatures to evolve were humans. Being the smartest species, we took over the world, with many still believing, it belongs to us. Earth had no boarders, no barriers, it was free for all to explore, for all to live as they wished yet as time went by, humans began to divide, over 190 countries across the globe. No longer do we believe we have a right to explore the universe, the galaxies, solar systems, planets or even our own hometown. We each live in a large mansion, many have spent our entire lives confined into our bedroom, on occasions we might visit the kitchen or the bathroom but we always return back to what we're familiar with, the bedroom.

What's so intriguing that keeps us stargazing, and what do we hope to find? Life on earth is fascinated by what awaits us in the far beyond, the places we cannot reach; most of us stare up into the night sky in awe, wondering what exactly it is we're looking at. Mercury, Venus and Mars are Earth's closest neighbours yet to the naked eye, they appear as tiny dots of light, helping brighten the night sky. A sky filled with millions of stars, some brighter than others, some containing life of their own, who look up into their night sky, believing earth is but another star, only there to shine.

In the past, earth was visited by others from above, which is a miracle on its own. As humans evolved, fire was discovered, brains developed, speech introduced, numbers calculated, history forgotten, land claimed, borders began separating and life was taken for granted. Religion took over, later replaced by politics and soon enough, the only thing we all believe to be true is, we're all ruled by one entity, we all follow one set of rules, we belong to a system. Hundreds of years later, not only did humans stop progressing, we began regressing; we began to fear, hate and stopped thinking freely, slowly we began reversing evolution. The sun is no longer worshiped; our new Gods are those whom are exactly like us, our leaders, we just choose to follow.

Modern humans have evolved many times on earth; unfortunately, we always end up reversing our evolution no thanks to war, greed and politics. Our early ancestors had no political parties, no society to live by, no rules to follow yet they thrived. Today here we are. 7.4 billion people now inhabit our world with only less than 1% controlling the way we live our lives. We are all puppets to injustice; our strings are being pulled for us and our words spoken on our behalf. As soon as we are born, we are given a first name, which is then followed by our family name, and in addition, we are given a social security number, this is how our system defines us. We immediately become part of a controlled community, one which shapes and moulds our way of thinking into that of a working citizen. We are taught to obey and follow rather than think and lead; we are meant to be clever enough to answer but not question, forced to work and not live life to its fullest.

We are led to believe that doing well in school academically will allow us to progress in life as individuals, yet we are all taught as one by the same process. School is supposed to prepare children for the real world, which is forever growing rapidly yet the education system doesn't seem to change as quickly; therefore, none of us are truly prepared for life. The real purpose of learning should be to help us build our future and according to the education system knowing your mathematics, languages, science, religion, history, geography, music, sports and computers prepares you for this. Apparently, being familiar with all those subjects helps you succeed in life; I'm not sure about you but I was completely unprepared for it. Granted some of these subjects are important for our human evolution but teaching children all this before they know who they are is pointless. School should help us learn who we're meant to be before trying to get us ready for who we're going to be.

I never understood who created our teaching curriculum? Who chose the classes we're forced to sit through? And who the hell decided children should wear ties in order to learn? Raise your hand if you know the answer and wait to be called, ask permission to move around, dress accordingly, remain silent, do as you're told and most importantly, this is all mandatory. What kind of childhood is this? What are we doing with their individuality, their uniqueness, their creativity, we're taking all this away from them. Energy, talent and freedom is being removed from children. They are spending over six hours a day learning, not through life but rather by lectures; education cannot be taught inside a building, education is taught by experience. As humans evolve, so does our learning patterns, and therefore it is important that our education system adapts alongside human evolution as should be the case with our chosen leaders.

As we grow older, we can count money but do we know how to take care of it? We speak amongst ourselves but are we truly communicating? We invent technology but are we inventing the right kind? In my opinion, not only does school not help prepare us for life, in fact it locks us down from becoming the person we're truly meant to become. By the time we finish school, we've spent our entire youth moulded into being part of an obedient society. We learn that we must follow one standard procedure or otherwise we'll fail at life. Learning should be a lifelong education but only when the right wisdom is being provided. The first and most important lesson is that one must study themselves, once a person has mastered this class, other subjects such as love, relationships and emotions will be easier to comprehend.

Most of us are lost in life; all we know from childhood is what we were meant to know, and now into adulthood, our quirky skills are lost on us to our future. It takes years for an adult to become successful; the main flaw we all share for taking so long is that we are forced to reteach ourselves with a different form of learning, one that suits us and productively helps our lives get better. We have elected leaders who control our history, our religion, our lands and our way of thinking—how is one supposed to properly progress life without all the information at our disposal available for us to study. We do not choose leaders to simply act on our behalf but to think for us too, otherwise each country would find themselves voting a lot more than once every four years.

As a civilisation we are still learning to evolve, with the reason for humanities delay being that we are not being taught what needs to be learned. It has taken human civilisation a very long time to evolve to where we are today; we cannot risk standing still or worse yet reverting to our evolution within time. Luckily, the world is waking up to this, humanity is slowly rebelling against the employment model, home-schooling is beginning to trend, we are reaching our limits, we're getting fed up, depression is opening our eyes. The lack of purpose is beginning to knock on our doors, many are willing to risk careers, people leaving on sabbaticals, people with work-related depression, people are waking up. Depression is consuming the world around us, and if we do not change our way of living, it will soon become a big part of our evolution. For worse or for better, we can change the world around us with everything we do, we all have a song to sing, if we only listened, we might each be able to do our own part in changing the world for the better.

Many people have awakened from their lone mentality; it's ridiculous that over seven billion of us, living in the same planet, have grown further apart from each other, even with the introduction of social media. What sense does it make to turn your back on others living around you on the same planet? The direction of cooperating, sharing, helping and togetherness should become our priority in the hopes of continuing to progress properly. The internet is more important than most of us realise, we are only now fully understanding its power. With the internet, the world opens, the barriers fall, the separation ends, the togetherness starts, the collaboration explodes and help emerges. You go after what you want, you bond to whomever you want, you explore wherever you may want to explore. With the introduction of the internet, the small are no longer speechless; there is a voice for all, the anonymous become acknowledged, the world comes together, and then the system may fall.

As children, we have no real concept of time; therefore, waiting for summer vacation seems to take an eternity but when you're older, summer returns in the blink of an eye. Children have no understanding of time to measure, except they begin to play with the concept as early as age four, when they first enrol in school. Children are forced to fall into a routine, one that is measured by time; although they might not be familiar with the various days of the week or even numbers for that matter, they do begin to realise that every five days they get two days off. Time is one of our most precious gifts and as we grow older, most of us begin to cherish it wisely. At the end of our lives, we recollect our past, regretting if we could only go back and take another crack at all the things we've left undone, we'd do them right.

We live our life from beginning to end, most of us considering the gift of being alive to be something of the norm, something that's expected to us in this unanswered mystery we call life. There must be a purpose; who put us here to begin with and why? Are we given life simply so we can find a good job, settle down with someone we love and raise a family? Surely there must be more to life than that or should I say, there must be a bigger purpose, a far greater reason for all our existence. Nobody really has the time anymore to take a moment to stop and wonder how us being here is even possible. Have you ever stopped to look around you, the glory that you see, will rise again each day, make sure you don't let it get away, enjoy every single moment.

What is your purpose in life, and are you living it the way you should? Consider whether this is the right life to lead, not if it's the life you should lead but rather the one you want, if not maybe it's time to make changes.

At the start of it all, you are born and at the end of your journey you evolve, what exactly happens when your life comes full circle? Do you think that is the end? Do you think we live for a mere one hundred years, give or take a few, only later to cease existing forever? I believe we live forever, maybe not in our shells, but our souls never deteriorate. Then why do our souls spend a few years living in its human shell, only to live on forever after without it? That is the test of life, one where you're in control, you lead the life you wish to lead, life is like a journey, who knows when it will end.

Life is the ultimate test, forget about graduating, acing your exams, trying to get your driver's licence or even making it to a million dollars! Life is that test which you should most want to pass because it is the one with the greatest reward and if you fail, you've only failed yourself. Self-control is one of the most important and difficult parts of one's journey through this crazy test we all call life. There are no shortcuts, there is no cheating allowed; if you wish to pass your test, you must simply study and learn using the tools, knowledge and gifts that have been provided for you, even before walking into your first class.

We lead the life we wish to lead, making the choices we want to make and even though we might try to lie to ourselves sometimes, we will always know which is the right and which is the wrong choice to make. We try to justify our actions to ourselves but like any test, everyone is treated fairly, nobody has any advantage over anybody else. Although many might not support this theory, we are all born instinctively knowing good from bad, right from wrong, pure from evil. Life is full of sweet surprises, every day is a gift; the sun will rise, your spirit shines, listen to the voice of reason guiding you in the night.

Chapter Two
Living the Movie

The Rock of Gibraltar is a British colony located in the Mediterranean, between Spain and Africa, we were once part of Europe, thanks to Brexit, I have no idea what we are anymore. Gibraltar has a population of approximately 30,000 Gibraltarians and one of these bilingual 'llanitos' is me. Growing up in Gibraltar, felt like spending a day on a rollercoaster, with only one loop to enjoy, after a while it tends to get monotonous. A person can actually drive all around the Rock in less than twenty minutes; it gets to a point where one wants to experience a new ride. However, we do have monkeys living on our Rock and roaming through our towns, this helps keep things interesting.

Greeks, Romans, Arabs, Spaniards and the British amongst many others have once inhabited this mighty Rock, yet those known in our history books to have first settled on the Rock were Neanderthals. How the Gibraltar Barbary Apes came to reside on the Rock is a bit of a mystery; they have populated our Rock since as far back as the 11th century, when the still standing Moorish Castle was first built. The same species of apes can also be found in South Africa, it's not hard to believe that they might have been transported here by ship many years ago and have continued to reproduce since. For those who prefer a more mysterious scenario, legend has it, there is a subterranean passage over fifteen miles long, which begins at Lower St Michael's Cave and passes under the Strait of Gibraltar connecting to Morocco, and perhaps these apes discovered this tunnel years ago and explored it to the other side.

Legend also states that if the monkeys ever leave Gibraltar, we will cease to be British, unless the monkeys left stealing every Gibraltarian's passport, I have no idea how this is possible. The origin of this legend dates as far back as 1704, when a fleet of Spanish Soldiers was preparing to invade the Rock from the eastern side. Apparently, the Barberry Apes, known only as monkeys, at the time were disturbed by the Spanish Soldiers and began making such a racquet, their uproar alerted the British Soldiers of the intruders. After a fearless battle and some monkey business, the Rock remained British, thanks to some noisy wild alarm systems.

Most Gibraltarians work average nine to five job, get married, have children, take out a mortgage, buy a house, pay taxes and devote their days to the profession that pays the most and is available at that current moment in their life. We divide our life into weeks, seven days and then we start all over, our life revolves around the system. Most people wait all weekdays for the weekend; we want those five days to pass by as quickly as possible, so we can enjoy our two days of freedom. Children and parents wake up as early as 8:00 am with an hour to spare, before spending most of the day either learning at school or working in an office. By the time our working day comes to an end, one is too tired to do much of anything, which does not consist of eating take-out, watching TV or changing into your pyjamas.

As a child, I dreaded the thought of continuing this pattern; I hated waking up early in the morning, only to find myself an hour later sat in a classroom, on the same chair all morning. Learning about history and religion, instead of eating cornflakes and playing hide and seek throughout the Rock. Every morning my alarm would go off, I'd hit snooze and go back to bed, five minutes later my mum would walk into my bedroom and remind me I had to get ready for school, I never forgot, I just chose to stay in bed. Who says these are the rules one must follow to raise a well-educated, well-disciplined ordinary human being?

Minutes later, I'd be sharing a bathroom with my dad, my mum and my two sisters, as we all tried to brush our teeth, comb our hair and sometimes ignore the fact that my dad was shitting on the toilet. Still half-asleep, I'd grab a bowl to eat my cornflakes but having spent that extra time in bed meant I was running late for school. No time for cornflakes; I'd make toast instead and hoped by the time it popped out of the toaster, I'd have found my shoes and my will to continue living. As I put on my shoes, whilst buttering my toast and grabbing my satchel, my cousin would call. Steven was ready for school and as we always did, we met at the top of the hill, which separated both our houses and together we'd walk towards an education.

Why did I have to go to school? Why did I have to sit in silence all day, wearing my uncomfortable uniform? I found it very boring and in all honesty, most of the things I learned there, have no use in my everyday life. No job I've ever applied for have needed me to know the names of all of King Henry VIII's wives or about Adam and Eve, the first two people to ever walk the earth. Sometimes going to school didn't mean you would learn the truth or that which was truly important. School for me was a complete waste of a good childhood yet for my government, I had been shaped into the little obedient soldier that believed what it is they wanted me to believe.

Friday always excited me, not only did it mean two days off school but it also meant a trip to the video rental store with my dad. It was in this video rental store that I came upon a particular movie, one I rented countless times, one that inspired me to, hopefully one day, leave my Rock and venture out to Hollywood. I loved watching movies as a child, especially the ones that portrayed different countries, as living in Gibraltar in the 90s was all I had ever known. Then came Saturday, the best part about it was waking up with no alarm; I'd wake up when my body was ready and felt much better for this the entire day. Instead of toast, I had enough time to enjoy not one but two bowls of cornflakes, whilst watching my favourite Saturday morning cartoon shows. Later that day, my mum would take me and my sisters to visit my grandparents, play at the park, a trip through Main Street, we always found something fun to do; second best thing about Saturday, at no point did I have to learn mathematics.

My dad is a taxi driver, when I was little I remember joining him on Sundays as he drove his taxi up the Rock of Gibraltar, guiding tourists along the way, whilst we stopped to watch the Barbary Apes and observe the sights. I had grown up climbing and playing throughout the Rock; the apes, which at times came down to town, would occasionally jump around on the roof of my house, forcing me to close my windows, I was used to all this. What I enjoyed most about these trips were the tourists, not only was I fascinated by them in their own ways but they were always happy, which made complete sense, seeing as they were on holiday. In my dad's taxi, I got to interact with people from France, Italy, Australia, America and all over the globe; as soon as I recognised the American accent, I'd always ask, "Are you from Hollywood?" At that moment, I still lived in my own movie; an idol of mine once said, "Life's like a movie, write your own ending, keep believing, keep pretending…" Does that apply? Can we decide what path we wish to take our lives?

At the age of six, I remember obsessively playing with my PVC figurines. I'd use them to create stories, I'd allow my imagination to run wild. Most weekends when we went to the market, my mum would buy me a PVC figurine of a character I was familiar with; that same day, I would introduce them into my PVC figurine stories. On occasions, I'd have an audience of two, my sisters, Stacey and Kaylie. Using our stuffed toys, I'd play out a story for them and on other occasions, we'd put on a show for my parents. As I grew older, I stopped telling stories with toys and put words to paper. At around age twelve, I was writing short stories but the way my imagination works, I prefer writing long, complex ones.

At age fourteen, I attempted writing my first movie script; it took me over two years to write, at the end of it all, it was ridiculously bad. Seven rewrites later, I wrote something I truly hope to one-day share with the world. As I grew older, I realised I preferred writing my stories in script form, since my childhood dream had always been to move to Hollywood. Perhaps, learning how to become a screenwriter might benefit me for the future I was hoping for. I was a young, naïve teenager, who believed I could easily lead the life I wanted; little did I know at the time, it's not that easy writing your own movie, although that doesn't mean you can't improvise along the way.

After a somewhat entertaining childhood, one I wish had been filled with more confidence, I had reached the first crossroads in my life. School was finished and now I had to decide, if I wanted to go abroad to university and continue my studies or did I want to begin tackling my dream straight away? Why waste four more years studying when I could start my adult life right now? I could start working, save up my money, travel to Los Angeles and become a famous Hollywood screenwriter, all before my friends graduated university, sounded like a great plan at the time. Since before I could even write, my big dream was always to become a screenwriter, but more specifically I wanted to write for a franchise I had grown up watching since childhood and this was no secret to those who knew me. Everybody believed my dream was foolish, impossible, non-practical and possibly even crazy. Some people were nice about it, some were mean, others made fun, one encouraged me but what they all shared in common was, they would always try and get me to check into reality, whose reality?

My whole life I've aspired to be a writer, more specifically a screenwriter but where I'm from that's as farfetched as wishing to be an astronaut, travelling across the galaxy, cliché as it might sound, we are who we want to be. Being open about wanting to become a Hollywood screenwriter in an isolated Rock, where a famous celebrity only stepped foot in once every ten years was apparently a laughing matter to those who knew me. We've come a long way since the early millennium but back then attempting a future outside Gibraltar, especially in Hollywood, was not only ridiculous but hopeless. My friends always teased me about this; I never took it too seriously, but I did begin to hide my passion. At one point, I'd eagerly share ideas and stories with them; when I realised they were mocking me for it, I began keeping my writing a secret, I tried hiding who I truly wanted to be.

My family on the other hand were a little more supportive but even they believed I was aiming too high; they never discouraged me but I always sensed the support was not there. I remember I was reaching the end of my school years, when it was time to apply for university, I decided my education was no longer needed, although I had the grades. I never really believed much in the education system; I believed if I put my mind to it, I could achieve anything I wanted to do and having good grades, for me was a complete waste of time. This is when I realised my family did not share my "life's like a movie" philosophy. My parents were angry at me, they wanted me to continue with my education, they wanted me to be a realist. They wanted me to do as everybody with the opportunity did and continue my studies, I was tired of learning, I wanted to start living, you can never aim too high.

I had figured it all out, I had set my mind to it, I had not spent my teenage years writing screenplays of all sorts, only to grow up to become a psychologist, a doctor or even a lawyer, that was not the life I wanted, my movie ended in Hollywood. This part of my life story is the one that has always interested me the most, this is the childhood dream that one tends to lose as they grow older and life gets in the way. Life got in my way, which is why it took me so long to complete my journey, it's only a childhood dream if you stop dreaming about it into adulthood, what you considered a dream as a child, should become one's plan as an adult.

When my friends left for university, I set out in search of work and it was a tough road but I eventually began working as a cable car operator. I spent my days taking tourists to the top of the Rock to meet the apes and back down again, all in less than ten minutes. I appreciated this job for the mere fact that I enjoy working with people from abroad. Tourists fascinate me; their stories interest me more than those who, as myself, have spent their whole lives confined to our small Rock. I enjoyed working plus it had the benefit that I might meet an American family, which came from Los Angeles, who might invite me to stay with them as I quickly attempted to achieve my childhood dream and become a famous Hollywood screenwriter. I might have been twenty-one years old but I was still very naïve when it came to the reality that is life, I had no idea what was next to come.

My first attempt at adulthood had begun, I was now a working man, I could afford to buy my own underwear, yet I had to remember, I had to stick to the plan, I needed to save up enough money to leave Gibraltar and travel to America. I opened a bank account, calculated how much I'd need to save up, subtracted my expenses, two years of this and I should be able to… A few weeks later, I bought a car. I was having a hard time saving up, I was trying to be fully dedicated to my plan but at the same time I was growing up. As much as I wanted to concentrate on my budget, I also wanted to enjoy life. It's funny, I spent my teenage years living on ten pounds pocket money a week, to buy anything I might desire; now I had gotten used to spending at least ten pounds each day, just on petrol. I might have been having a hard time being a responsible financial adult-in-the-making but I had become a completely new person, that was what I most cherished from this new experience. I began finding confidence I didn't know I had in me, for the first time, I was in my element. I wasn't in school, I wasn't sitting down quietly, I wasn't following the rules, I wasn't learning what didn't interest me, I was doing what I enjoyed, I was happy with the person I was becoming.

Every day, I got to interact with hundreds of tourists as we spent ten minutes inside the cable car getting to know each other. Then another fifteen minutes at the top of the Rock, admiring the views, playing with the apes and providing them with historical information and then another ten minutes on our ride back down. The history of Gibraltar, that's something we never covered in school, I had to learn this on my own and what helped me the most was remembering my dad's Sunday taxi tours when I was younger. I was always impressed at how confident the apes were around my dad. When they saw him, most of them would run up to him excitedly, just as me and my sisters did, when we were young, to see him back home from work, minus the fleas. When I started working at the cable car, all this began to make sense to me. I too developed a much stronger relationship with the apes than I had ever had. My dad takes tourist up the Rock every day and has been doing so for almost thirty-five years; he's bonded with the apes, just as I was now doing too.

Growing up the apes were always just there, I never paid much attention to them; most of the time, they were a nuisance as they would come down to town and jump on the roof of my house. On one occasion when I was young, I had just been given a PlayStation for my birthday. A few weeks later, I had left some food in my bedroom. Two apes entered through my bedroom window, I heard the noise and went upstairs. When I entered my bedroom, the two apes made a run for it out the window breaking my new PlayStation along the way. I never left food in my bedroom ever again or left the window open, when I was not home for that matter.

My dad used to perform what I considered the best trick ever, he would hide a treat in his hand, cross both arms over each other and have the apes guess which hand he had the treat in. I was soon able to perform the trick myself, I remember I couldn't at first; each time I tried, all the apes would pounce on me at once, knowing I had treats on me. I was comfortable with the apes jumping on me but the first time I tried to perform this trick, I wasn't ready for ten of them to pounce, I screamed, ran and hid inside the cable car. The embarrassing part was, I had a group of tourists with me, that was an awkward ten-minute ride back down to the cable car station.

I remember at the beginning, the apes all looked alike to me, I even had a hard time telling apart the males from the females but as the months went by, I slowly began to recognise each ape individually. There's around three hundred apes living on the Rock; they're broken up into five clans which are scattered throughout. The cable car brought tourist directly to the top of the Rock; these apes were not the ones who would enter my bedroom and break my belongings. These were another clan, one made up of around sixty apes, these are the ones I became familiar with. The thing I always found most interesting was the fact that apes, like humans, will feel uncomfortable keeping eye contact with us until they become more familiar with you; eventually, we were able to play who blinks first, I never won.

One day whilst making my rounds to the top of the Rock, I was approached by a tour guide; apparently, she enjoyed the way I interacted with tourists. She recommended I apply for a new position which had become available within the Gibraltar Tourist Branch as an information officer, a section of the Gibraltar Developing Company. This moment was exactly when my life decided which direction it was going to take me, this was the start of my story, I still didn't know it, but this was the day I first came in contact with my bully, the day I met Shale.

Shale was my first bully in life, but soon as the problem escalated others got involved, including many government officials and Unite the Union, all of whom play a big part in my story. I've lived my whole life confined to my little Rock known as home; we're a small country yet big in power and sadly like most countries those in charge, control all of it, and sometimes it's not always used for our benefit. This is not just a Gibraltar problem, it's a world-wide one, but I'm not here to share Gibraltar's story, I'm here to share mine, my own personal eight-year experience within a failed system, a story I'm sure most can relate to.

Chapter Three
All Work and No Play

Many of us believe we work to live, but the reality is we live to work. We all want to travel the world, but most of our time is spent travelling from desk to desk. Work life and personal life is hard to balance, and as the years pass by and prices go up, finding that perfect balance won't even be possible. Life is made up of moments, not careers; we all strive for that perfect career, whilst missing out on many great moments in the process. At the end of one's test, it is these moments that make up who we are, not the way we earned our living. We work from the early hours of the morning, almost until the time it gets dark; at this point, one is too tired to enjoy life properly. We all need time to unwind, recharge and reconnect; annual leave has led us to believe, this is all the time we need, this could not be further from the truth. We all deserve the chance to quit our jobs in order to appreciate life to its fullest, but how is that possible for our survival in today's society?

I applied for the job at the Gibraltar Tourist Branch, went to my interview, where I was met by a group of individuals, which included Shale (Head of The Gibraltar Tourist Branch), Beverly (Human Resources) and Ricky (Head of Tourism) amongst others. I was asked a series of questions, your standard interview questions: Why does this job interest you? What makes you think you're qualified for the position? Have you had any prior experience? Do you still smoke marijuana? I too was caught a little off guard but in all honesty, it was a question they had every right to ask me, Clara, Tableta, Paki... I had tried them all. Gibraltar is located next to the straits of Morocco, we know our cannabis, it's not that difficult to come across.

Cannabis, also referred to as marijuana, is a greenish-grey mixture of the dried, shredded leaves and flowers of cannabis sativa, the hemp plant. The main active chemical in marijuana is THC (tetrahydrocannabinol), it is a psychoactive ingredient. The highest concentrations of THC are found in the leaves and flowers. When marijuana smoke is inhaled, THC rapidly passes from the lungs into the bloodstream and is carried to the brain and other organs throughout the body. THC from the marijuana acts on specific receptors in the brain, called cannabinoid receptors, starting off a chain of cellular reactions that finally lead to the euphoria or high that users experience. Certain areas in the brain, such as the hippocampus, the cerebellum, the basal ganglia and the cerebral cortex, have a higher concentration of cannabinoid receptors. These areas influence memory, concentration, pleasure, coordination, sensory and time perception. Therefore, these functions are most adversely affected by marijuana use.

Back in the day, there wasn't much for the youth of Gibraltar to do. Most of us spent our days smoking up the Rock, and most of us were caught doing so. In today's society cannabis is becoming much less taboo; in some countries, it's even beginning to be legalised. There is no denying all of its medical benefits but back when I was a teenager, all I knew was, it was time to get high. I smoked my first joint when I was fifteen years old; it was disgusting and that one puff left so much smoke in my lungs. I was suffocating and then the beach began to spin; I closed my eyes but everything was still spinning, afterwards I got the whities.

My friend Antony and I had ridden a canoe to another beach, one you could only arrive to by sea. A group of friends of ours from school were there too, and as we began getting closer to shore, I realised they were smoking. I had already tried cigarettes before this, didn't much care for them but if everybody's smoking cigarettes at the beach, I will too. Before anybody realised I was actually a nerd who was writing a movie back home whilst covered in sunscreen. What I found strange was, they were all smoking from the same cigarette; had their packet accidentally fallen in the ocean, and all they had left was one? I didn't care why they were all smoking from the same cigarette, better for me, I honestly didn't want to smoke a full one, this way I'd look cool without being a fool.

As the cigarette came towards me, I realised it smelled differently, and there was a lot more smoke coming from it than that of a cigarette. This cigarette looked like it was on steroids but I was trying to fit in, and so I puffed and I puffed and quickly realised this must be hashish. I ended up vomiting inside my canoe that day on our way back to the other beach, the sun was making it so much worse. After throwing up inside the canoe, we had to jump into the water and turn our canoe around for a quick clean. As I emerged from the water, I was expecting Antony to yell at me but as soon as we had tipped our canoe around, we both broke out laughing. I thought I was drowning but the giggles kept hitting us hard, then for some reason a shark started singing around us, wearing a sombrero. We got back on our canoe and were determined to share this experience with our other friends.

Soon enough smoking cannabis and drinking alcohol on the weekends became the new normal. My friends and I would meet at an old abandoned bunker nicknamed the Nipperish, used during the time of the war as a defence fortress; we used it to smoke and drink. I like the Nipperish for so many reasons, even after I stopped smoking, I still used to go up there alone many times. It had a great sight of Gibraltar, Spain and Africa, three different countries, all in one view; it was breathtaking and was only a five-minute walk away from my house. It eventually became a memorial to one of our dearest friends, who sadly passed away in 2008. I lived the closest of all my friends, this was where I had grown up playing hide and seek when I was little; I considered this my back garden, my happy place. We celebrated many birthdays up there and best part was that all throughout this area, located at different bunkers, were other groups of people. Sometimes we'd all get together and just dance our cares away, leaving our problems for another day, all along the Rock.

Thanks to our musical stoned Rock parties, I had a police record that smelled a lot like marijuana. After I left school and started applying for jobs, I realised it was a bit embarrassing.

I was used to being asked that question during job interviews; in fact during my interview for the position as a cable car operator, I was also asked the same question…did I smoke marijuana? I answered honestly, and they respected me for it, and I was hired. Imagine going for a job interview and being asked do you drink alcohol? "I do" is probably everybody's response but does that mean they're an alcoholic? I answered my hopeful new employers truthfully, I still smoked but assured them it was only after working hours and would not affect my job, in other words, "I won't be coming stoned to work." The reality was I really didn't smoke as much at that time, most of my friends had gone abroad to university and those of us who had stayed behind began working and slowly drifted apart. No longer did I meet up with friends to smoke, drink and party; the last time we had all been together at the Nipperish was back in 2008. After one year of staying away, we all got together and returned to the Nipperish to draw a picture of our friend Ashby, who had passed away that summer.

My friends and I had started growing up and because of this, we had left our old childish ways behind. No longer did we go out partying as we used to do, no longer were we wasting time during the day getting high, we had responsibilities now. At this point in my life, I'd usually only ever smoke cannabis if I sat down writing at home and truth be told, I also remember always sparking up a joint whenever a new episode of *Lost* aired on TV. There was so much shit going on, how can one not get high watching *Lost*? I did understand where they were coming from, they had seen, through my vetting, that I had been caught by the police on a few occasions, all incidents related to cannabis, they wanted reassurance this would not happen again, it never did.

Two weeks later I received a phone call, informing me I had been successful, I now worked for the Gibraltar Tourist Branch as one of ten information officers based at a different location each week. I truly had enjoyed my time at the cable car yet this new job provided me with a higher salary; it was a government position and most importantly, I was still dealing with tourists. Would this be the job where I'd save up enough money, meet an American family, move in with them and become a Hollywood screenwriter? Apparently not. I said goodbye to my monkey pals and begun working inside an office, alongside human colleagues who soon enough, I was able to tell apart from one another. I soon learned their names, these co-workers already came with names of their own and did not pounce on me when I was eating candy. My new colleagues soon became my new friends, and those of us who were younger would get together after work and share a drink at the square.

I was soon getting the hang of my new job; it mostly consisted of tourists approaching me and asking for information about Gibraltar. It was usually the same questions, most of them wanting to know how to reach the cable car station or find a taxi. I was based at a different office each week; in total we had three main locations, our main tourist office based at the Square, at the end of Main Street, where Shale was permanently situated. Our second office was located at the Frontier, next to the airport, on occasions we would have to spend some time at the airport terminal when flights arrived into Gibraltar. Our third office was located at the Coach Park, near the cruise terminal, where at times, we were also situated. In other words, any entrance into Gibraltar either by land, sea or sky, we were there, ready to greet tourists and welcome them to Gibraltar.

I enjoyed my new job, I still got to interact with tourist; although unlike my dad's taxi or the cable car, I didn't have much time to socialise with them, other than provide them with the information they needed. I also felt like I was back in school again, going from classroom to classroom each week, sitting down at a desk all day, wearing an uncomfortable uniform, repeating the same information over and over again. I missed my time at the cable car, I missed my monkey friends, I missed wearing a tracksuit, I missed being out in the open, I missed interacting socially as opposed to just formally. On the bright side, my new job offered more money and was a government position, isn't that what we all search for in life? I was finally finding my rhythm at the Gibraltar Tourist Branch and was praised by Shale for doing such a wonderful job, so little did I expect, what was about to happen next. Only a few weeks after I had resigned from my cable car job and began working for the Gibraltar Developing Company, all at their request, I was met with the first piece of shit, life forced me to step on into adulthood; I was suspended.

One day I was asked to attend a meeting at the main office, where I found myself in the presence of Shale, Beverly and Ricky. According to them, I had lied on my application form, where had I lied? I had no idea and when I asked them, they responded by telling me, I was not privileged to that information. They placed a letter of resignation in front of me and asked me to sign; they were nice enough to allow me to resign rather than be terminated from my position, which would show up on my record. I really didn't want this on my record, especially since I hadn't lied and believed this dismissal was unfair yet who was I to argue with them, I was just a boy out of school trying adulthood for the first time. If these three individuals who are above me are allowing me the chance to escape free from this mess, why don't I count my blessings, grab the pen and sign. I requested a copy of my application form, and at this moment Beverly got up from her chair, looked down at me, she appeared to be furious yet managed to keep her calm. Beverly urged me to sign the letter, I was not allowed a copy of my application, as this was their property, they were doing me a favour, one which could go away if I did not act now. I couldn't bring myself to sign, therefore I didn't and there began a sequence of events, which not only paused my movie for eight years but made everything much harder, to the point where at times, I just wanted my movie to end midway.

Since I did not sign the resignation letter they had prepared for me, where apparently, I claimed I had lied on my application form in order to get the job, I was met with a temporary suspension. I was told to expect an official termination letter in the mail, sometime in the coming few weeks. What had just happened? I wasn't exactly sure what lie they were talking about, but I did have an idea what this was all about. I was having a hard time gaining access into the airport terminal, apparently whoever was in charge of the Gibraltar Airport at the time, had performed their own vetting on me. Seeing as I had a history with cannabis, I wasn't being allowed access into the departure lounge, where I was meant to greet the tourists.

Fair enough, to each their own, I understood this person was just doing their job; I wasn't an addict, I was no criminal but on paper, all they saw was a past attached to cannabis. As much as I understood this, it still made me feel bad; luckily, there was always more than one of us based at our frontier office. When the time came to do our rounds at the airport, I simply stayed behind and someone else would go in my place. I knew this must have been the reason behind my dismissal, yet I had been completely honest in my interview about everything. The only reason they had asked me those questions was because I granted them access to my police records, they were aware of all this but hired me anyway, and now they had regretted their decision.

I joined Unite the Union hoping for their help, they were not able to do anything for me; they weren't even able to retrieve my application form from human resources. This was something I was desperate to get my hands on, as I did not understand where I had lied on my application and according to them, this was the real reason for my termination. I found it strange that Unite were not able to retrieve my application form and in reality it could get the access. At that moment, I still hadn't realised who the good guys were, and who the bad ones were. I went by the rules, I was honest about my past yet for some reason, these rules were not applying to me. I should have been more aware of Unite's intentions; perhaps had I opened my eyes earlier, they wouldn't have fucked me over six years later.

Before my termination letter arrived through the mail, I was able to retrieve a copy of my application form on my own merits and was surprised to find a note on the top corner of the form. This was not written by me yet if someone were to read this application, believing I had written that piece of information, then I could see where all the confusion had come from. I had three charges and someone had written down two of them, above my signature; on the same page, I had confirmed everything was accurate. They had left out a third charge, making it seem as if I was only informing them of two charges.

Long story short, I was able to prove I had not written that and in fact, it was revealed that Beverly from human resources herself had tampered with my application form. Beverly claimed it was a note she had made, simply as a reminder, and apparently Shale and Ricky were aware that she had written this and not me. If this was the reason why everyone was led to believe I had lied and these three knew I had not written that in the first place, then why did they not speak up? After winning my appeal, I was allowed to return to work yet I was now on probation and was to be carefully evaluated, the perfect opportunity to try and get rid of me all over again.

I found it strange that Shale, Beverly and Ricky seemed to have lied to me in order to get me to resign by luring me into signing my resignation, allowing them to get rid of a mistake they had made. At the same time, why had none of them faced a disciplinary hearing for having lied against me, to the point where I was out of work for several weeks? If I was able to get my job back simply by retrieving a copy of my application form, then why weren't Unite able to do the same for me? These were actually serious questions I should have put more thought into but at that moment, I was just happy that my life was back on track, back to saving up and hoping to venture far out from my fragile Rock and into the world of show business. Life was heading in a different direction for me; I might have got my job back but I was about to lose a lot more, little did I know, I had just made three new enemies. The worst part was, my new enemies were also my superiors; they didn't want me working for them anymore, and so began the years of bullying that followed.

Government had made a mistake, and they tried to get rid of the problem they had created, the problem being me. The longer it took for them to resolve the problem, the bigger it got, to the point where it became so complicated, I have to write a book just to share my story. Our governments don't necessarily decide to go against their citizens, but if they make a mistake and you are the face of it, then you can be sure they'll do whatever they can, not to fix their mistake but rather hide the fact that they ever made one. I had no idea how difficult the next few years would become; I wanted to quit many times along the way, in the end, I'm glad I didn't.

Back in 2007, I had remained behind and not gone off to study abroad alongside my friends as I planned to get a head start with my career as a writer. I wanted to save up money, make connections with people from around the world, travel, accomplish my screenwriting goals, live life, and hopefully like everybody, eventually settle down, find love and start a family. Four years later, all my friends returned having graduated from university; they all had their degrees to show for their time well spent and well deserved, and what did I have to show for my first four years into adulthood? I had no confidence, suffered from depression, anxiety, low self-esteem, social phobia, constant déjà vu and had now developed epilepsy.

At this point in my life, I could only feel one emotion, all I felt was anger, which sadly I welcomed. Any feeling was better than living life as an emotionless zombie, who doesn't even want to be here but is too afraid to do anything about it. I was broken, I had endured bullying for four years; although for a very long time, I was in denial about it all, yet sooner or later I had to open my eyes. Gibraltar, as most of our world, is full of bullies; the sad part is that these bullies are no longer in school. These bullies are able to overpower us not because they are bigger or physically stronger but rather because they are in a position of power that they can abuse for their own benefit, a topic that I think applies throughout the world.

I hated the person I had become, I was finding it very hard to live with myself, I felt weak, worthless and I knew if I resigned, I would have felt completely defeated, not by them but by me. Having not resigned and putting up with their bullshit, was the only strength I had to show for myself, yet how could a little bit of bullying get me to such a dark stage in life? A little bit of bullying each day for over four years will do that to a person; I had never really experienced bullying at school, I had got into an occasional fight or two, fallen out with friends but I was never bullied constantly by anyone. Now as an adult I was experiencing this, it was the hardest time of my life; I can only imagine how school kids who go through this experience must feel. I felt so small and useless, clueless and lost; I couldn't seem to understand why. I felt so invisible as though I were the only one lying in bed awake at night.

Chapter Four
A Tour Through
Workplace Bullying

Bullying at work takes many forms of abuse, such as shouting, swearing and ridiculing. Constantly humiliating, regularly criticising, attacking and persecution through threats and fear, all forms are part of bullying at work. Exposure to bullying at work has been classified as a significant source of social stress within the workplace, a more crippling and devastating problem for employees than all other work-related stress put together. Clinical observations have shown effects of exposure to workplace bullying such as social isolation and maladjustment, psychosomatic illnesses, depressions, compulsions, helplessness, anger, anxiety and despair. Although acts of aggression and harassment occur fairly often in everyday interaction at work, they seem to be associated with severe health problems in the target, when they occur on a regular basis. To be a victim of intentional and systematic psychological harm, be it real or perceived, by another person produces severe emotional reactions such as fear, anxiety, helplessness, depression and shock. Bullying leads to pervasive emotional, psychosomatic and psychiatric problems in victims.

When I was at my worst, I searched the internet for inspirational stories regarding bullying, stories I could read to give me not only hope but strength too. I was reaching out for help with the only little bit of confidence I had left. I didn't want to speak to anyone, I didn't want to start a conversation, I just wanted to read something positive from one victim of bullying to another. I never came across anything that spoke to me. I never found the perfect story to help me escape reality yet find the strength I needed once I reached the end, to walk out the front door and face my fears, this is what I hope this book can achieve.

I remember it all started as soon as I returned back to work after my unfair dismissal, apparently during my temporary suspension, my colleagues had to cover my weekend shifts during my absence; I was forced to do their weekend shifts upon my return. This all seemed reasonable enough at the time, it went on for months and still I was blinded; for some reason, I did not see this as unfair, I was just grateful to be back at work. It was all harmless at first. I had returned a little shy and less confident in myself yet working even harder than before to prove myself to everybody because for some reason, I felt as if this was all my fault. When I returned, I was pressured to play catch up with those who had started at the same time as me. Shale excluded me from group outings, shouted at me in front of tourists and ridiculed the way I pronounced the word 'monkeys'. Apparently, it's pronounced 'mankeys', it's a silent 'a' disguised as an 'o'. I began to realise I was being forced to cover many holidays and was being over worked, on occasions more than three weeks straight without a break, something which did not happen with others. I tried my best to reach their high standards of professionalism but upon my return, it felt like they expected too much from me.

Shale began making things difficult for me, whilst sometimes also humiliating me in the process. If I arrived at 9:01 am, I would get called into her office and told off for coming late. I began arriving at 8:50 am, hoping to avoid any confrontation first thing in the morning. Shale would then approach me as I ate my breakfast and would tell me to stop eating and to go outside and start working. I would inform her that it was still not nine but according to her, as soon as I came in through those doors, I had to begin working, even if it was before opening hours. Ironically, if someone else had also come early that day and were in the process of eating breakfast, then Shale would also allow me to eat mine.

Soon enough Shale began coming on many surprise visits, whilst I was based at different locations, hoping to catch me out doing something wrong. On weekends, Shale did not work, and she believed I was more laid back when I knew she was not working and always hoped to catch me out. Shale would always find something to complain about, if it was not the newspaper open on my desk then it was my can of drink, visible to tourists; there was always a problem or so she believed.

One afternoon, I received a phone call at the frontier office. Shale had found herself short staffed at our main office at the Square and needed me to come over. I wasn't happy about this; today I was supposed to finish at 3:30 pm but having to cover at our main office, now meant I wasn't going home until 5:30 pm, but this was part of the job. On my way there, I was wondering what had happened, there were five information officers there that morning; I wondered why some had left so early. When I arrived, I found they had all left, I was all alone in the office with Shale; I hated being alone with her. I asked where everyone had gone and she grinningly informed me, she had sent them all out to visit a new cave opening at the top of the Rock. I asked Shale when I'd be able to visit the new cave and she informed me, that after working hours I could visit any cave I wished.

At first, the mental bullying I was experiencing at the hands of Shale was nothing but petty, silly things but when you are ridiculed and singled out by pettiness each and every day, it begins to affect your health, no matter how strong you try to be about it. At this point, I was still handling it all quite well, even after all the injustice I felt I had experienced and was still experiencing. Although, I think I was trying hard to live up to their expectations; Shale soon recommended my probation period be extended even longer than it already had and my evaluation by her did not look promising.

After over six months, I finally began to realise, I was being treated unfairly; I wasn't simply being paranoid about the situation, this was actually happening. I had begun dreading going into work every morning and especially worried if I was based at the same location as Shale, which generally happened to be one week with and one without. It was just before Christmas, it was pouring down, it was one of those days you're glad you're indoors, even if your bully is in the next room beside you. I was asked by Shale to deliver invitations all around Gibraltar, apparently inviting different companies to a Christmas party being hosted by the Gibraltar Developing Company. Information Officers are always based at one location at a time, it is not in our job description to run errands. Especially since the Gibraltar Developing Company have their own errand boy whose sole purpose is to do these jobs for them, yet this did not occur to me at that moment.

Shale handed me a stack of invitations and as I waited for the car keys, she informed me the car was broken and I would have to deliver all these invitations by foot. I went to grab my tourist branch appointed raincoat and was told by Shale I was not allowed to wear it during working hours. I needed to have my jumper and badge visible at all times around Gibraltar, so tourists could recognise me and ask for my help if needed. Yes, you are reading this correctly, my big bullying example has to do with a raincoat, it's more to do with the psychology behind the event than the event itself. For the longest time, I believed this was all my fault, this is when I finally realised I was wrong.

For the last few months, I had played nice and put up with all of Shale's requests and outbursts but today was going to be different. I wasn't going to walk out of my office, into the pouring rain without my raincoat. I wasn't necessarily standing up for myself, had it not been raining the way it was, I might have just walked out that door without my raincoat but the way it was pouring, I finally stopped doubting myself. I knew this was not right, I grabbed my raincoat, walked out the door and as soon as I did, I wished I never had to go back to that office again. When I returned later that day, Shale called me into her office, she gave me a verbal warning and told me if I ever disobeyed her again, I would face a disciplinary hearing at our main office alongside Ricky and Beverly.

I went home that day, wondering if I had crossed the line by disobeying Shale and not leaving my raincoat behind and delivering their invitations in the rain on foot. Now, I know better but when you're broken, all one does is doubt themselves. The weird thing about bullying is that it takes a while for the victim to realise they are in fact being bullied (or to at least accept it). However, someone observing from the distance, would be able to give you a definite answer by the end of the first day.

The next morning, my life was still shit, it was still raining, the car was still broken, Shale was still my boss, and they still had more invitations for me to deliver. Again, we argued over my raincoat and this time I asked her why I was having to do this. Did the Gibraltar Developing Company not have someone specifically employed for this? Apparently, the errand boy was out sick and so it was up to us to cover for him; I then asked why I was the only information officer forced to do this task, especially in the pouring rain.

I left the office again that day wearing my raincoat, it was a small victory, looking back now, sadly wearing my raincoat, against her wishes in the rain, whilst delivering their invitations was considered a win for me. As I walked around Gibraltar, getting wetter by each invitation I delivered, I could not stop thinking to myself, had I been rude by questioning why I was doing this as opposed to the errand boy? As much as that was bothering me, the fact that I also questioned why I was the only information officer doing this made me feel terrible; I was basically implying Shale send out one of my colleagues into the rain on foot as opposed to me.

That was always the hardest part and Shale played this card many times. Not only would she make me feel bad for not being a team player but on every occasion she could, she tried to turn the entire staff against me. Luckily, my boss might have been the biggest bully I had ever faced but at the same time, my colleagues were the nicest group of people one could hope to work alongside. They knew what was happening, they knew the kind of person I was; gladly, Shale never managed to turn them against me, although eventually she did end up getting me to hate myself. It was knowing that my colleagues would also be there in the office with me that many times helped me get out of bed in the morning and on my way to work.

An example of this comes on the third day when once again I was asked by Shale to deliver invitations, this time a colleague of mine stood up and offered to deliver the invitations herself. I'll never forget Chelsey's act of kindness; it was not the fact that she was willing to deliver the invitations on foot in the rain for me, it was the fact, that in her own way, she was standing up for me, against her own boss. This was the exact moment I knew I was being bullied, this was not in my head. Shale agreed to this but not before handing Chelsey the car keys and informing her to come back in an hour as the errand boy needed the car. If you're wondering, I never faced a disciplinary hearing for walking out with my raincoat on the second day; obviously, they could not officially discipline me over this as legally they were in the wrong. I spent a whole month nervously waiting to be called into the main office for my disciplinary hearing, one amongst many other promised disciplinary hearings that never came.

Shale once yelled at the staff, when we run low on paper, we must report it, so that more paper can be purchased. I informed Shale that I had already mentioned this to another colleague of ours, who had in fact already gone to collect the paper. Shale's response to this was by immediately accusing me of blaming Nikolai for the fact that we had run out of paper. I tried to inform her that I was simply explaining that the paper was probably on the way, yet when Nikolai arrived Shale quickly informed him on who was blaming who for what. I constantly had to explain myself because of Shale, most of which needed no explanation from me, my colleagues knew what was happening.

On multiple occasions, Shale had tried turning the staff against me; this particular time she tried to do it with everyone at the same time. Shale had given everybody two secret free hours for our hard work during December, with a great amount of tourist to deal with, what a nice boss. We could use these hours to leave early or accumulate a full day of working hours and therefore use it to take a day off. I called Shale later that day, to ask her to log down two extra hours for me, as was always our procedure, which I had accumulated the day before working at the cruise terminal.

Shale refused saying that I shouldn't be greedy, as she had already given all of us two secret free hours for all our hard work. I once again thanked her for this but reminded her, I had actually worked overtime at the cruise terminal the day before. Long story short, she gave me my two hours after she cancelled everyone's two secret free hours and informed the entire staff that they were losing their hours because I was being greedy.

I remember Beverly came into the office one day to speak to Shale and found me outside our door smoking a cigarette. We all took turns smoking outside but today Beverly was in a bad mood and she didn't like me. Beverly suspended me right there and then, in front of everybody. I was humiliated, no warning, no disciplinary hearing, I was simply suspended. I got home and began crying; this was becoming a normal routine for me, I never used to cry and now the slightest thing would get me going. The worse part about this was I knew I couldn't win either way, I knew there was no record of this suspension. If I didn't show up the next day, I'd probably get in trouble for not coming to work and if I did, I'd probably get in trouble for showing up when having been suspended.

The next morning, hoping not to give them the ammunition they craved, I went to the main office and asked Beverly if I should go into work that day or not. Beverly yelled at me for not being at my proper location as work had already started. There comes a point, where the victim has to realise there is no right answer, there is no way out of what the bully is intending. This is one of the things which took me longest to realise, it took me a few months to actually admit to myself I was being bullied but it took me years to realise, you can never please your bully.

I came to realise Ricky was not in fact necessarily a bully; he was simply somebody caught in a situation he preferred to pretend was not happening. Which in return allowed the bullies to feel they could get away with doing what they were doing. The problem was that Ricky was in a position of power to stop this, he was their superior, he should have acted like one and dealt with the situation rather than turn a blind eye. Ricky moved away from tourism a short while after, Darcello was his replacement. Now, I truly was in hell;

this was the male equivalent of Shale. Once Darcello showed up, and Shale and Beverly knew they not only had his backing but his blessing, things started to get out of control.

I knew Ricky silently knew what was going on and realised I was not the bad person Shale was making me out to be, but with Darcello, I was a blank canvas. I hoped I could meet with him before Shale painted a bad picture of me. A week later, I found myself in my first meeting alongside Darcello, and to my lucky delight, Shale was present too. Darcello informed me, if I continued to claim that I was being bullied by Shale, they would have no choice but to let me go, he advised me to stop complaining. At this same meeting, Shale said she wanted an apology from me; even though, I felt I was not in the wrong, I did not want to give Darcello the wrong impression, as he had just said, I should forget everything and move on. Hoping to be mature about the situation, I apologised to Shale but then she began complaining that this was not a proper apology. Shale wanted one in front of everyone, she deserved a public apology. Darcello agreed that I had to apologise in front of everyone, something that never came into fruition. Since this day, Shale knew she now had the full backing of her superior (unlike before), and at that moment, her bullying became her full-time job.

For the past few weeks, Shale had been making a very big deal about how badly I was apparently conducting my tours. To be honest, I was having a hard time remembering past knowledge but was nowhere as bad as Shale was making me out to be. One day I'm told by Shale, if I did not improve, she would be forced to have me conduct a full tour for her and the students inside her office. I told her nobody had ever had to do that before, I found that to be humiliating on my behalf. Shale responded by telling me that nobody had ever been as bad as me giving tours. What she forgets is she hired me because she liked the way I gave my tours, whilst working at the cable car. On another occasion, I was forced by Shale to sit on a small child's school desk, which she had placed opposite her own desk; this desk was not only too small for me, next to me rested a perfectly normal sized desk. I was forced to sit there and study notes based on Gibraltar information; this was a power move, Shale's favourite way to spend the workday. Shale was crushing my spirits, I was losing my confidence, I felt useless compared to others, belittled every time I spoke, I had become Shale's bitch.

I had taken the afternoon off and was supposed to leave at 2:30 pm. According to the clock in our office (which is the time we always went by), it was already 2:30 pm. I approached Shale and informed her that I was leaving; she informed me it was not 2:30 pm yet. I told her that the clock outside was indicating it was but according to Shale the clock outside was wrong. When she looked at her own clock, it also showed 2:30 pm. I pointed this out and looking defeated, she told me not to go anywhere and checked the time via telephone. Suddenly Shale smiled at me, somehow, she had found her win; she put the call on loudspeaker, where I heard the operator say it was 2:28 pm. I didn't want to argue, I told her I'd start getting ready and I'd wait those two minutes before leaving. At this point, thinking she had nothing to lose, Shale instructed me to stay standing where I was for two minutes, she did not want me to move or speak, just stand still for two minutes. When I asked why, she responded by reminding me that she was my boss and apparently, I do as she says. I looked at Shale and could not believe the point we had reached. Workplace bullying at its worse; this is something I would have expected a school bully to utter but not a woman in charge of tourism.

I did not stay standing motionless in front of her for two minutes and instead walked back to my seat. I faced a disciplinary hearing, when I asked Darcello what I should have done, he informed me, I could either put up with it, resign or they could fire me. As we all know bullies come in many forms, shapes and sizes, mine just happened to be my boss using her superiority against me. This became a game to Shale, how could she bully me without breaking the rules. Shale's main tactic was always to try to get me so angry that I would lose it to the point where they would have a proper reason to punish me. I never gave them that reason, I developed epilepsy instead, whilst being broken down.

At least once a week, hoping to crush my spirits, Shale would present me with a report, covering problems I had caused in our office in the days past. She would always remind me that this had been added to my file, if I ever wished to apply for a new job, this file would not help my chances of succeeding much further outside the Gibraltar Developing Company. I felt that if I left, nobody would want to hire me, my vetting hadn't helped me in the past, the addition of a bad work record would only make things impossible for me. At that time, I was still paying off my car, I had started paying my parents rent, I got used to buying my own food, my own clothes, I had become self-responsible, I couldn't afford losing all that. Those negative reports written about me always destroyed me; when Shale handed them to me, I'd play down how much they truly affected me. When I reached home and read each report properly, most of the time, I'd simply go straight to bed. I kept every report, I didn't know why I was doing this at the time, these reports made me feel so bad about myself and so worried about my future. I should just have tossed them all out and never read them again but I needed them, I needed to read them. I was torturing myself, in the end, the best thing I did was keep those reports, never throw away your evidence.

Chapter Five
It's a Bully World

Bullying is unwanted and aggressive behaviour that involves an imbalance of power which is repeated, slowly dehumanising a victim over time. The bully will use superior strength or influence to intimidate their victim, every injustice we feel by those of greater power is a form of bullying. Bullies aren't just found in school, work and home, most of them are found in positions of power. As we become older, we realise money is life, our parents were right, money doesn't grow on trees. This is why most of the population will do whatever needs to be done to fill their pockets, mainly at the expense of others. When you want something, which is affecting you, to be changed but your voice is not being heard and you continue to suffer because of it, that is bullying.

At the very beginning, the first thing I ever did to try and put a stop to my bullying was privately speak to the bully herself directly. As terrified as I was, one day I walked up to Shale's door and knocked to get into her office. Inside my head, I was knocking to open the door into hell, I was terrified of what was waiting for me on the other side yet I never expected this to happen. I approached Shale and knew I had to be very careful with which words I used. I had practiced at home the night before but at that moment, I didn't even remember why I had even knocked in the first place.

I knew the word 'feel' would be very important here; I had to make it clear that I felt bullied and was not calling her a bully directly. I remember this day very clearly, as soon as I told Shale how I felt, before even responding back to me, she had already picked up the phone requesting Beverly and Ricky to come down to our location right away; I was being disrespectful to my superior. Shale told me to wait outside, I embarrassedly walked outside and sat next to my colleagues, nervously waiting for the principal and his assistant... I mean Ricky and Beverly to come into the office and scold me.

Ricky and Beverly were both located at the main office, whilst I was located at various other sites, most of the time alongside Shale. This in return allowed her to bully me on a daily basis as opposed to the other two. As soon as they arrived, the four of us locked ourselves in Shale's office and I was quickly instructed by Shale herself to repeat what I had just said to her. I informed Ricky and Beverly that for the last few months, I had felt bullied by Shale and that's when all hell broke loose. That was the day Shale stopped hiding the fact that she had become my bully. Before our meeting was over, they informed me, if I ever accused Shale of bullying again not only would I be suspended but I would also be facing legal action in a court of law. Seven years later, I took legal action against my government.

The main fear I constantly had was that I would lose my job, I was still young and naïve. At that point in my life, not obeying instructions and actually wearing my raincoat in the rain made me anxious that if I complained, I would lose my job. Now, I also feared that if I spoke out again about how I felt, not only would I find myself unemployed and penniless, I would also be faced with legal action, where I might be forced to pay them in return. I went home that day, knowing I had made things worse; at least I had said something about it, I had spoken up for myself, I stood up to the bully, at least I did in my mind. Somewhere along the lines during our meeting Shale jumped to the conclusion that I was claiming that all my colleagues felt bullied by her. I was quickly becoming familiar with how the mind of a bully works, when a victim is finding their courage, tear them down quickly. Shale called me out on it during our meeting and I quickly tried to explain myself. I was complaining that I felt bullied and singled out, my concerns did not concern anyone else. Many times, in the past, Shale had tried to turn the staff against me, not only would this continue to crush my spirits and hopefully get me to resign but it would also give the impression, I was hard to work with. The difference between a workplace bully and one you would find in school, is that in the workplace, being adults, they tend to be cleverer but at the same time, they must always cover their tracks. If this escalated any further, Shale hoped to argue that my problem was with everyone as opposed to just her and so she tried to make it seem that way.

The next day, all tourist information offices were closed as Shale wanted to have all her Information Officers located at the Square for a meeting, alongside Ricky and Beverly. Shale began by addressing everyone, telling them she had heard of problems within the office regarding bullying and that I had claimed we all felt this way. As was becoming a routine with me, I was forced to apologise to my colleagues for the inconvenience and to further explain that I had not mentioned them during my initial meeting with Shale, this had nothing to do with them. My intention was not to blow this up as it had, all I wanted was to approach Shale and try to solve this matter between ourselves but she was the one to involve everyone else.

How many people could Shale turn against me? Although my colleagues knew exactly what was happening, never the less because of me, they always found themselves in uncomfortable situations. In a sense, Shale was their bully too; Shale used them for her own manipulative desires, this was not constructive, we all worked together, why try to turn us against each other? Why try to turn everyone against me? Shale addressed the staff once again, wanting to know how many of us felt bullied by her, other than myself. Nobody wanted to keep eye contact with either of us, this felt childish, ridiculous and then suddenly Roger spoke up. He too felt bullied by Shale, I was so proud of my friend; it's easy to call out the bully behind their back but to their face, few people have courage.

We were all in shock, especially Shale and myself, I knew others felt the same but I didn't think it had escalated to this point. Shale had just dug her own grave, instead of speaking to me privately and trying to fix the situation, she made a big scene, hoping to prove me wrong and accidentally proved me right in the process. I will never forget the look on Shale's face after Roger stood up to her, my smile just increased her anger; this was something that had been going on for the last few weeks. Shale's hatred towards me was so strong that I believe she despised coming to work; being the boss, she would lash out her anger and frustration throughout the office. The Gibraltar Tourist Branch was quickly becoming the saddest place to visit within Gibraltar, the tension between Shale and myself was unbearable. It was affecting everybody who worked with us and in my case, everyone at home too.

It's easy to see people being bullied around us and turning a blind eye, even if to a point the bullies' actions affect us too. When we think about bullying, we tend to think of children in school; sadly as I've grown older, I've come to realise, the biggest bullies you'll ever come across, appear into your life once you've grown up. My colleagues and I ranged from the ages of twenty-one to sixty-five and still found ourselves confiding in each other, our fear of those who held power over us, in our case, our boss.

The funny thing is Shale was our boss, she was in charge of us and most of us had no respect for her, that is why it was so easy to gossip about her. However, when it came to each other, the citizens of Shale's country, her workers, we respected each other, not once would we gossip about another colleague amongst ourselves. Again, I felt I had travelled back in time, back to school, except this time I was sporting a beard and had less confidence in myself than I had in me ten years ago. This was me and my friends all over again, complaining about our teacher, waiting for school to be over, to continue on with our lives. This was exactly the life I was hoping to avoid into adulthood, whilst I was still in school.

At this point in my life, I remember thinking a lot about my time in school; in first school, there wasn't much bullying of any kind from what I can remember. Boys and girls played together, most of us were just happy to get a sticker from our teachers to show off to our parents, at the end of the day. Simply finger painting, eating paper, peeing on the floor, being different, unique, that kept us happy and nobody ever made fun of each other for that and certainly never bullied each other over anything either. Once I entered middle school, things began to change; for starters, people looked down on you, if you started finger painting and eating paper. In other words, if you did anything out of the ordinary, you were ridiculed for it. Secondly, groups began to form between girls and boys, and bullies began appearing within both groups, in our heads we belonged to a world made up of males and females.

Then I entered comprehensive school and realised life was far more complicated than I first anticipated. No longer were there just a group of boys and girls but each group now had its own sub-category. Jocks, cheerleaders, nerds, bullies, goths, skaters, artists, musicians, stoners, clowns, sheep and everybody else in between, which in reality is all of us. We all feel like we don't belong in a single category, we feel like this because we don't belong in just one, we belong in many. Although I had my group of friends back in school, I always considered us the outsiders and easily labelled other groups, I wonder if people from those groups considered themselves outsiders too?

Back in school, I remember this quiet boy, he was always rather dirty, had a weird smell, was never one to keep eye contact for very long and usually hang around with his younger brother. Sadly, because of this some kids made fun of him and at times his brother too. I got on well with this kid but I never stood up for him. One day as he was walking home from school, I remember two other kids started pushing him around, his younger brother started crying and that just made the two kids enjoy what they were doing even more. I looked at my friends, I considered us to be the group who would stand up for others but in reality, we weren't, we did nothing, I did nothing.

If I were to get involved, I probably wouldn't solve the situation, I'd just paint a target of ridicule on my back. I did nothing that day and for years this poor guy found himself bullied by a group of idiots with others, like me, who were just as bad for allowing this to happen in front of us. When I was older, I found out this friend of mine had terrible parents. They neglected both him and his younger brother, who he normally took care of after school as his parents spent most of their days at the bar getting drunk.

I also remember a girl who used to cry over anything and everything; she was a nice girl but cried at least once a day. She was never really bullied by anyone in school physically but mentally we would all laugh as soon as she started crying. Others went as far as calling her names over it and many of us made fun of her, behind her back. Again, as you grow older you begin to realise everyone has their own story to tell, their own book to write, their own movie to film, their own game to play, their own song to sing and most importantly their own demons to fight. This poor little girl was abused by her mother every single day, her mother had anger issues, which she would take out on her daughter by slapping her silly for whatever reason.

These things all happen in front of us, if only we were to take the time to stop and understand where different people are coming from. I had the excuse that I didn't know better back then, I was just a child myself but now I have no excuse, I'm an adult and I promised myself I would never turn a blind eye on anyone, who I think is being bullied. Now in order to realise this, one must do something we are not used to doing much these days, one must listen to what the other person is saying, even if words are not being spoken, emojis are always visible.

On occasions, students would join our tourist information team and train alongside us before going back to school or continuing with their studies abroad at university. At first, Shale had started out as my own personal bully but as time went by, her power over control went to her head. I was and will always be her favourite victim but she had now become a bully of power. Not only did you have to do as she said, in every sense of the word but if she smelled your fear, she would thrive on it. Shale always reminded our students to always wear their tourist badge, stating they were students, on occasions as has happened with all of us, sometimes a student would forget their badge. I understand asking them to be more responsible but tearing them down for a simple mistake, especially if it has only happened once, is certainly not a way to motivate students getting a taste at life into adulthood for the first time. I remember me and another colleague trying to console a student who had broken down in tears. Vanessa was scared to tell Shale that she had forgotten her badge at home, and that was the first time it had ever happened to this poor girl.

One Saturday morning, I was based at our office at the Square with no other information officers but in the company of eight students. Shale gave me very strict instructions that she wanted all students to patrol Main Street in groups of two. I was in charge, they were my responsibility, whatever they do wrong, I did wrong, as Shale always pointed out. That morning I sent the students all out, whilst I dealt with a storm of tourists, two cruise liners had come in that day, Main Street was filled with tourists, maps were flying everywhere. Every once in a while, a pair of students would return back to the office, claiming they had walked all along Main Street. I tried to juggle things as best I could and honestly our office was full of tourists, their help every now and again was very welcomed.

After a while, even though I believed it would be better for them to continue helping me, I knew Shale might pop around as she had done in the past, hoping to catch me out. Once again, I would send the students away, others would return and I would listen to their complaints. I would deal with tourists, I would send another returning group back out, I would make copies of leaflets which had run out, I did the best that could be done in that situation. All eight students were very helpful, although two of them did fool around a bit more than others but nowhere to the point where they needed to be told off. They were simply reminded to approach a tourist or make copies, and they would do so efficiently.

The following Monday, I was called up by Shale, wanting to know how the students had performed during the weekend. I told her they had all done very well, in my opinion they all had. Shale then began to inform me, that one of the student's complained that there was not enough work for him on Saturday and that they had all been inside the office at the same time. I tried explaining to Shale how I tried to juggle everything whilst still doing my work. Shale said she wanted a full report from me based on each individual student and began giving me names and I began giving her a report on each one. I knew how Shale's mind worked, the last thing I wanted to do was give her ammunition to attack any of the students, who had all worked very well. What I did inform her of was that two of them needed a little push to get going, I felt as if she already knew this and didn't want her to catch me out, I was paranoid that this was her trap.

Shale then called me back and put me on trial against Gene and Alistair, saying she had them in front of her and they were giving her a different story. I was not angry at Gene and Alistair, I knew how Shale worked but I was very angry with Shale. Not just by the fact that I had been put on trial but she had involved these two students in our little game of cat and mouse; it was no longer a one-man show. Shale wanted a report, she forced me to give her one and then she used it to stir up trouble. I was very humiliated by this and later apologised to Gene and Alistair, who apologised back to me, even though neither of us were to blame. The sad part about all this was that I was already broken, life had already ruined me but for these students, this is the first taste at adulthood they were experiencing.

On another occasion, I was based at the cruise terminal with another student. I went outside for a cigarette, keeping an eye on the counter at all times, in case it got too busy for him alone. I then saw a tourist approach the counter angrily and started yelling at Maurice. I threw my cigarette away and went back inside, where I stood behind the tourist listening to his complaint, which had to do with the taxi drivers. Maurice rightly informed him that we did not have anything to do with the taxi service, but he could sign a complaint form and we would pass it along on his behalf. The tourist kept yelling at Maurice; I stepped in and again informed the tourist that we could not help him at the moment but if he filled out a complaint form, our boss would get back to him eventually.

The tourist then told me this had nothing to do with me and to step back, he wasn't dealing with me, I informed him that Maurice was a student and that now he was dealing with me. By this point, I had already made my way back into the office, dealing with the tourist over our counter as he stood in front of our entrance. The tourist continued to insult me and went as far as trying to punch me. I stepped back and in the heat of the moment yelled out at him. I told him to step back as he tried coming into our area. We never ended up fighting, we did get into a screaming match, the tourist never managed to lay a hand on me. Had he done so, I probably would have been in the wrong as I would have punched him back to wherever he came from.

The outcome to all this, I was questioned, Maurice was questioned and the tourist was probably given a care package. Even though Maurice's version of events matched those of mine, I was still in the wrong, I should have not got involved, I should have let the student handle this on his own. I never quite understood where Shale was coming and going from. When I asked Shale what I should have done in regards to the tourist trying to smack me, she replied by telling me, I should have just taken the punch, that would have been the professional thing to have done.

At this exact moment, I knew I would never win with my bully, even if a tourist was aggressive with a student, and I stepped in and almost got punched for helping, it was still my fault. Again, the worse part about all this wasn't that I got in trouble, it was the fact that yet again another student was caught up in our battle. I remember speaking to Maurice about this after work and him apologising for the fact that I had faced a disciplinary hearing over this. I assured him this was not his fault, we began talking and he confided that he felt as if he was still in school, he thought that when he started working, he'd be treated as an equal, none of us are.

Bullying either at school, work or even at home can be very dangerous both physically and mentally. This is a big theme in my story. After so many years, I've become very passionate about standing up against bullies not just in the workplace but between humanity as a whole, I hate bullies. I would love no less to try and put a ban on bullying worldwide but that's not happening anytime soon, especially since bullies never like to listen. My aim is to help those who will listen, those who will read, the victims, I want to help those being bullied, not only realise it but hopefully find the courage they need to fix the situation, rather than fall victim to it. Everyone matters, even the smallest can make their biggest dreams come true, we can change it all for the better, with everything we do, even you, even me, even them.

Chapter Six
The Great Depression

Depression in actuality is a modern-day disease, one rapidly increasing by generation, which also affects animals and even plants. Today's youth live a very different life to those of our ancestors; massive, rapid advances in society and sudden changes in environment do not help. The world is getting more complicated each day and evolution within the human body does not happen as rapidly. Our ancestors were not on social media yet that did not stop them from socialising with one another. Humans are social creatures; we've always worked in groups, as teamwork is an essential part of surviving. Many people no longer have close friends, we interact on social media but not face-to-face, we need physical interaction to build trust and grow relationships. This is why many of us build close relationships with our fellow workmates, although one might socialise with friends, it is rare to surpass the time one spends surrounded by colleagues at work. Bonding with other humans even releases certain hormones that reduces stress and anxiety, which helps fight depression.

In the past, depression was described as a chemical imbalance in the brain; a lack of the neurotransmitter serotonin was to blame, the feel-good chemical that gets our brain happily drunk. Brain cell growth and connections play a very important role in the phenomena that is depression. The longer a person has been depressed, the smaller their hippocampus becomes, a section of our brain that controls memories and emotion. The cells and networks literally deteriorate over time as depression increases and the hippocampus gets smaller. Social isolation will literally cause your brain to shrink, social interaction is that important, both in fighting depression and evolving as a person. When this region of the brain is regenerated and new neurons are stimulated, it allows one's mood to improve; it's not simply a weakness, which someone should get over.

When I returned back to work after my unfair dismissal, I had spent four weeks suspended, it was the first time I had ever felt lost in my adult life. At that moment, I didn't believe I'd be returning back to work, at least not until I got hold of my application form. I was so embarrassed; every time I run into a friend or family member, they would ask how my job at the cable car was working out for me. I'd reply by informing them I was no longer at the cable car, I left for another job, eagerly they would ask me where I was working now. I'd inform them, I left the cable car to begin working as an information officer and when they'd ask me if I enjoyed my new job, I'd say yes. In reality, I had found myself suspended just for a few weeks and my previous job was no longer available. I was back to where I started, exactly after I had finished school over a year ago. My colleagues were aware of everything that had happened, they also knew the facts behind this. It was now out in the open, my cannabis history was a topic of conversation amongst many.

At the beginning, when I first felt Shale's hatred towards me, I convinced myself I was being paranoid, we had never discussed what had happened, I just returned to work and started working as though it were my first day all over again. As time went on, I began losing the energy that once got me out of bed in the morning and off to work. I began to feel just as I did when I was in school, I wasn't eager to start my day anymore. Every time Shale yelled at me in front of the staff or tourists, I'd simply continue working as though nothing had happened. My colleagues around me would do the same, between them they spoke about these incidents but with me, at the beginning, they never did. Probably because I was trying to pretend that this wasn't happening, or more specifically, I was trying to convince myself that this was normal. It was normal at school; perhaps, I had misjudged adult life and this pattern of teacher and student continues throughout one's entire life.

Every morning at 8:00 am, my alarm would sound and for the life of me, I could not get out of bed. I'd stay lying there, looking at the alarm, waiting for it to be 8:30 am where finally the worry of arriving late kicked in. No time for breakfast, instead a quick shower, a search for my tie and in less than ten minutes I was ready to go. I'd say goodbye to my parents as they left for work together, Stacey and Kaylie made their way to school, I locked up, got on my motorcycle and drove to work. I always arrived there at 8:55 am, hoping to avoid any confrontation with Shale, I would wait outside, if she were not standing there waiting for me already. I would smoke a cigarette, and at 8:59 am I'd walk in through those doors, nervous of what might be waiting for me inside.

I tried dealing with the situation as best I could and mostly allowed Shale to walk all over me, obeying her silly commands in the hopes of keeping things civil. This worked against me because this made Shale believe she could treat me however she wished and get away with it. On one occasion after being accused by Shale of stealing a tourist's camera, I remember I was so frustrated, so angry, but I couldn't yell at her, otherwise I'd be giving her exactly what she wanted. I was trying to remain calm but as I sat back down at my desk, my colleagues were looking at me with pity. I felt so humiliated, so ashamed and worse, I felt tears begin to form.

I couldn't believe this, after everything I had been through at the hands of Shale, this accusation was petty yet I had finally broken. The water dam in my eyes was no longer working, tears were starting to flow through. I quickly got up and made my way to the bathroom, locked the door and immediately began crying. What was happening to me? I couldn't remember the last time I had cried, I don't think I had done so in the last ten years but all of a sudden, I couldn't control myself. Suddenly there's a knock at the door, I felt physically sick, thinking it might be Shale, I couldn't handle her again just yet, I needed time to pull myself together.

Fortunately it was not Shale, it was Chelsey, I quickly wiped my tears away. I was surprised how easily I was able to stop crying at the thought of someone seeing me, when just a few seconds ago I had no control over the water works. I opened the door, smiled at Chelsey and we sat back down at our desks, ready to hand out the next map. As I sat there greeting tourists, I was very professional but the urge to interact and be social with them was gone. No longer did I speak to tourists about my desire to write; in fact, I hadn't written in a very long time. My childhood dream had slowly slipped away from me and I hadn't even realised, luckily one can never leave the magic.

I didn't want to accept it, as hard as it was to accept I was being bullied, it was even harder to accept the fact that I was literally depressed 24/7. I had more or less given up hoping for change, after over a year of daily bullying. I was not only broken, I was used to being that way. I had become a victim and worse part was, not that I continued to allow it but rather, I learned how to accept it. I would burst out crying for no reason, as simple as it always seemed to control my tears, for the first time, I had forgotten how. I slowly began losing touch with my friends, not only had I isolated myself, I had done so by pushing people away, mainly the fact that I had become so negative.

I'd return home from work broken, at first, I was able to quickly snap out of it, a few hours after returning home. After two years, I soon began going to bed the same way I felt throughout the entire day. After work, no longer did I meet up with my colleagues for drinks, instead I'd drive straight home and once there would lock myself in my bedroom. For some reason, I couldn't handle doing anything after work, at least not until I came home and breathed. I needed to be alone before I began to interact socially after a day's bullying. I'd log onto my computer, visit Facebook, check my emails and watch a random funny YouTube video. I'd always plan to do something afterwards but bit by bit, all I ever did was stay at home. At times, I'd go for a quiet spin in my car up the Rock, I would then park my car and admire the views of Spain and Africa in the company of my monkey friends.

Slowly, I began isolating myself from the world. I lost my passion to socialise and in doing so rediscovered my passion for writing. When a person is being bullied, they tend to be so broken, that not even speaking with friends, family or even a psychologist seems helpful; in fact, it seems even more stressful. My escape from bullying was by writing, most days after work; once I was at my worst, all I would do was write. Not only would I escape my mental torture by working on my screenplays but soon I also began jotting down everything that had happened to me so far. I found that writing about my problems was very therapeutic, you're letting it out, some might wish to call it a diary, I was writing a book. Locking myself in my bedroom, away from the rest of the world, allowed me a lot of time to ruminate, look back at everything that had gone wrong in my past. If I was going to isolate myself, at least I needed to find an engaging activity to keep my focus away from the negativity, television, music, video games, nothing was working for me anymore.

Honestly when one is broken and simply wants to be alone, writing about your problems can be very relieving. It's a great way to get one strong again, to hopefully speak about their problem with others, rather than simply feel at ease writing about it. I began working on my life story, especially after I began suffering seizures. I had lost my short-term memory; fearing I would lose it all, I decided to write down everything that had happened to me so far, in case I was never able to remember it again. Those who do not enjoy writing might prefer reading and will use that as their escape, when you are sad and depressed, locked away from the world for as long as you can, it reaches a point where not even television will ease your mind. Having to use one's mind to read a story rather than watch one, allows for the victim to easily concentrate on the obstruction rather than the problem they are trying to forget. I was so embarrassedly broken, I've lacked confidence most of my adult life and that is what I most regret. I hope this story can help those in similar situations to realise this much earlier than I had.

My parents had picked up early on that I was having problems at work, it took me a while to open up to them but my mum knows me better than I know myself, she knew something was not right. My dad on the other hand believed I was making too much of a fuss over nothing. According to him, I should just go to work and be grateful I had a job to go, even if I was unhappy. As the months went past, my mum noticed I was barely going out after work. I spent most days locked in my bedroom, I was sleeping a lot, I was losing weight, I had no appetite, eventually someone finally suggested I quit and find a new job. Hearing my mum utter those words, made it feel like a real possibility, but every time I thought about my work record, that hope quickly disappeared. Eventually, my sisters, my grandmothers, my cousins, my friends, Pepe who works at the kiosk down the road from my house, everyone could tell I was depressed. When I explained why, just as me, nobody really knew what advice to give, other than to resign and find a new job or the way I saw it, give in to my bullies and run away.

At first, I never wanted to discuss my bullying at work situation with anybody but soon enough it was the only thing I could speak about. On the rare occasions that I would meet up with friends, I would spend the entire afternoon complaining about my job, how much I hated Shale and how shit life was. It was always about me, about how bad I felt, what Shale had done to me that day, I was obsessed, and in return, this bored others and to a point, even kept them away from me. Throughout school and even during my time at the cable car, I was always known for my jokes. I was always the one trying to get people to laugh, even if my jokes failed terribly at times. Now, I had become such a serious person, many did not recognise me. I didn't even recognise myself, but at the same time, I couldn't remember how or when this change in my character actually occurred. I now realise it was a slow transformation, one that began the day I returned back to work at the Gibraltar Developing Company, when I began to work my cares away.

At this point, I was feeling so pathetic, I did not have the confidence to mingle with anyone I was not familiar with already. I believed I acted very awkward all the time, I could barely look at people in the face when I spoke to them, let alone keep eye contact. I usually spoke to others whilst looking away from them, whilst trying to get through the conversation as quickly as possible. This reminds me of a visit I made to the grocery store one day after work. I hoped to buy some bread rolls before going home, and as I entered the store, I came across an old friend. I had gone to school with this girl. I had always had a very big crush on her but never said a word about it. I hadn't seen her in over seven years; there was no way I could pretend not to have noticed she was there, as I had been doing lately with everyone I recognised in town. As I walked in, our eyes met and she begun to make her way towards me. I was having a difficult time conversing with people, let alone a girl I had a crush on since middle school. I was terrified of what words would come out of my mouth.

"Nicholas," she said grinningly, what was I to say? Should I mention her name too? Should I tell her I've come hoping to find warm rolls for my tea? Should I inform her how sad I feel due to work? Before I could decide on what to say, I realised I had taken my eyes away from her, I was now looking at a fine selection of cheeses. Making a huge effort, I was able to lock eyes again and begin a conversation; unfortunately as soon as I did, my voice came out hoarsely, I had a cough stuck in my throat. I should have excused myself, coughed, cleared my throat and continue my conversation but instead, I continued talking to her as though I were imitating the Cookie Monster. Suddenly as I spoke to her, phlegm spat out of my mouth and landed right on her shoe. I hoped she hadn't realised, but she immediately looked down at her foot in disgust. I nervously coughed in her face and then bent down towards her shoe, not before hitting my face against her knee. In a panic, I disgustingly used my sleeve to wipe away the phlegm, I should have just taken the extra five seconds to grab a tissue. As I stood back up and found myself face-to-face with her again, I realised I wasn't that hungry. I turned around and without saying a single word, I walked back out of the store.

My confidence was at an all-time low. I did not go out to celebrate New Year's Eve, I could not deal or face so many people at the same time. As midnight came around, fireworks began appearing in the night sky, I stayed sitting by my computer, should I get up and look at the firework displays? This had always been my favourite part about the New Year when I was young, the fireworks that only came once a year, how could I not get up and admire the view? I didn't watch the fireworks, I kept on writing instead. I hated the fact I hadn't gone out, I just wanted the night to be over with, a new year, a new start, hopefully things would get better for me in 2010. I checked on Facebook and read everyone's New Year messages, whilst looking over their photos celebrating the occasion. Everyone was happy, everyone was excited to be around others, and my friends were all getting ready to meet up. I couldn't handle this, I switched off Facebook and continued writing my story, well into the New Year. This is not the life I wanted, not only had I wasted two years of my life, I had actually used that time to destroy myself in every sense, both emotionally and physically.

When I was young, I never could fall asleep when I laid in bed, I'd turn on my right, then moved to my left, faced upwards, crossed my legs, one hour later I was still lying awake. My mum would peak into my bedroom, find me still awake and would tell me to go to sleep, what did she think I was trying to do? For some reason, I could never fall asleep easily. I came to the conclusion that this was because I wasn't excited to start the day. I had now fallen back into that same routine. I'd lay in bed, time would pass. I'd soon check my alarm clock and would realise, I'd been in bed for over three hours, where had the time gone? As I continued to look at my alarm, I'd worry that my night was passing me by and I had yet not fallen asleep. I had to wake up early for work the next day, I had to fall asleep soon, I had already wasted over three hours trying to do so, the fear of not being able to fall asleep, only kept me awake longer.

The only times I had ever been able to sleep properly, up to that point in time, had been during my brief occupation working at the cable car between finishing school and starting at the Gibraltar Developing Company. Summer holidays from school were always the best, that was the only time in childhood that I slept like a baby at night. Was it the fact that I was excited to start the next day or the fact that I had tired myself out playing at the beach that same day? Sleeping is very important to our health, as boring as it once was for me, rest is essential in order to move along progressively in life. I had started taking on an abnormal sleeping pattern, I'd go to bed in the afternoon, wake up two hours later and work on my screenplays. By the time I went back to bed again, I could not get to sleep, when I eventually did, I had to wake up only a few hours later to start my working day. Physical activity is very important, not too long ago humans were busy in fields tending the crops all day, hunting food, building shelters; they would exercise for a minimum of four hours a day. In today's age, how much exercise does the average human get in a week? I for one was not getting any exercise, I spent most of my days either sitting on a chair, resting on a sofa or lying in bed. I was tired all the time yet unable to sleep most nights.

When you exercise, imported neurotransmitters such as dopamine and serotonin have increased activity levels in the brain. These are the same neurotransmitters that cause depression when they are at low levels, these are the same chemicals anti-depressants hope to create in the body. Why take medication when a simple walk through nature can provide you with the same effects and a nice tan? I still lived five minutes away from the Nipperish and on occasions, would visit the green area. My friends no longer came here; out of fifteen of us, I was the last one visiting. I sometimes felt silly as though I were the only one unable to move on and let go of my youth. Soon enough I realised, I had grown up in this area for the last twenty-three years of my life, this was my happy place. It was bitter sweet as every time I visited, I'd feel happy yet at the same time sad. After admiring Ashby's memorial picture, it always made me realise, how lucky I was to be alive but what a waste of a life I was leading. If I continued ahead from the Nipperish, ten minutes later I'd reach a clan of apes, some of who still recognised me from my time at the cable car. Although most of the apes I had become familiar with, resided at the top of the Rock and my path only led me midway. If I continued further away from the apes, I could walk back down to town through a different pathway with just a steep hill walk back up to my house, after a relaxing stroll through nature.

When I was young, I lived with my parents, sisters and grandparents in one big house, something I remembered very well was that my grandmother Mama Angela suffered from depression. Depression runs in my family and I was not going to give into it. I'd arrive from school to find Mama Angela asleep in her dark bedroom. Curtains blocking the light from entering her bedroom as she slept the whole day away, only to wake up and watch television during the night. Mama Angela was on a strict medication routine where she had to have a certain number of pills at certain times of the day, if her medication was not balanced, she would have terrible side effects.

Valium is considered the 'fix it' drug when it comes to anxiety and depression but it doesn't fix the situation, it merely stops you from feeling the pain. I understand relying on Valium perhaps after the loss of a loved one, a tragic accident in the family or maybe even whilst figuring out why you are anxious, if you're still unsure why. A shortcut for life if you will but only for a short period of time. After a while, you have to stop taking this magic pill and face reality; although by that point, you're so hooked on it, even your body believes it needs this in its system to survive. This was not my story, I knew where my depression came from, I knew why I was anxious. I didn't want to rely on Valium to fix my problems, I wanted to rely on me. This was not the outcome I was after, the last thing I wanted was to become hooked on pills, I needed to face my problems with a clear mind. You may be experiencing depression at any given moment in life, that doesn't mean it's part of who you are; depression comes and goes but you are always here.

Chapter Seven
A Mess over Stress

We all experience stress whether we realise it or not, it happens every single day of our lives, you can't live with it, you can't live without it. When life seems to be too much to handle, when demands start to exceed our perceived ability to cope, stress sets in. Stress is a condition that arises when there is a gap between what you need and want to do over what you feel you're able to do. Stress starts as a feeling towards certain reactions to situations, it's the body's way of making you more alert and ready to take on a challenge. When a person is stressed, they tend to be edgy, nervous, constantly anxious and at the same time irritable, angry, dizzy, weak, lightheaded and many times even violent. Everyone needs a little stress in their life to perform better but too much stress can break a person, not just in mind but in body too. You grow with stress but like depression, you can also grow out of it; if we learn to manage our stress, we can live much happier lives. The sad part about all this is that stress is not always something that can be avoided in today's society.

Stress doesn't just happen in the mind, our whole body can be affected by it, when you encounter a perceived threat or face a stressful situation. The hypothalamus, a tiny section in our brain, sets off an alarm system in our body when under stress, through a combination of nerves and hormonal signals. These systems prompt your adrenal glands to release a surge of hormones, increasing adrenaline, which increases your heart rate, elevates blood pressure and boosts energy supplies. This natural reaction is called the stress response, it enhances a person's ability to perform better, when balanced properly under pressure. The stress response helped our ancestors survive in the past, when out hunting or being hunted, but at the end of the day, they were able to switch off. Today's generation might not need to hunt or fear being hunted but stress is all around us and we can't switch off; instead, we buy fidget spinners in the hopes of masking our anxiety.

Working for a bully meant stress slowly crept into my life and eventually moved in with depression, helping destroy me from inside out. I was lucky growing up, I had a very easy childhood, my parents were always there for me. I had a close family to support me and I was always well behaved at school, never missed handing in my homework on time. The only stressful time in my life I remember as a child was leaving my homework for the last minute over the weekend. My bedtime was at 8:30 pm and at 7:00 pm, I liked to sit in front of the TV and watch *The Simpsons*; sadly, my homework was never done by that time. I'd watch *The Simpsons*, whilst stressing over my homework, which most of the time, due to lack of concentration, I got wrong, D'oh! Stress as a child is simply a word you hear grownups speak about; for the longest time, I thought it was a form of Funko Pop! as everyone seemed to be collecting it.

At first, Shale's bullying made me very angry, but I would always keep my anger to myself. The greatest way to relieve stress is by punching your bully right in the face, obviously that was not an option for me. I kept the anger buried deep inside me, I did not let go of it, I did not rebel, I did not shout, I didn't even cry, this was my biggest mistake. If I've learned anything through all this, it's that it is very dangerous to keep your anger bottled up for very long, eventually you'll explode; if not, your health will begin to suffer. Obviously, we cannot all go around hitting others to release ourselves from our anger but shouting, crying and even a little rough sex, does help release parts of it. Anger is mostly released when one is stressed, if we can manage our stress, we can control our anger.

After two years of bullying, stress now lived with me constantly. I would go to bed with it and then wake up in the morning still covered in stress. I was constantly anxious, my nerves had gotten the best of me. I remember it got to a point where my finger would tremble as I tried to guide tourists along a map. The tourists would actually ask me if I was alright, I'd take a deep breath and concentrate on controlling my finger. I've always been a nervous person, even before all this ever happened; my parents tell me all the time, that as a child, I drove them crazy, I probably still do. I speak very quickly, I'm always fidgeting and constantly on the move. I remember when I was thirteen years old, my grandparents surprised my family with a trip to Disney World. I was so happy and excited, Disney World is every kid's dream, especially when all you've ever known is a giant Rock, with Hollywood being located in the same country. Suddenly my parents, my sisters and my grandparents broke out laughing, all whilst looking and pointing at me. What was happening? Was this a joke? Had my grandparents just pranked me? Was I going to the dentist instead? Did Mickey Mouse not like me? Apparently, I was so nervously excited that my eyebrows began to twitch at a very fast pace and I could not control them, no matter how hard I tried.

I've realised that when I'm excited, my eyebrows twitch but when I'm stressed, I lose control of my hands, they begin to shake uncontrollably. Once during a Christmas work dinner, which I could not believe I had attended, I found myself sat next to Shale. I realised my hand had begun shaking; I was trying to hide it, but soon enough I'm asked to pour the wine. As I grabbed the bottle, I realised I couldn't perform this simple task, my hand was out of my control, I ended up spilling the wine all over the table. It was starting to get embarrassing, many times tourists would ask me to take pictures of them, this soon became something I dreaded doing. My trick for controlling shaking hands was by clenching my fists tightly and breathing in through my nose deeply and out my mouth, until I felt the muscles in my fists relax.

A constant pain, just above my left eye would begin throbbing every once in a while. I'd close my eyes, breathe deeply through my nose and out my mouth, eventually the pain would pass. Growing up, I always heard how concentrating on your breathing helps reduce stress. I used to think it was an expression used simply hoping to make one feel better but it does in fact work very well. I used to be a smoker at the time, it usually took me two seconds to breathe in and out, I didn't have time for breathing, I'd concentrate on it, if I ever took up meditation. The truth is we're all breathing all the time, but in reality, we are not breathing properly, we breathe too quickly, which does not allow enough air to fully reach our lungs. I decided this technique of deep breathing worked very well, the difference between ordinary breathing is that instead it's over in less than two seconds, this is how we've been doing it our whole lives. I decided I was going to concentrate on my breathing at all times and not only when it was needed, it might sound stupid and it's much harder to achieve than you might think. If you can rewire your brain, extending the process of breathing from two seconds to four, I promise you will begin feeling much better for it.

Chest pains were something I always associated with elderly people, but at twenty-three years, I was already experiencing severe chest pains myself. My heart would begin racing, my breathing techniques no longer worked, and soon enough, I found myself having a panic attack. I remember the first time my mum tried helping me with a panic attack, she ran into the kitchen and brought out a plastic bag, she wanted me to breathe into it. I was convinced that didn't work, my mum had been watching too many movies. Surprisingly enough, during a panic attack, when natural breathing techniques no longer seem to work, breathing into a plastic bag is actually very helpful. It forces us to rebreathe the carbon dioxide we just exhaled, this increases the carbon dioxide levels in our blood, which in turn, slows our breathing rate and helps us relax.

By the third-year, crying had become as normal as blinking to me. I've never been one to cry but as of that year, my eyes had become a waterslide, which I could only control when around others. I was constantly crying when I was alone and was perhaps more embarrassed about this than the bullying itself. I was not releasing my anger, I was not shouting, I was not yelling, I was keeping it all inside. This anger had to be released and finally it had turned into physical tears, hoping to escape through my eyes. When a person cries, hormones from the brain trigger a tear response from the glands in our eyelids, crying is an emotional response sent from your brain, exposing your sadness to those around. I've always hated myself for crying, I felt it was a sign of weakness, it's your body's way of healing, one needs to get over their ego and allow yourself to heal, listen to what your body is telling you.

I was tempted to resign each morning. I had now been suffering from severe insomnia for over a year. I could not go to sleep as every time I closed my eyes, I knew the next time I opened them, I'd have to get ready for work. I had also stopped using my car and motorcycle, I was mostly travelling back and forth on foot now. Many times, whilst driving to and from work, I would feel this sensation of déjà vu then accompanied by a feeling of depression so strong that my body would become paralysed as though the depression were sitting on my shoulders, weighing me down physically. This went on for months, I had begun seeing doctors because of it, they offered me two alternatives, Valium and a medical certificate of absence due to depression and anxiety. I accepted the second but refused the first.

Valium is a prescription medication used to treat anxiety and depression. It belongs to a group of drugs called benzodiazepines, which work by reducing the activity of nerves within the brain, common side effects includes tiredness, drowsiness and weakness. I knew what the problem was, I was overstressed, I needed to change my situation, I should have removed myself from the problem but truthfully, I feared more the failure than the stress. After everything I had witness my Mama Angela go through, I was not about to fall into the same trap; I was determined to relieve my stress naturally and not medically prescribed. If I truly wanted to get rid of my stress, I should have resigned the moment my health was put into question by my superiors.

Both Shale and Darcello began questioning the authenticity of my medical certificates. Shale began complaining that they usually came with a stamp and mine didn't. Darcello suggested to me, that I did not even visit my doctor, how did I hand in medical certificates for stress? According to both of them, I was clearly not stressed and simply hoping to find an excuse to miss work. When I did hand in a medical certificate, Shale would always be quick to announce to everyone, that I was once again away on stress, so they should get ready to cover my weekend shifts. I was not taking holidays, I was taking leave because I was stressed, losing my mind, having panic attacks and becoming very ill yet I was made to feel as if I was not a team player. Every time I returned from being away on stress leave, I would cover the weekend shift for all those who had covered for me in my absence. Most times whilst I was away on stress, Shale would phone my house, making sure I was at home. I could not seem to get away from my bully, not even in the comfort of my house, it reached the point that I would panic every time the phone ringed.

I decided to ask my doctor to write a letter for me, so that I could prove to both Darcello and Shale that I did in fact go to visit a doctor every time I handed them a certificate. With my letter, I went to Darcello's office and informed him, I had a letter from my doctor, proving my medical certificates were real. Darcello would not accept my letter, apparently my doctor hadn't spoken to either himself or Shale, "How had he come to the conclusion that I was stressed?" I am as confused as you. Darcello denied to accept my letter and I was forced to leave and mail it to him by post, hoping to make sure it was added into my file.

My Mama June is a very religious woman. The last time I read the bible, I ended up writing a sci-fi action movie; we're both on different pages, when it comes to God. Mama June would always remind me, that she had prayed for me and urged me to do the same for myself, it would help me feel much better. The problems I was facing, had to be tackled in an office, sitting in a room, praying to someone I've never met, asking for help, did not seem like the most constructive use of my time. Mama June however once told me, if I did not feel comfortable praying, I should just meditate, I should think quietly to myself and so I did. Just like writing when you pray or rather meditate, you're also acknowledging your problems, you are confronting them head on, even within your own thoughts but the secret is, our thoughts have more power over us than we're aware.

This was my first introduction to meditation, many people always recommended to try it, yoga too, I never quite understood the difference. Yoga relates to the body, it is a physical act of healing one's physical pains, whilst meditation concentrates on healing the mind, a mental act to achieve final goal of recognising supreme power in one's inner self. There is no way to practise yoga yet alone properly meditate, if one is constantly stressed. In order to achieve results, one must learn to let go of their anxiety, their anger, their fears, their bullies. I could not find the courage to resign, as much as I practised meditation, all it did was help me relax, not achieve a greater understanding of myself. Mama June was the reason I first took up meditation, and I was the reason she can now be found on Facebook.

Insomnia had become my new late-night habit, and I couldn't seem to crack it. I would lay awake in bed all night at times, going to work the next day feeling exhausted. Sleep deprivation is our most silent killer, bears don't seem to have this problem, perhaps hibernation should be carefully looked into. When I did manage to fall asleep, my brain would go into overdrive. I'd spend the whole night dreaming, so vividly, that the next day, I'd wake up feeling as though I had spent all night watching television. Even when I slept, I woke up tired, my mind was working non-stop, even when I did manage to rest my body. When we sleep, we're not only resting and recharging our bodies, we're resting our minds too, recharging our brain, allowing it to cool down. In my case, my mind had found a mind of its own, my head was in constant pain, I could not put my brain in shut down mode, not whilst meditating, not whilst sleeping, not even when binge watching *Prison Break*. Lack of sleep can cause one to feel ill, hallucinate and if gone on for long enough, can even begin to affect one's memory.

My short-term memory soon began to fail me; it became very difficult for me to remember telephone numbers, new names, list of items. If it had not been locked in there before in the past, chances are I'd forget seconds later. The stress hormone cortisol can hurt your memory, messing with your sleeping pattern also plays a part. Sleeping is the time when memory consolidation happens in our brain, if we do not sleep properly, our brain can't rewire itself properly either. Soon enough every form of interaction in my life became a challenge. I could not open the door to leave the house, my anxiety would not allow me to face the world. When I finally found the courage to open that door, I had forgotten where it was, I was planning to go.

I had already spent almost two years unable to sleep at nights, dizzy, light headed and severely depressed but as of late, it was all becoming much worse. I would constantly be waking up at night, always dehydrated and had to walk downstairs to the kitchen for a drink. I'd go to the kitchen for a glass of water and as I tried to make my way back to my bedroom, my legs would collapse on me. Slowly my vision would fade inwards and would later find myself waking up on the floor a few moments later. I was having mild seizures but was unaware of this; in fact at the time, I wasn't even realising I was blacking out, all I knew was that somehow, I was losing my mind. Slowly, I was losing control of the one thing I cherished the most, the tool I used to write, create stories, escape reality; over long term if your mind and body are constantly on edge, you may face health problems.

The rising rate in suicide is alarming, as depression grows and stress increases, sometimes taking your own life, might seem like the only way out. This is where psychology fits into the equation, always speak to someone when you're feeling this low; when thoughts of suicide sneak into your mind, make sure you start talking with anyone willing to listen. The danger with suicide is that many of us do not realise we are tempting with the idea until it is too late. If you start wishing that you were dead yet knowing you would not have the courage to go through with it, this is when you must realise, you need help. The more time you spend wishing you were dead, the stronger your depression becomes until finally, what you once wished would happen, turns into something you actually hope to make happen.

Many of us turn to anti-depressants when we feel depressed and anxious, the unfortunate part about pharmaceutical medications are the side effects, especially the one that might cause suicidal tendencies, which happen to be most of them. Every medication my doctors prescribed for me had dangerous side effects, what's the point of taking something, which you hope will make you feel better yet might have consequences that make you feel worse? Medication is not the answer, when helping to deal with suicidal thoughts, speaking, exercising, reducing depression and anxiety, meditation not medication, that is the key.

Chapter Eight
Introducing Epilepsy

Epilepsy is the world's most common serious brain disorder; it isn't a one-off diagnosis, it can severely damage people in terms of their capacity to live meaningful, independent lives. Epilepsy is a neurological disorder that effects the nervous system, a disturbance of electrical energy in which brain activity becomes abnormal, causing seizures or periods of unusual behaviour, sensations and sometimes loss of awareness. Over sixty million people suffer from epilepsy worldwide, half the time the cause behind it is unknown. Epilepsy can develop in any person at any age; it is usually most common between babies and the elderly, when one's brain is most vulnerable. Something as simple as lack of oxygen reaching the brain, can cause one to develop epilepsy, as well as many other factors including kidney failure, tumours, strokes and even stress. Epilepsy is a result of injuries and chemical imbalances in the brain, anything that injures the brain can lead to epilepsy, it doesn't always have to be a physical bang on the head.

Not only does stress produce new hormones and chemicals sent to our brain, it also plays with the sizes of different regions in our brain too. Stressed endured seizures are all too common, stress causes you to feel depression, suffer insomnia, over think, none of which is good for a healthy mind. A person who suffers from epilepsy, usually claim stress as the main trigger for their seizures; however many times, those who do not have epilepsy can suffer a similar experience. Psychogenic Non-Epileptic Seizures can occur not by abnormal electrical charges in the brain but by psychological stress factors the patient is not fully aware of.

Thoughts and feelings have impact on our physical being, unresolved stressors usually manifest as physical symptoms, headaches, skin rashers, ulcers, shaking blackouts that resemble seizures and even tears fall into this category. The subconscious brain (below consciousness) does not treat time the way that the conscious brain does and all psychological issues can live on.

Perhaps, something happens today to bring back feelings from yesteryear, which can result in Psychogenic Non-Epileptic Seizures from unresolved and psychological tension dating back to your past.

Remembering is mental time travelling, picturing something already seen. Déjà vu is the feeling of having a strong sensation that an event, experience or person currently being experienced in the present has already been experienced in the past. Neuroglial dysfunction can also play a role in déjà vu. I came to realise that this was one of the earliest signs my body was using, to warn me of what was to come. By late 2011, my déjà vu sensations had become an almost daily recurrence and were each time stronger than the last. The strangest thing about all this, was when I'd feel a sensation of déjà vu in the present, regarding something I had never experienced in the past, my brain was sending me confused mixed signals.

On one occasion, I remember feeling a sensation of déjà vu as I walked past where I once used to live, when I was first born. My parents and I lived in a small house, located at the bottom of a long row of steps, leading up to what locals refer to as 'the jungle'. By the time I was three years old, after Stacey had been born, we all moved to my grandparent's house, where we stayed for many years. I was only three when we left that house. I didn't really have any memories from there, and I literally never passed through the area after that. The day I finally did, I felt a sensation of déjà vu which made me feel very sad, I suddenly burst out into tears. All my déjà vu sensations were always accompanied by sadness and soon enough, I could feel these sensations, not only affecting my brain but taking over my body too.

On other occasions, I remember driving my motorcycle back home, I drove along Queens Way, a road I travelled every day, on my way to and from work. Every time I reached the end of the road, before turning at the roundabout, I'd pass under a specific tree, shedding its leaves through autumn, this visualisation always caused me to experience déjà vu. My body would begin to weigh me down, a strong feeling of depression came with this sensation. A depression so intense that it seemed to weigh me down physically and almost paralyse me; it got so bad once, I had to park my motorcycle on the side of the road and walked home. I never understood why I always experienced déjà vu at the same time and spot every day, if I did not travel that road, I did not experience any sensation. What was more confusing was that other than having driven and walked by that area hundreds of times, it had no significant meaning to my past and isn't that what déjà vu is all about?

Each time my déjà vu sensation got stronger, I felt as if my brain was gaining weight, I probably shouldn't have eaten so many McDonalds upside down. The heavier my brain began to feel, the faster my body begun paralysing on me; luckily, my sensation would pass before I completely remained without the ability to move. The most common way to experience déjà vu is by reliving something from your childhood, unremembered until you actually experience it again. Examples of this include running into an old teacher, roaming your school corridors, an old toy you once played with or watching the opening theme song from a childhood show you once watched.

Insomnia had now taken over my life but when I did manage to sleep, constant dreaming would keep my mind awake all night. Soon enough, I began waking up at night feeling dizzy, disoriented, dehydrated, confused and a tingling sensation all throughout my body. Many times, after struggling to find the strength to get out of bed and make my way to the kitchen, my vision would begin to fade and blur. My remedy, when feeling like this, was always to lay on the kitchen floor, the cold tiles against my skin always made me feel better. Other times, I would blackout on my way back to my bedroom. At this point in my life, all this was new to me; never in a million years would I have thought, I was experiencing epileptic seizures, I thought that only happened when exposed to flashing lights. Some times after waking up at night, I'd end up throwing up, I knew stress was not good for the body but I never expected it to affect me this much. I was unaware at the time but I was experiencing mild seizures during my sleep, when my brain was most vulnerable, when I had no control over it.

Seizures are a result of epilepsy, it occurs when a burst of electrical impulses in the brain escape their normal limits. They spread to other regions of the brain and create an uncontrollable storm of electrical neuron activity. The electrical impulses can be transmitted to the muscles to cause twitches or convulsions. There are six main types of generalised seizures, all involve loss of consciousness and normally happen without warning. My first big convulsive seizure occurred at a restaurant in London; when I woke up, I was told what had happened to me, I didn't believe them. I had never had a seizure in my life, I had no idea what my waiter was talking about. When I returned back home to Gibraltar, I informed my family what had apparently happened, we shrugged it off, as if the waiter were probably confusing this with a simple British panic attack.

That same year my youngest sister Kaylie and her boyfriend Nicky had given birth to my nephew Aiden. Finally, some light in my mostly dark and depressing world; at that point in life, all I ever felt was anger and sadness, finally feeling love and joy, every time I was around my nephew was a welcome change in emotion. One day when they came home to visit, the three of us were sat in the living room, whilst Kaylie held Aiden I was busy making funny noises, keeping him entertained. That is as much as I can remember, according to Kaylie, I suddenly froze, continued staring blankly ahead, a few moments later I collapsed onto the floor. I began trembling, twitching, moving my arms and jaw in ways that one cannot imitate unless under a seizure, finally I began bleeding from the mouth.

The next thing I remember was two men were looking down at me, with one of them pointing a flashlight into my eyes. I was furious, who the hell are these two? Get away from me! How did you get into my house? I was told to calm down, who the fuck are they to tell me to calm down? I had woken up disoriented but mostly angry, I had never felt anger this strong before. I realised Kaylie and my mum were crying by the corner, Aiden was in his playpen, an ambulance was waiting outside and my dad arrived through the door. What was happening? According to the paramedic, I had experienced a form of seizure, perhaps my waiter had been right back in London, maybe I should go back for a second course. It was time to go to hospital but I wasn't going anywhere, all I knew was that I had been playing with my nephew and now two random men wanted me to leave with them in an ambulance? Eventually, I did end up going with them, they took me down to hospital and along the way, I suffered another seizure.

I woke up the next day in a hospital bed, *Where am I?* I had no idea, all I knew was I needed a cigarette and for some reason I was fuming. Again, anger had taken over my body and I had no idea why but soon enough, I began to realise my tongue was in agony. I looked in the mirror and realised, my tongue was covered in holes. A nurse then came into the room and explained I had suffered multiple grand mal seizures, a term used for seizures that take control of one's whole body, I was being kept for observation. Apparently during my seizures, a scar had appeared on my brain, excuse me? Were they saying I now had physical damage done to my brain? The anger that took over me was like none I had ever experienced before, I knew whose fault this was, I knew why I was so ill, I wasn't going to let my bullies get away with this.

Waking up from a seizure has many mental and physical side effects but for me personally, having bitten my tongue to shreds during my seizures was always the worse part, the pain was intolerable, I'd hate to be a shark in that position. Every time I spoke, I could feel the air passing through these holes, why people get tongue rings, I'll never understand. The pain was always most intense as soon as I'd wake up from a seizure; three days later, my tongue would heal properly and unfortunately for many, I was able to speak again. My kidneys were tested, my brain had been scanned, blood had been taken and after a few weeks my results arrived, everything seemed healthy, other than my new cool brain scar, the cause of my seizures could not be determined.

Three MRI scans of my brain showed a minimal pathomorphological alteration in the paraventricular region of the right temporal lobe exact in the hippocampus region, a pulse of electrical neurons had fried a small section of my brain. This new scar on my hippocampus, probably contributed to the epileptic seizures I was experiencing, as well as related symptoms. Including memory dysfunction and emotional instability as well as *déja vu* episodes, everything which stems from this region of our brain. As my seizures progressed, my memory began to fail me; at first, I was simply suffering from short-term memory loss, soon enough my long-term memory began to suffer too. Most of what I had learned in school is now lost to me, does this have to do with epileptic attacks or the fact that what we learn in school, is not something we really use much once we leave? At one point, I remember waking up after a seizure and unable to remember my parent's names. I knew they were my parents, but I couldn't remember their names. I knew that was something I should know because I was embarrassed to ask them...Stanley and Eileen! A few moments later, their names came to me.

After I was first hospitalised, my mum became my new shadow; she was terrified of leaving me out of her sight, for a while she even missed work to stay at home with me. It reached a point that I felt suffocated, if I were going to have a bath, I would need to tell my mum, and she would sit outside against the door, playing on her computer. One day, I finally told her, she had to stop worrying so much about me, she replied that if I were to see myself during a seizure, I would understand why she was so worried and protective.

A few days later, my mum went back to work; a few days after, I had another seizure. By this point, I more or less had an idea when a seizure was preparing to take over my body. First my palms would become sweaty, I'd begin to feel as though I were drunk, light-headed, a tingling sensation would begin at the back of my head and slowly move to the top of it. Eventually, my vision would become blurry from the outside in and seconds or minutes later, I would have a seizure. I had many false alarms, mistaking panic attacks for upcoming epileptic attacks; however, this specific day I had a feeling this was no false alarm.

I knew if I called my mum at work and told her I felt as though I might have a seizure, she would come straight home. I was hesitant to call her at first but I finally did and after that, again I have no idea what happened. According to my mum, she arrived home to find me lying on the floor, next to our fireplace and I was turning blue like a whale, I had stopped breathing. My mum says she'll never forget that image; she thought I was dead, a dead whale in front of your fireplace is never pretty.

Again, I woke up in a hospital bed, having no idea how I got there, this time I was officially diagnosed as epileptic. Just another problem to add to my list of life fails, another obstacle to stop me from achieving the life I wanted. How was I supposed to live my life, if I was afraid of having a bath in case I had a seizure and drowned in my own watery filth. Worse yet when experiencing an epileptic seizure, a person can lose bowel or bladder control and shit or piss themselves in the process, talk about embarrassingly inconvenient. I now lived my life worried that I would begin shaking in town and start bleeding through my mouth and shitting through my ass in front of a live audience.

If I went to the beach, I had to take a swimming buddy as my greatest fear was always drowning during a seizure. My peaceful strolls through nature, towards the Nipperish soon became something I aimed to do as quickly as possible, as this was generally a secluded area, if I blacked out there, it would probably take a few days until somebody found me. Writing was no longer an option, my memory, my concentration, no longer allowed me to create stories. I was completely losing my independence, my life, my future, at least I had bullies, who kept me motivated to get through this, I wanted justice.

Growing up, I had never spent a night at hospital apart from the time my tonsils were removed at age six. In the last two months, I had been hospitalised twice and every time I woke up, I didn't remember why; as time progressed, I had many more visits to the hospital. At first when I'd visit the doctor, all they had to go by was my experience; they all suggested I reduce my stress, in the hopes that these stress endured episodes would stop, eventually I became epileptic. The difficult part was we couldn't figure out how to stop my seizures and although not every day did I have a physical seizure, as I explained to the doctors, I felt my brain seizuring out all the time. The sad part about all this was that at the time, the neurology specialist only ever visited Gibraltar for a few days, once every six months. I couldn't wait that long for the specialist's next visit to Gibraltar, I felt as though I was losing my mind by the second. My eyes have always been sensitive to light, but it gradually reached a point where I couldn't step foot outside without my sunglasses, otherwise I'd be forced to close my eyes, at times light became so bright.

Grand mal seizures are normally followed by a so-called postictal recovery time, which can take minutes to hours. During the recovery time, the memory can be affected partially. Symptomatic epilepsies due to lesions in brain areas, in which one has to localise their memory centres, the temporal lobes, hippocampus, parts of thalamus, can lead to longer memory restrictions after seizures. Memory loss can be a late consequence after decades living with epilepsy and antiepileptic medication.

I tried different forms of medication, nothing seemed to work. I began taking Lamicital (lamotrigine) and slowly began to see improvements. It took a while to begin taking effect on my brain; at first, it left me drowsy the whole day, I had to take two tablets in the morning, I felt stoned all the time. By the time the effects started to wear off, I had to take another two tablets at the start of the evening, I'd go to bed feeling drunk. I'd spend my whole day unable to concentrate, feeling nauseous and worst yet all whilst at work. Eventually by early 2013, after almost a year of playing around with the right dosage of medication, I found an alternative solution.

Lamicital is an anti-epileptic medication, also called an anticonvulsant, it can also be used to delay moods in adults with bipolar disorder and manic depression. The only downside with taking Lamicital, is that like all prescribed medication, it can come with some very nasty side effects. In this case, you had a life-threatening rash, brain inflammation, behavioural changes, depression, anxiety, restlessness, hyperactivity, suicidal thoughts…was it worth taking the risk? I was already so broken, I didn't want anything fuelling me to do anything stupid, anything cowardly but at the same time, I needed these seizures to stop. Lamicital helped me control my seizures but as is my thought process, I did not want to rely on this forever, I wanted to fix myself naturally, I wanted to cure my epilepsy.

If you ever begin to feel a seizure coming on, if time allows always try to find the person closest to you. Breathing, we all do it all the time, we do it without thinking, it is that important but in order to hopefully prevent or reduce a seizure, one must concentrate on their breathing. I always found it most helpful to lay with my back against the floor, with my knees bent, allowing my feet to remain touching the ground. I would then begin to breathe deeply, for around five seconds and then back out through my nose again. This didn't always stop the seizures but at times, did slow it down long enough for help to arrive.

If you find yourself in the presence of somebody experiencing a seizure, protect them from injury, keep them from falling, guide them gently to the ground but most importantly do not hold them down. Try to position the person on their side, to allow fluid to leak out the mouth instead of being swallowed, make sure to clean them if they lose bowel control, it's all very embarrassingly smelly. During my two years living with epileptic seizures, my neurons were all over the place, creating fake hallucinations and allowing for lucid dreaming. I considered it a spiritual journey yet at the same time, one could argue, that I was simply losing my mind.

Chapter Nine
The Dreaming Connection

Dreams are visions but only mental illusions and dreams have nothing to hide, whilst we are sleeping, at a certain point, the subconscious mind is able to communicate with the conscious mind. A unique type of electrical activity occurs during a certain stage of a person's sleep, neurotransmitters are sent from one part of our brain to another. Activity most of us are never awake to experience, therefore unable to control. Dreams are successions of images, ideas, emotions and sensations that occur involuntarily in the mind during stages of sleep. The scientific study of dreams is called oneirology; dreams can last for a few seconds or as long as thirty minutes, all of us under its spell, we know that it's probably playing within the magic.

A healthy sleep cycle progresses in various stages, each with distinctive brain wave patterns. During the earliest phases of sleep, we are still relatively awake and alert, groggy, one may experience strange and extremely vivid sensations known as hypnagogic hallucinations. We can also find ourselves experiencing a slight jerk in body, these are our muscles getting ready to shut down. The next phase releases surges of electrical activity as our brain tries to disengage from the waking state and descend deeper into sleep. The brain produces what are known as beta waves, as the brain begins to relax and slow down, slower waves known as alpha waves, followed by theta waves are produced. Slowly, our body temperature begins to decrease, our heart rate slows down, our breathing becomes more regular, our blood pressure drops, our muscles relax and we become less responsive to noise and activity around us. We are achieving the goal of meditation, to relax, slow down one's body and mind, whilst we are falling asleep.

REM sleep is the final stage of sleeping, our body becomes relaxed and immobilised, our brain activity becomes more rapid and our eyes begin moving rapidly behind our eyelids, we experience Rapid Eye Movement (REM). During deep sleep is when our brain waves are slow, strong and synchronised. Most dreaming takes place during the REM stage, when blood flow to the brain increases, electrical activity parallels a state of high alertness, and the eyes move as though scanning a scene. On average, it usually takes the body ninety minutes to reach REM sleep, this is why one can never give up on meditation after twenty minutes, it takes time to relax your body and achieve a free state of mind. During our night cycle, we do not always remain in this stage of sleep, the phases of sleeping can begin to work in reverse, which is why most of us, find ourselves waking up in the middle of the night. You can't get out of the car whilst in fifth gear, you slowly have to shift gears until you are able to stop the car and step out safely. This is why sometimes people can experience being paralysed upon waking up, their mind has awoken before their muscles are active.

The neurotransmitter acetylcholine is a common factor linking sleep, dreaming, learning and memory. Brain wave frequencies soon become similar during REM sleep as they had whilst we were awake and alert. In both states, electrical activity is high and the brain appears to be actively processing information. When asked what a person dreamt, the results are usually unreliable; we normally forget about 95% of our dreams, ten minutes after having it, if you wake up hours later, you probably don't even remember you had been dreaming. This is why we tend to remember nightmares (bad dreams) more often than not, these are the visuals that wake us up soon after. Strongest felt dreams are anxiety, anger, fear, this wakes us up; when we have nice, calming dreams, this puts us into a deeper sleep of peacefulness and relaxation.

The subconscious mind only becomes accessible whilst we are sleeping, during deep meditation, a part of our brain that can only work, when the body has shut down and we no longer have control of our conscious mind. When the subconscious mind begins to activate, it begins sorting out memories from our pasts. Our brain is performing a form of reverse learning, getting rid of information that is unnecessary. Brains can be overrun by unneeded useless connections, unnecessary thinking you don't need whilst awake. Your brain is taking the time to do, what many don't, it is rebooting our computer, cleaning out our memory files, in order to continue working properly. Dreams result from our brain's need to create memories in order to function properly, whilst removing others in the process.

Many times, whilst dreaming, it is the last time we experience something that has ever happened to us yet since we're sleeping, we don't even remember experiencing the final thought. These electrical impulses created by the subconscious mind are detected by our conscious mind, which freaks out, has no idea what is happening, and like all of us teach it to do, it tries to rationalise what is being processed. Our brain tries to make up a story from what we're familiar with, what is stored in our daily memories, that is why dreams seem so weird, it's like playing Chinese whisper inside the brain. Dreams are always so absurd because the visual is coming from your conscious mind, the animator, whilst the information, the story is coming from your subconscious mind, the writer. The two are working together to tell you a story, that is why you should always look behind the visualisation and always focus on the meaning, when it comes to following your dreams.

Imagine buying a new phone yet all your contacts, pictures, files and information are stored in your old phone, on a simple memory drive. A person can remove the memory drive from their old phone and insert it into their new phone, hoping to retrieve their past information. Sometimes if your new device is too advanced, you will have a hard time unlocking all those contacts, pictures, files and information, you hope to remember. This does not mean this information is not stored inside your phone, it simply means you can't access it, not without a little rewiring. If we're lucky, maybe some pictures manage to sneak their way through, some files might open, some contacts might show up but in order to restore all that information, you have to work at it.

For the longest time, I was no longer experiencing dreams or at least not remembering even parts of any of them. I'd stay hours awake at night in bed, hoping to fall asleep; when I finally did fall asleep, the slightest noise would wake me up again. By morning, I had probably woken up two or three times at night. I was never reaching deep sleep, my mind and sleeping pattern barely allowed time for REM sleep to take over. When you have trouble reaching REM sleep, this allows you to forget, REM sleep is when the mind is asleep, not just the body; if one does not fully reach this phase of sleeping, the mind will suffer. Mood disorders and an irregular sleeping pattern keep a person from reaching deep sleep, which results in mental disorders. Dreams keep us healthy, sleeping is important, dreaming is healthier, you are in a deeper sleep. Dreams had become a thing of the past for me, until I developed epilepsy and began dreaming in ways I never had before.

Normally when one dreams, we are unaware of the fact that we are dreaming, no matter how crazy a dream might be. You might be dancing the tango with a crocodile on the wing of an aeroplane and yet until you wake up, you do not realise you were just dreaming. I remember one of my earliest recurring nightmare as a kid, having a green slime monster chase me through my bedroom. On occasions, my head would come detached from my body, I would nervously call my body to pick up my head, hoping we could make a run for it, before the slime monster caught up to us. Even after waking up, I still wasn't sure if this was a nightmare or not, I would always touch my head, making sure it was still sitting on my shoulders. Dreams can feel very real yet sadly most of the time, we are not aware of the fact that we are simply in a dream.

In this nightmare of mine, which felt so real, my point of view did not come from my eyes, I was in fact watching myself as if I were sitting on a sofa, watching a television screen. A slime monster was chasing me, my head was on the floor, my body was moronically kicking me out of its way, as it tried to pick me up, yet I still thought it was real. Fair enough, dreams are tricky, now the fact that I was seeing my own head rolling on the floor should have triggered something into realising, this was not reality. This happens to all of us, once we wake up, if we remember the dream, we feel idiotic for not having realised, it was only a dream in the first place. Other times a dream can be so soothing you wish it had been real, especially when you dream about those you love who have passed away.

One night, whilst I was sleeping, I finally began to dream, I was very excited, I hadn't recalled a dream in over two years, this excitement I was experiencing within my own dream. I was completely aware this was a dream, the moment it began, I looked around and found myself in a garden, one I had never seen before. I began walking around, the energy of happiness and excitement flowed through my whole body. I knew I was walking around in a dreamt-up garden, anything could happen. Although I knew I was sleeping, it all felt so real and very familiar, a sensation of déjà vu came upon my body, I was experiencing déjà vu whilst I was sleeping, my conscious mind was reacting. This place looked familiar, almost unreal, it was too soon to know where but it was a place I felt close to my soul.

I was giddy like a child, fruit trees grew all around, flowers were large and blue, leaves were green, sky was orangish, water was purplish, I could see life moving below the river. It was a visual I had never experienced before but still remember as if I had returned from that dream only yesterday.

When I finally woke up, although the dream had seemed so peaceful, I now realised I was covered in sweat and completely dehydrated. I had just experienced a mild epileptic seizure just prior to my dream. At that time, I was still unaware that a few months later I would suffer grand mal seizures, I wasn't even aware I had developed epilepsy. During my early days of epilepsy, after my mild seizures in bed, I would remain completely unconscious, I would immediately reach a state of REM sleep. Unfortunately, my dehydration would immediately cause me to wake up soon after, worse part being my muscles were still in REM sleep, they were inactive, I was paralysed. All I could do was remain in bed, thinking about my dream, wishing I could go back there someday, waiting for my muscles to begin working again, allowing me to start moving. The fact that I was reaching deep sleep so quickly and waking up from it even faster, without shifting gears, meant I was not only conscious during my dreams, I was able to recall them very clearly.

When a person reaches a state of REM sleep, the production of many different chemicals within our body causes our muscles to stop working, you can dream about flying, running, fighting and your body doesn't move. Our muscles become locked in order to protect us from reacting to our brain, seeing as the subconscious mind is in control. This is why people sometimes sleep walk, their mind is in a state of REM sleep, their subconscious mind has taken over but the muscles are still awake, allowing your subconscious mind to control your actions. The opposite involves your mind waking up before your muscles, you can be completely conscious without the ability to move, your muscles are still in REM sleep, causing you not to regain movement for a short while.

As the nights continued, so did the dreams, sometimes I found myself in different places, interacting with different people and experiencing different sensations. Every dream was different, although to me, most of them appeared to be different areas, of the same location, the colour of the sky never changed. What all my dreams shared in common, was how lucidly I experienced each one. When I'd wake up, I would remember each one so vividly, as though I had just finished watching an episode of my favourite show on television. I'd remember the faces I spoke with, every little detail from a scar to a beauty spot, and most of these people I had never met in life, I had no idea who they were.

The moment my dreams began, I immediately knew I was safe in bed, I would remember the fact that I had gone to sleep and not woken up yet. Immediately, I would recognise that the place I was at was not one I had ever seen before. If I was in a garden, I'd know if it was one located in Gibraltar or not, it never was and so my mind knew, I was not in Gibraltar. Since I was aware of the fact that I lived in Gibraltar and had just gone to bed, I was able to determine when I was dreaming. The biggest trigger of them all, was the fact that every time I experienced a lucid dream, my viewpoint as is the norm would always come from my own eyes as opposed to watching myself on a television screen. I was also starting to experience normal dreams throughout the night as well, the dreams where you barely remember what happened, have no control over your actions and makes complete sense until you remember it when awake.

Whilst in a lucid dream, you can make conscious decisions of where you want to go and what you want to do, within your surroundings. At times, a person experiencing a lucid dream can even create their own surrounding, choosing where they wish their dream take place. As much as I tried, I usually always found myself in the same unique places, garden, beach, open desert and other locations which were familiar to me. Examples included a restaurant I was familiar with from a specific movie and even a farm, I had only ever seen in pictures. Only on few occasions was I able to decide what direction to take my dreams in but most of the time, I was forced to experience a dream I had no control over, other than knowing it was all but a dream.

Being aware that you're in a dream makes the experience more unreal, you are experiencing real emotions and thoughts, which you can feel as if you were awake. You're experiencing visuals and actions your conscious mind cannot comprehend, an example might be riding a dinosaur or flying over the moon. Imagine if suddenly aliens landed on earth and began communicating with us in our native language, that is how I felt, most of the time during my lucid dreams. Being conscious in a lucid dream, gives you the advantage of truly enjoying when a loved one who has passed away, appears within your dream. This is why dreaming of my grandfathers was my favourite kind of lucid dream, especially from what I can remember, since they had passed, I had never dreamt about either of them before, and now they were both sharing my lucid dream.

Grandpa Alberto and Grandpa Arturo had joined me in the garden; the emotions took over and in my dream, I began to cry with happiness. I literally felt like I was experiencing somebody from the dead coming back to life and having the chance to say everything I missed on telling them the first-time round. The only downside was that although they were both standing there and I was communicating with them, they didn't seem to be following my conversation with me. Grandpa Arturo would continue to ask if I had written my letter to Sean Connery yet, he reminded me not to take time for granted. Grandpa Alberto kept reminding me of an ornament I had brought back to him from Disney World, excitedly reminding me that I had once visited America in the process. I missed them so much, at the time Grandpa Alberto had passed away seven years earlier and Grandpa Arturo had also left us five years ago, I hadn't spoken to either of them, since I began working at the cable car, it had been many years, which I wanted to catch up on.

Grandpa Alberto would take me for rides; I sat in front of him as he drove his motorcycle, I loved these rides. I was always used to travelling in a car, riding on a motorcycle, even if only around the car park, allows you to feel the wind against your skin, it was so exciting for me back then. Growing up, I also used to sing "I want to go to America". I wanted to visit Hollywood but since that didn't make too much sense to people, I excited myself over Disney World, I wanted any excuse to travel to America. Thanks to my Grandpa Alberto and Mama June paying for our trip, my family and I were able to finally visit America. We didn't go to Hollywood but I did spend a lot of time at MGM Studios and at the time, as a kid, that was close enough for me.

My parents and I moved in with my Grandpa Arturo and Mama Angela once Stacey was born and most of us stayed living there for twenty-four years after. My grandparents lived on the first floor and my parents, sisters and me lived on the second floor but that didn't stop me as a child from spending most of my time downstairs. Grandpa Arturo used to watch me play with my figurines in his patio, and as I grew older, he was aware that I wanted to become a Hollywood writer. Gibraltar was once a very secluded place, Hollywood was a fantasy and nobody truly motivated me to achieve this dream except for Grandpa Arturo. I remember the first time Hollywood made me blush, Grandpa Arturo wanted to help me write a letter, to send to someone in Hollywood. I literally felt so embarrassed, I joked around and we never wrote the letter. It was one thing saying I wanted to be a Hollywood writer but when someone actually tried to help me, it finally felt real and that made me nervous. As the years went by, every time I told Grandpa Arturo that I wanted to be a Hollywood writer, he would suggest we write a letter, specifically one to Sean Connery.

Grandpa Arturo was a marriage registrar in Gibraltar in his earlier years and one of the few times a celebrity graced our Rock at that point in time was 007 himself. Sean Connery had come to Gibraltar to get married and Grandpa Arturo happened to be the one who performed the marriage. People in Gibraltar were not used to being around celebrities, Sean Connery's arrival made everyone excited. Everyone wanted pictures of the newlyweds, who simply wanted to enjoy their first day together as husband and wife. Whilst Mama Angela was busy in the kitchen, she received a call from Grandpa Arturo, who asked her to prepare some tea as he was bringing guests over to the house. Little did Mama Angela expect that Sean Connery would be walking into her living room a few minutes later. Sean Connery and his new wife enjoyed a little peace, away from their screaming fans, hiding out in my grandparent's house for tea. Grandpa Arturo always wanted to help me, the only connection he had to the world of Hollywood was through having performed Sean Connery's marriage.

I was so depressed at the time I began having lucid dreams, that escaping from my life in Gibraltar was always something on my mind. I had started writing again, I had my screenplays ready, all I needed to do was travel to America again, more specifically Los Angeles, where hopefully I could start my new life. The meaning behind these particular dreams was not to revisit Disney World and write a letter to Sean Connery, my subconscious mind was expressing that I travel to America and write emails to as many people as I could before I got there. Disney World represented Hollywood and contacting Sean Connery represented finding an agent. As my lucid dreams continued, both my grandfathers continued to show up in them, these dreams only consisted of people I knew who had passed away and other faces I did not recognise. During my lucid dreams, I would never experience it with someone who I knew alive and well in the real world, but only those roaming the other realm.

Once I was officially diagnosed as epileptic, I began to do my research; through my dreams, I found a pattern that warned me, a few days earlier, when I was going to experience a grand mal seizure. At night, whilst I slept, I would suffer mild seizures, which would then keep me unconscious for a short period of time, playing around with my stages of sleep, allowing me to experience lucid dreaming. When I had these types of dreams, a few days later, I would experience a grand mal seizure. Tiny seizures throughout the course of the night, in my case, eventually led to a big one a few days later. Every time I began dreaming lucidly, I now made sure to increase my medication, remain in a safe environment for the next few days and concentrated on my breathing techniques, hoping to avoid the attack all together. Dreaming began to become very interesting to me as did the idea of meditation, imagine being able to visualise your thoughts as clearly as you would when dreaming yet whilst being awake. Meditation allows you to reach the dreaming world in your mind, without falling asleep, therefore allowing you to control a lucid dream. Soon enough, these brain malfunctions that allowed me to dream lucidly began causing me to hallucinate and hear voices throughout the day.

Chapter Ten
Brain Malfunctions

Have you been half-asleep and have you heard voices? Calling out your name? Who might it be? The voice might be one in the same. Voices began speaking all around me, I could hear them as clearly as one would, whilst speaking over the telephone. The thing was I didn't recognise any of these voices, who were talking to me? I would look around if I were outside, and find nobody was actually speaking to me. If I were in my house, I'd begin to play hide and seek with the voices, they're great hiders, I never found any of them. As time went on, random people would walk up and start speaking to me, as if though I were supposed to have known them yet some did look familiar. These people looked like us but some didn't necessarily dress as fashionably as we do today, we must follow the science as opposed to ideology.

I had become a crazy person and I knew it; all I wanted to do was talk to somebody about this, anybody who was real but I knew I couldn't share. I had been complaining about bullying for the last three years. I was constantly depressed, anxious and quite honestly, very negative to be around; the last thing I had to do, was give anyone a reason to lock me up in a mental hospital. Something I came to realise, as long as you're questioning your mentality, you have never actually gone insane, it's once you don't question it, that you've totally lost it. The human brain is the most complicated tool in the world, give humans a super computer and we'd be lost without the manual. Unleash the super computer in our minds and we would have no idea, how to handle that sort of meditated power we are controlling, therefore what we see, makes us crazy. Though the mind is being distorted to a certain degree, the cause of the hallucination is more important than the hallucination itself.

A hallucination is the perception of a noise, smell or sight that is not physically present, it is sensation without stimulus. The difference between the subconscious and conscious mind is, you are in control of one and not the other. When we dream, we experience mostly visuals that depend on our conscious mind, we may hear words, but we understand most of the dream through pictures and people from the past or present. When we are awaken, our mind switches from visual thinking to audio thinking, at school we're taught mostly through lectures rather than visuals. People who grew up watching black and white television tend to dream in black and white. A dream's attention span is roughly the length of a television show, which is as long as we've programmed our mind to concentrate on one thing at a time. Musicians generally dream through song, with many great musicians throughout the years actually finding inspirations for songs through their dreams. The world around us affects our memories and ways of thinking. If we feel fear, our mind will interpret that usually as a visual you're familiar with from daily memory; for me, as a kid, it was a slime monster.

Hallucinations occur when the subconscious mind does not completely switch back to the conscious state. While hallucinating, the sensory regions of the brain are overridden by the hippocampus, where our memory is stored. The memory areas of the brain's memory are now in charge and call upon the sensory areas to deliver a hallucination, using what we're familiar with in the awoken world. Hallucinations have long been associated with mental illness because many people become confused as to what they are seeing or experiencing. Mainly hallucinations do occur in mentally ill people, most commonly in people with schizophrenia, bipolar disorder, psychotic depression, PTSD, delirium, dementia and epilepsy but anyone can experience them. Hallucinations can be a factor of lack of sleep, drugs and prolonged meditation, not all causes are related to psychological disorders.

Mushrooms are considered a very healthy antidepressant but like certain types of fish, toads, plants, teas and other drugs created at Mother Nature Laboratories, they cause you to hallucinate, your mind plays tricks on you. Although at the same time, you are using increasingly a lot more brainpower, why would you become dumber when fuelling your brain? Our brain is like a piano, if you have no idea how to use your instrument, you'll make terrible noise. Vivid colours, people turned into objects, apparitions, giant surroundings and even trees chasing you, whilst a talking frog asks for directions to your house, hallucinations come in many forms. Many actually take man-made drugs to enhance their experience of euphoria, but when you jump from first gear to fifth gear, you'll have no control of what's happening to your vehicle. Meditation is key, it allows you to experience the activity within the subconscious brain, whilst still being alert and in control of your illusions.

At first it was all very confusing, it started off with voices, mainly calling out my name, and as the days past, I began recognising the same voices over and over again. Soon enough, I stopped writing for a while, the words on the screen would slowly become smaller, and as I looked away from the screen, so did my surroundings. Sometimes people and things would begin to appear smaller or bigger and other times as if slowly they were disappearing further into the distance, I should have gone to Specsavers. A few months before suffering my first grand mal seizure in London, I suddenly became popular, random people would come up and talk to me, for no apparent reason. Generally, they never continued a conversation with me, they were determined to say what they had to say. Sometimes they would provide wisdom on how to fix my problems, other times they'd share their own concerns and on few occasions, they'd interact with me properly.

At the beginning, I genuinely believed these people were actually there, I'm embarrassed to think of the many times people saw me talking to myself and I was unaware, soon enough I realised, they were simply illusions. One night, as I went out to throw the rubbish, I found an old woman standing around the area, minding her own business, I believed she was waiting for me to leave, to sort through the rubbish. As I approached the rubbish area, she smiled and began talking to me. I felt sorry for her, she didn't look well, I hoped maybe by speaking to her, I'd find a way to help, if she needed it. As we began talking, I realised she was not following our conversation, I tried to follow hers but we just couldn't make sense of each other. At that point, one of my neighbours approached me and asked who I was talking to. At that moment I first realised, I saw dead people, either that or I was hallucinating, I didn't know which one I preferred.

How can a hallucination feel so real? How many times had they happened? And who were all these people? Why was I not hallucinating about people I knew in real life? Why not characters I was familiar with from movies and television? Why only random chatter boxes? Why was I not hallucinating about Wonder Woman! I was determined to touch one; the next time I believed someone was a hallucination, I was going to see if I could feel them actually there. I couldn't justify to myself how these 'real' visuals were not actually there, at this point going crazy wasn't even on my mind. I was simply interested in explaining to myself what it was I was seeing, I knew they weren't real but couldn't convince myself that they were not there either.

Very few times did I hallucinate about animals, but the first time I did was one of the scariest moments I've ever experienced in life. One day after work, I needed a little bit of fresh air before locking myself in my bedroom all afternoon. I decided to go for a walk up to the Nipperish. Along the way, I found myself face to face with a bear, I had not hallucinated about animals before then, it did not cross my mind, that this could be a hallucination. I immediately felt my heart begin to race and a tingling sensation all throughout my feet; suddenly, I began to run and if that weren't bad enough I started shouting too. I run past a group of tourists on my way down and yelled, "There's a bear, run!" but as I continued to run past them, I realised they were not screaming and running behind me.

As I continued running, I was trying to turn my head back around, I wanted to see where the tourists were but the fear did not allow me to move my head and look behind me. Finally, I glanced back and not only realised the tourists weren't running but nothing was chasing after them either. I had never felt so embarrassed in my life, now I was hallucinating about animals too? For the first time since my hallucinations started, I began realising that the actuality to all this was, that I was losing my mind. I became very embarrassed about everything, the voices, the illusions and now even lucid dreaming felt crazy. Every time someone felt like a hallucination, I'd begin to ignore them, to a point when I walked through town, I began ignoring everybody. I didn't know who was real and who wasn't, I wasn't going to embarrass myself by talking into thin air in front of an audience.

People continued to approach me, at times whilst I was sitting in the kitchen having a snack, they wouldn't leave me alone. As the weeks went by, I began recognising some of these illusions that were appearing before me, although I had no idea who they were, some of these people had appeared in my dreams. This both made sense and completely lost me at the same time, was I now dreaming whilst awake? If I were to imagine dreams as images then those same images were now appearing before me as illusions. Who were these people? And why was I dreaming about them? Why had my mind created detailed new faces in my dreams, and now why was it projecting it in real life? How does this even work? I was lost and the few times I asked my imaginary friends anything about this, they never responded with an answer.

I was basically now dreaming whilst awake, a form of day dreaming yet this was not only taking place inside my head, it was starting to affect my social life too. When we dream, we do so very vividly but when we think of an image inside our heads, whilst we're awake, it is not as clear. Everyone can sing, everyone can draw, everyone can dance and anyone can visualise vividly within their minds, visual thinking, all you have to do is practise. When a person daydreams, they are lost in both a semi-sleeping state and a high alertness to their surroundings yet during a daydream, the imagery inside your head is much clearer, than once you're fully awake. This doesn't mean we need to be asleep to connect our minds to HDTV, all you must do is concentrate. Imagine painting a picture, it takes time, the longer you visualise the same picture in your mind, adding details, the clearer it becomes. At this point, for some reason, I felt as though a television screen were constantly playing inside my mind, I could see everything so clearly, both inside and out.

What was happening to me? I needed answers but couldn't find the courage to ask anyone the question, not even my family. At this point, I still wasn't aware I had epilepsy. I had no idea how the brain worked, I was convinced I had achieved a sixth sense, I could see ghosts, who was I going to call? It was all too much, I had recently felt the weird sensation of experiencing life after death through my dreams, interacting with my grandfathers. Now I was having to admit to myself that the phenomena that are ghosts, actually did exist, all I needed now was to get abducted by aliens. We can be aware inside our dreams, we can hear voices that aren't there and ghosts exist, which now opened up the question of life after death. It was too much, happening too fast, not simply to try and understand but accept, for years I'm led to believe one way but now I was forced to start believing another way.

I've always been very open minded; ghosts, aliens, Santa Clause, I believe in all of them, but actually interacting and experiencing with any, would however still feel very unreal. When we're young, we're brought up believing one religion and many of us also believing in Santa Clause, the Tooth Fairy, the Easter Bunny, imaginary friends, aliens and even Big Foot himself. As we grow older, we learn Santa Clause is not real and the Tooth Fairy has her own night job that keeps her busy. We're also led to believe by most that aliens and ghosts, are nothing more than ideas in movies and even if we believe, we still doubt. What is real and what isn't? It's all very complicated to understand but if you're given an answer, one tends to accept it easily.

However, many of us are never told not to believe in God any longer, we continue to believe in God into adulthood yet at the same time, sometimes doubt. Had nobody ever told us Santa Clause was not real, would we still believe in him today? How can we believe in religion but not believe in spirits? How can we believe in science but not believe in life on other planets? I find it fascinating that all religions are so different yet so similar, all at the same time; instead of arguing over which one is correct, perhaps we should all compare notes. I should have compared notes with someone, maybe I would have found my answer sooner but at the time, I was convinced, I could communicate with the dead. Now all I needed to do was prove first that these illusions were in fact people who were dead, I needed familiar faces, who I knew had passed away, so that I could confirm my new sixth sense.

Once again, I woke up dehydrated and covered in sweat, I felt so dizzy and again my muscles were locked, this was getting frustrating. After what seemed like an hour but probably only just a few seconds, I was able to move again and soon I was able to get up. I needed a glass of water but could not find the strength to walk downstairs to the kitchen. Everyone was asleep, and eventually, I left my bedroom and began walking downstairs. Walking down the stairs in this house, meant I had to walk past a window, that viewed out into our patio, the one my grandfather used to spend his days, when he still lived with us. Walking down the stairs, a small orange light in the patio caught my attention, I quickly looked out the window and over one of the chairs appeared to be an orange glow. At first, all I could see was an orange spec of light hovering above the chair, but as I kept my focus, I began seeing Grandpa Arturo, sitting on the chair, smoking a cigarette, as he always did, when he still lived in that house.

My muscles hadn't locked up on me but literally I could not move, I felt a shiver down my spine, my hands began to tremble slightly and all I could do was stand there, looking out the window. I wasn't scared, I was just in complete shock, seeing Grandpa Arturo once again, sitting on his chair, smoking a cigarette in his patio, was an image I never believed I'd see again. Interacting in my dreams with him had seemed normal up until then, but now, I didn't know what to think, this seemed impossible. Finally, in my mind it was confirmed, these illusions, although perhaps not real, all represent dead people. Up until this moment, I had considered my illusions simply hallucinations, now my mind began to accept them as ghosts, which only confused me even more.

I wanted to approach Grandpa Arturo but if I've learned anything from watching movies, it's that by the time he leaves my view, whilst I continue to walk down the steps and turn the corner into the patio, he would be gone. I began walking down the stairs slowly, I wanted to run but my legs would only move slowly. As I turned the corner, facing into the patio, I realised Grandpa Arturo was still there, he hadn't disappeared. This was very strange, it's the first time I looked away from an illusion yet was still there when I looked back at it. I slowly walked up to Grandpa Arturo and as weird as it felt, at the same time I had already been dreaming about him, I felt as if I had just spoken to him days earlier.

I wanted to speak to him in our patio but for some reason I couldn't, I was waiting for him to speak to me first, as I waited I reached out to touch him, my hand went straight through him, it felt as though nobody were there. I suddenly realised, I was smelling the smoke from his cigarette and all this time, whilst I'm standing there looking at him, all I can think about, is the smell of his cigarette. Slowly, the orange light, which rested at the tip of his burning cigarette began to fade away and with it, so did Grandpa Arturo. All I wanted to do was run upstairs and tell my mum I had just seen her dad smoking a cigarette in the patio; instead, I grabbed my water and went back to bed. This was something I had to keep to myself, I already had no confidence around others, talking about visions, voices and dreaming would only make me appear insane and feel worse.

Everyone is born naked yet we spent most of our lives covering up wearing clothes, trousers, shirts, dresses and shoes, this isn't part of spirituality, so why were my ghosts wearing clothes? That part didn't make sense, not that I wanted to start seeing naked ghosts or anything but the clothing always had me thinking. Seeing as they were dressed eventually convinced me of the fact, that they weren't ghosts but rather hallucinations caused by my own brain and nothing more. Our daily memories associate people with clothes, I doubted very much that my Nike shoes could go to heaven but they could be a projection of my mind. This is why many who claim to have seen ghosts, never claim to see them naked, our conscious mind is taking part in these illusions.

Why can someone see a ghost in a certain room whilst others can't? Whatever is going on is happing within the control of the person's mind, that doesn't necessarily mean they aren't communicating with others. This theory of mine was confirmed a few months later when I went to visit Mama June, as I walked

89

through the car park Grandpa Alberto drove past me riding his old motorcycle. Grandpa Alberto asked me to join him on his motorcycle, believe me I wanted to, just as I did when I was little, but I knew he was not there, I was going to look foolish if I tried to get on. Before I could decide what to say, Grandpa Alberto drove away, slowly fading, the further away he got from me.

A ghost riding a motorcycle, wearing clothes? These were hallucinations but the fact that they all followed the same pattern, led me to believe there was still more to them than I had figured by then. Everyone I either dreamt or hallucinated about were dead, probably even the animals, why was I not experiencing any of this with anybody who was alive? I was eager to experiment, if two people having a lucid dream at the same time, whilst thinking about each other, could they interact inside their dreams and then speak about the same experience when they were awake? Dream Telepathy is the ability to communicate telepathically with another person whilst both are sleeping, is this actually real or again something simply out of the movies?

I was trying to make sense of everything that was happening, whilst hoping to follow the science behind it. After I started having grand mal seizures and was diagnosed as epileptic, it all started to make sense to me. I was suffering mild seizures at night, which kept me in and out of consciousness, reaching various stages of sleep in an abnormal rhythm, which allowed me to dream lucidly. As my illness progressed, these illusions began to manifest in real life, all which happens to be a side effect of epilepsy. It was all starting to make sense to me, until one day I looked down and found myself dead in bed.

How can one see their body unconscious below them? Perhaps, this was simply a dream I was having, one where I was looking down at myself whilst sleeping, that made sense. This also happened to be a lucid dream, as I floated above myself, I couldn't stop thinking about the fact that this was an Outer-Body Experience dream. A few moments later, it all ended and I woke up with blood inside my mouth, I had suffered another grand mal seizure whilst in bed. A few hours later, when I recalled what had happened, I wasn't sure what to believe out of it, all I knew was, if it ever happened again, I was going to jump out of my window and fly to the stars.

I had opened my third-eye, close your eyes and yet using your brain you are still able to see whatever it is you wish to picture. Our third-eye is nothing more than our mind, the window into our soul, where one will dream, hallucinate and see everything clearly, even with both eyes shut. This all sounds completely crazy, what was happening to me? I just wanted to write funny movies in Hollywood not become a philosophical government protestor, attempting a spiritual journey using only natural remedies to cure my seizures. What kind of life was I living? Who wrote this movie? It certainly wasn't me, this wasn't what I had signed up for as a child, I wanted to write my own ending but as is life, obstacles got in my way and moved me in a different direction.

Chapter Eleven
London Calling

Moving right along, hoping for good times and good vibes, with good friends I can't lose, opportunity only knocks once, I needed to be ready to reach out and try it. In summer of 2012, something positive did come out of my negative life, I always believed it happened at the worst possible moment. Looking back now, I realise it was probably the perfect timing, as it was when I most needed hope, life was throwing me a bone. During my time with depression, anxiety, mild seizures, hallucinations and strange dreams, I had spent most of my time locked away in my bedroom. Fixing my screenplays and writing email after email, hoping to get somebody's attention. I was tired of waiting for an American family to come to me, I decided to start emailing as many people in Hollywood as I could. Hoping that eventually, I would stumble upon someone, who might be able to help me achieve my dream.

Talking to people was my biggest challenge at this time but writing to them, from the comfort of my own bedroom, able to edit my words, think carefully before I spoke, that I could handle, I lost myself in emails. Becoming a writer somewhere far away from Gibraltar was my only escape, it was the only thing that helped me wake up in the morning, thinking that one day, I might lead the life I wanted and not the one given to me. I knew I wasn't going to chase my dream, I was having a hard-enough time walking out the door just to go to work, let alone get on a plane and travel to a different country, to attempt a childhood dream. I was determined to get on that plane though, not just to follow my dream but I was hoping, that somehow, I could also leave my hallucinations behind me as well, I hoped this was a solo trip.

One night I had gone for a walk up the Rock, I reached the Nipperish and looked out across the ocean, over at Spain and Africa, I just wanted to be anywhere but Gibraltar. This had become a normal routine for me, I knew I would not be sleeping most nights, rather than laying restlessly in bed, I would go for a quiet midnight walk through nature. That night I was particularly sad, it wasn't just about the bullying anymore, it was the fact, that I was losing my mind, my short-term memory was failing me, I was seeing and hearing people who were not actually there, I was completely broken. I returned home that night and as I always did, before going to sleep, I checked my emails, hoping someone would have responded to one of my letters. I knew it was a long shot but I had nothing to lose, probably had I not been so desperate, I would not have written such personal emails to total strangers. I was hungry for adventure, I was fed up with my life, if I didn't get some excitement soon, I was going to lose my mind.

To my surprise, someone had actually replied. I received an email from a person who unknown to me at the time, would soon become very special in my life, and not only for the reasons I first thought. Shale was my devil, Cristina is my angel, not only because she helped me fulfil my childhood wish but because she is a genuine example of how a kind gesture from a stranger can make all the difference in someone's life. I was ready to give up on life, I never had the courage to end it but every time, when I went to bed, I hoped I would never wake up. Cristina's reply alone not only gave me strength to try and live again but it allowed someone so broken, they could not even leave the house for groceries, to actually believe enough in themselves, to get on a plane and travel to another country alone.

Two of my idols were apparently visiting England to promote their new movie and were filming adverts for it inside a hotel room, somewhere in London and I was invited to meet them. This sounded very strange, somebody was playing me, I was sure Shale, Darcello and Beverly were playing a practical joke on me, get me to fly all the way to London, only to find myself alone, in hotel Room 209. Bullying changes people, it makes them trust less, overthink more and shut others out. I had been doing that for the past few years, this time I was not going to overthink it, I was simply going to do it. I have no idea how I found the courage to get on that plane, before then I had only ever left Gibraltar on two separate occasions, in the company of my family when I was young. Now here I was about to get on a plane, for the first time in years and travel all the way to London by myself, in an attempt to achieve my childhood dream, whilst broken, losing my mind and writing around invisible people. Was this actually happening to me? I couldn't believe it and at the time, I was so far gone, I seriously believed I had fallen into a coma, living the life I wanted simply inside my head. As my parents pointed out to me numerous times, I wasn't in a coma, this was happening.

The best part about going to London alone, was not only did I get to be by myself away from everyone I knew, most importantly, I was off work for two weeks. It was a bully free holiday with the added bonus, that if things went according to plan, I would meet two of my lifelong idols and hopefully find a way to escape my prison. As I boarded the plane and began my journey, I could feel my nerves starting to kick in but unlike back home, this nervous feeling was actually nice. I couldn't believe it, after over three years of feeling nothing but hate and anger, I was starting to feel excitement. When you do not feel a certain emotion for such a long time, and then suddenly welcome it back into your life, it is overwhelming. The last few years had been an emotional roller coaster of suffering, but 2012 was shaping out to be a great year for me. Not only was I excited about my trip, three months earlier my nephew Aiden had been born, which meant I had also began feeling love again. Little did I know, I was about to start suffering grand mal seizures and would soon be forced to resign from the Gibraltar Developing Company for other reasons.

When I arrived at London Airport, I was very nervous; I had never travelled by myself, where was I supposed to go? At the same time, I was very happy, since the night before I had not heard or seen a single hallucination. I was still under the impression that these were ghosts, I truly hoped I hadn't smuggled illegal ghosts from Gibraltar into London. I eventually arrived at The Leafless Tree Hotel and was instantly greeted by Abdul, who informed me not to order dinner, there was no kitchen anymore. I truly hoped Abdul was real, by this point I wasn't sure who was real and who was a hallucination. I had been travelling all day, I needed a nice warm shower, the bad thing about cheap hotels, having to share bathrooms with other guests. As I walked through the hallway looking for the shower, I saw an old man roaming the corridors. I arrived at the communal bathroom, I opened the door and found myself in a room so small, I had to make sure I had not opened a wardrobe instead.

I locked the door, stripped naked and jumped into the shower, hoping to get this out of the way as soon as possible, after realising that this hotel required you to bring your own hot water. England was freezing and so was my shower, I missed my bath back home with warm water, but at least I felt alive again. All of a sudden, I realise the old man walking outside had now joined me inside the bathroom, the odd thing was, I had locked the door, and had not heard it open since. The old man just kept walking around, I continued looking at him, I was trying to find the words to speak, but I started to believe, it might be a ghost. I closed my eyes and began washing my hair with shampoo, I was going to count to five and open my eyes again, usually if I did not focus on the hallucination, when I looked back they were gone. I counted to five, opened my eyes, the old man was gone, I felt terrible, I had brought my illness to London. I was going to meet my idols soon, I couldn't have voices and hallucinations getting in my way, I needed to concentrate.

The day I met my idols was probably the best day of my life up to that point; sadly, the day before was probably one of the worse I had ever experienced. I had already spent two days in London and on the third day, I explored Oxford Street, where I realised there were more shops in one street in London, than houses all across Gibraltar. This was a new world for me, a bigger one, I felt like if I were walking inside a movie, as these images I was experiencing, I had only ever done so through television. I spent most of the day walking up Oxford Street and soon enough, after a short bus ride, I found myself near Kensington Gardens. I hadn't eaten all day and was beginning to feel very light headed, I felt drunk, I had no idea why. I came across this particular restaurant, it appeared to be a sports bar, the place was packed, over fifty people easily filled the room, some even leaned against my table, as I tried to eat my bread rolls around their asses.

I started to feel a little hot at first, by the time I had finally ordered, the room had become an oven, I was boiling. I had already removed my jacket and my jumper, all I could do next was remove my t-shirt and start stripping. My bangers and mash finally arrived, I had so many things around me, I felt suffocated. My laptop was on the table, my iPad inside my laptop case next to me on the bench I was sitting on, most bothersome were all the bags full of toys, souvenirs, clothes, everything I had bought through Oxford Street. Suddenly at that moment, England scored and everyone began to cheer, causing me to heat up like a barbecued rib on a grill. I could not breathe, I felt suffocated and I felt so hot, even the heat coming from my mash potatoes was making me sweat. I was actually really hungry and thought that maybe if I ate, I'd feel better. I took the first bite of my sausage and mash, right then I realised hunger was not the problem. I started burning up, I sipped my cola and then England scored again, everyone cheered, for once in my life, I didn't want England to win.

The next thing I know, all my shopping is scattered throughout the floor, my food is stained against my clothes, I'm lying on the floor, being looked down upon by a waiter, whilst a crowd of people look on. My first thought was I had been hit from behind, had this waiter knocked me out? Everyone kept looking at me, I was very confused. I began to get up and the waiter quickly urged me to stay sitting on the floor. Apparently, I had just suffered a seizure, an ambulance was on its way to pick me up, I was determined not to let that happen. This had been my first ever grand mal seizure, having a stranger tell you at age twenty-five that you've had a seizure, is not something you believe at first. I was also very angry for some reason, little did I know at the time, this was a side effect from waking up after a seizure. I had come all this way from Gibraltar to meet my idols and that was supposed to happen the very next day. I was not going to let some stupid hospital stop me from living out my dream because I had to stay with them under observation. I collected my items and whilst everyone looked on at me, I began to throw up, this was so embarrassing; in a drunken fashion, I respectfully made my way out the door.

The fresh air will do me good, or so I believed, I was completely wrong, as soon as I stepped outside, everything felt much worse. Everything and everyone was moving too fast, the cars, the people and the noise; I could not handle so much chaos happening all around me. Everybody was looking at me, someone even commented on how pale I looked and honestly, what I really felt like doing was just lying down on the ground and letting this all pass. Once again, I felt the urge to throw up, I did a little but managed to stomach down the rest, I knew that the state I was in, if I started to throw up in the middle of the street, I'd be arrested or sent to a hospital.

Luckily, I realised that Kensington Gardens was just opposite the road from me. Feeling as if I had been drinking all day, I made my way to the other side of the... *HONK!* A car almost ran over me... *HONK! HONK! HONK!* Another car almost ran me over, thankfully I got to the other side. I looked around and found people playing football, others cycling and most importantly, others simply lying down on the grass. That's exactly what I wanted to do and here I could do it, without calling attention to myself. I placed all my possessions on the grass next to me, removed my coat but as I began to lie down, everything just started spinning again, soon I actually began feeling much worse.

Everything I had been holding down since the restaurant was coming back up and this time, I couldn't stop it. I looked around and noticed a beautifully decorated rubbish bin nearby. I picked myself up, ran towards the bin and just started letting it all out. Whilst I was throwing up, I kept reminding myself that this wasn't home anymore, I couldn't leave my possessions unattended. Suddenly, I saw a guy from the corner of my eye pick up my laptop, and started walking away. I quickly turned around and as I continued throwing up all over myself, I also began yelling and chasing after that asshole. Before he began to run, he dropped my laptop to the ground, I was able to pick it up, whilst I kept throwing up at the same time.

At this point, I couldn't care less who saw me, everyone was looking at me in disbelief. I knew if I wanted to meet my idols the next day, I had to get back to my hotel room as soon as possible, before I brought any more attention to myself. I smelled, my heart was racing and everyone was staring at me; on the bright side, I did feel a little better now yet I was in no state to walk home. I had no idea where the hotel even was but at the same time, I knew that as soon as I stepped inside a taxi, the mere motion of being inside a car, would make me throw up again. At this point, this was a risk I was going to have to take and so my taxi driver.

"TAXI!" Luckily, it didn't take long for a taxi to stop and as soon as I stepped inside, I knew I'd be leaving the car by force before I reached my destination. Before the car even began to move, I felt like I was going to throw up all over again. The taxi driver began driving and as soon as he took the first turn, I knew I was in more trouble than I had first thought. I placed my right hand in front of my mouth, knowing that as soon as I started talking, I was going to throw up. I pleaded with the taxi driver as best I could to please open the window for me but as I began speaking, I started throwing up again.

Like an idiot, I tried to hold my vomit back with my hands, when I finally realised that wasn't possible, I brought out a bunch of plush toys from their bag and used it as a bin. My taxi ride ended with the taxi driver pulling his car over to one side, yelling at me, he thought I was drunk, and after chucking out all my bags and possessions onto the floor, he drove away. Seeing as I had used one of the bags to throw up inside, I now found myself walking through

London, covered in puke, holding a bunch of stuffed toys as I tried searching for my hotel before I blacked out.

I couldn't walk straight, this was the equivalent of not being able to walk back to my bedroom after waking up at night, except this time, I was lost in London. People kept staring at me, which in return embarrassed me to approach them and ask for directions; every time I tried to make eye contact, they would look away. A lady finally walked up to me and asked if I was okay, she placed her hand on my shoulder, this confirmed she was real and hopefully so were her directions back to my hotel.

As I tried looking for my hotel, all I knew was, I needed to buy sunglasses in London as soon as possible. I could not open my eyes, the sun was too bright, and London isn't usually known for its sunshine. Something I soon came to realise after three days in London was how much I missed the sun. Gibraltar in a sense is a small tropical paradise, the sun visits us a lot throughout the year, bringing us its warmth. I felt as though my body was missing some form of nutrition, literally a flower without sunlight. On rare occasions when the sun did shine, those few minutes standing in its rays made me feel better, and at the same time reminded me of home.

I finally arrived at my hotel a few minutes later, I had felt weak before, usually during my late night wake up calls but this time, I found myself not even able to think. The next day, I was meant to meet those who I had grown up watching since I was three years old. I had waited over twenty years for this opportunity; now that it was here, I didn't feel like I could go through with it. How did I ever convince myself to come to London in the first place? All I wanted to do was get on a plane and go back home, I missed my bullies, instead I cried myself to sleep that night, until someone woke me up.

That night, as was the cases with me most nights, I ended waking up, as soon as I did I realised someone was sitting at the foot of my bed. I felt the same fear I had felt, the time I hallucinated a bear on my way towards the Nipperish. Back home, I was used to hallucinations showing up in my bedroom, but in a different country, alone in a hotel room, I had no idea what to believe; fortunately, I quickly recognised the face. My friend Ashby had never appeared in my dreams, I had never hallucinated about him either. Since Ashby had passed away five years earlier, sometimes I thought about the possibility of seeing him, now that it was happening, I couldn't believe it. It seemed like the longer I was experiencing hallucinations, the more unreal they were starting to become, probably the fact that when I recognised the person, in my head, it only confirmed the fact, that I was being visited by ghosts.

Ashby didn't speak to me much, he kept repeating the name 'Germaine', she was my friend, she was the girl Ashby left behind when he passed away. I hadn't seen Germaine in a few years, she had moved to England after his death. As I lost myself in my thoughts, I came to realise Ashby was no longer there, we didn't have much of a conversation but it was good to see my friend again, even if only an illusion. Before going back to bed, I thought perhaps I should email Germaine and find out how close we both were to each other. I emailed Germaine that night, the next day she had replied, she was living in Edinburgh and we arranged to meet up a few days later.

I went back to bed that night and couldn't fall back to sleep, I was so excited about the next day, I hoped the promise of excitement was one the night would keep. When I was little, my dad used to take me to the video rental store, now those same celebrities from my VHS tapes were going to be talking to me the next day. This was a childhood dream I always shared with everyone and nobody thought I'd ever achieve, yet I had, I was about to meet my heroes, two of Hollywood's biggest stars. A few months later, I would find myself with a new ambition in life and again people made me believe I'd never achieve it, knowing I had done so once before kept me trying.

Chapter Twelve
It's Not Easy Being Normal

A wise man named Jim Henson once said, "If you care about what you do and work hard at it, there isn't anything you can't do if you want to." I had spent twenty-two years waiting for this moment and today it had finally arrived, either that or someone had played a huge prank on me. Cristina seemed like a genuinely nice, helpful person, I didn't believe those people existed anymore, I wasn't sure what to expect from Room 209. It had all been so sudden, so random, I wasn't completely sure if I could trust Cristina, best decision I've ever made in life, trusting Cristina. This was not only the best week of my life, this was a week of my life being given back to me, for the first time in years, I was living again. I was under the impression when my trip ended, that the best part had been living out my childhood dream, turns out one of the most important moments was learning about Upper Cervical Care.

I left my hotel early that day, Abdul was very excited for me; for the first time in a long time, I was giving out positive vibes. I was meant to meet my idols in Room 209 of The Soho Hotel, I had no idea where that was and left early that day, hoping to find the hotel, with time to spare. Once I found The Soho Hotel, it all suddenly became very real for me. There was a bellboy standing outside the hotel, I had never been to a hotel with its own bellboy, standing guard outside the entrance, how fancy. I approached the hotel, walked straight in and was immediately greeted by the receptionist, who asked me who I was here to visit. This was insane, I was about to speak out the names of my childhood heroes, not out of interest but out of necessity. I was about to find out if all this was actually about to happen, and according to the hotel receptionist, it was all very real.

I arrived outside Room 209, I could not stop staring at the number pinned on the door, all I had to do was knock, but I couldn't. As excited as I was, three days away from my bullies had not cured me, I was still a total mess. I lacked confidence and apparently, as I would soon realise, having no social skills in the presence of being starstruck is a terrible combination and first impressions mean everything. As I knocked on the door, I quickly remembered I had chewing gum in my mouth, what a disaster, I could not greet them with chewing gum in my mouth, how disrespectful of me, these are legends, I got really nervous and before the door opened, I swallowed my gum.

My idols did not open the door for me, in fact they weren't even in the room, although scattered throughout were around a dozen people and production equipment, inside a bedroom? Had I been tricked into making a porno? I was greeted by a guy around my age, this made me realise I wasn't a young kid wishing on a dream anymore. I was actually at the age where I could work in show business, if I played my cards right; unfortunately for me at the time, I wasn't playing with a full deck. I was greeted by the production team, who were helping set up for the interview, all of whom were very nice, fortunately since I did not recognise any faces, I felt comfortable speaking to them. This might go better than I had expected, in that moment I had my confidence back, I wasn't being awkward, I was actually socialising properly and then the door opened.

My idols had finally arrived, they were not on a television screen, they were not on the covers of my DVDs back home, they were right in front of me, at least I hoped they were real. They were forced to introduce themselves first because I had all of a sudden forgotten how to speak, was this my lack of confidence? I don't think so as just seconds ago I was socialising properly, I was literally starstruck. Somehow my chewing gum had found its way back into my mouth again but nothing was going to stop me from making a good first impression, I quickly re-swallowed my gum and extended my hand towards them.

We had already been shaking hands for almost a minute, it was getting awkward, I needed to say something, anything, I asked them to give me a second to breathe. The first impression I made in front of my childhood heroes was to ask them, to allow me time to breathe, this wasn't going as I had hoped. I was honestly still in shock and very nervous whilst speaking to them, the only reason I was actually able to get through our conversation was because they both made me feel very comfortable speaking with them. In my head, I felt as though I had known these two all my life, to an extent I had, but to them, I was simply a new fan, they were meeting for the first time, who was making a fool of himself every time he spoke.

They were so professional, after over twenty interviews, they began recording short advertisements for their new movie, which had recently been released on DVD in the UK. These clips were no longer than twenty seconds each, yet they kept reshooting and reshooting, they were dedicated to get this right, I was very proud of their passion for their work. As I stood there, it was all starting to sink in, my dream had come true and not once did I look down at my watch. This was a job I could wake up in the morning eagerly to get to, this was a job that seemed to satisfy at the end of the day, this was work that could make millions of people happy. I came to realise at that moment that working is not always boring and unfulfilling, it's not having the right job that does that to a person.

I made so many friends on this trip, the people behind the camera are just as wonderful and talented, everyone made me feel welcome, especially my new friends Bill, Steve and Debbie. I could not believe I had spent an entire week watching behind the scenes at interviews and meet and greets. I had never travelled in a limo in my entire life; in a week, I rode inside a limo four times, I couldn't believe this was happening. That week of my life was special for many reasons, not only did I achieve a lifelong dream, in the process I had enjoyed life for the first time in years, this was the true gift Cristina had given me. Not only did I start feeling better, I had got a taste of the life I wanted to lead. I was going to try and change my life, I was tired of being a victim at work, a victim of stress, a victim of mental illness, I was going to figure myself out.

My ghost friends had started appearing out of nowhere a few months earlier, I never expected them, now that they were here, I had got used to it. This experience however, I had been waiting for my whole life, now that I was experiencing it, I wasn't believing it. I was eating lunch with two celebrities, who had inspired me to write even before I knew my alphabet properly. When you experience one of the best days of your life, during your worse years, it makes the memory truly special. At first, I couldn't even speak to them, I had never been in the presence of anyone famous and the first two celebrities I met, were the ones who had inspired me as a child, to follow my dreams and continue living my movie in Hollywood.

Bill is such a talented artist and very fun to talk to, this was my first experience dealing with someone from Hollywood, and thank goodness, he was so patient because as much as I tried not to, I was coming across as insane. Bill had nothing but nice things to say about Cristina, a name so important to me, yet did not have a face to go with the name. Bill had much knowledge about screenwriting in Hollywood, he gave me many tips on how to succeed with my dream and in return, I was a blabbering idiot. I was actually opening doors, making connections and whilst I was busy enjoying life, not a single hallucination bothered me, which I had hoped would be the case. These were the people, I was hoping to work for in the future, I had no patience for a full time mental illness.

Steve was just as wonderful, he worked very hard at what he did, he was always loyal in his performance, this meant the world to me. Steve's dedication was one of the reasons I had been inspired by his work for so many years. Debbie was someone I wasn't expecting to meet on this trip, it was a surprising pleasure to get to meet her as well, she too was dedicated to her work, in fact, she was always very busy, at times she could not join in our conversations, whilst making sure everything was ready for the next take. Everybody I met was professional, motivating and nice, it wasn't something impossible to come across, I just hadn't been looking in the right places back home.

On a different occasion, I met up with Bill, Steve and Debbie for lunch, we were going to a Thai restaurant, as we approached the area, we came across a window with rabbits on display. Dead rabbits, inside out, hanging in plain view, is this supposed to make someone hungry? This is not something I was used to seeing back home, I was starting to realise my little bubble known as Gibraltar, had sheltered me from most of the outside world. I vowed that day, if I ever worked at a pet store, I would care especially well for any rabbits we might have. I had lost my appetite but that wasn't important, I was not really going to eat, I was on my way for what one might call a 'business lunch', I was about to eat noodles with big time named producers.

At the restaurant, I slowly began to panic, I had started hearing voices just a few hours earlier; luckily, they stopped by the time our business lunch had begun. Now that I truly had to concentrate on my conversation, all I could think about was the fact that I might start hearing voices throughout lunch, in front of a bunch of Hollywood producers. This time it was me alone, who was getting inside my head, I couldn't stop thinking of what might go wrong instead of concentrating on what was going right. As we entered the restaurant, the producers were already sat at a table, we joined them and I immediately realised how out of place this all seemed, I felt like a clown and a fool.

As much as I wanted to be there, it didn't make sense, I was nobody, my bullies had convinced me back home that I was worthless. Now that I had the chance to prove them wrong, I was in fact proving them right. I couldn't even decide on what to order from the menu, back home, you couldn't find this kind of food, it all seemed so weird and having seen dead rabbits just a few minutes ago wasn't helping me find my appetite. I had to start speaking about my stories, I had to start cracking jokes, I had to seem present, I had to go back to Gibraltar and start all over again, I was not making the most out of this opportunity. I was so close to finding what I had been searching for my entire life yet still so far away at the same time.

Then came the most awkward moment of my entire life, trust me on this, if you ever mispronounce a word during a meeting with potential investors, never repeat the word in the following sentence, just to correct yourself. If you do so and mispronounce the word again on the second time, then just shut up, otherwise you'll appear as I did, at the end of that lunch. I have no idea why but during our conversation, I actually pronounced 'Thai' as 'thigh'. I quickly realised my error and once again decided to bring up the word Thai, hoping to correct myself. "This thigh food is delicious," I said. "I've never eaten thigh food in my life," I then said, hoping to correct myself, but I didn't.

"I need to tell my family about thigh food when I get back home." What was wrong with me? Every time I tried to correct myself, I only made it worse, why could I not pronounce the word 'Thai'? After several failed attempts, it wasn't even the word 'thigh' that was embarrassing me anymore, it was the whole sentence. "I'm going to write a movie about thigh food when I get home." What the hell was wrong with me? I couldn't even pronounce the word, how on earth was I going to write a movie about it? I needed to stop talking or at least start pronouncing properly. We left the restaurant later that day, the producers didn't seem that interested in what I had to say any longer, if I'm totally honest, neither did I. Whenever there's a dream worth dreaming, and you want to see that dream come true, there'll be plenty voices talking, forget all about it, it isn't worth the trouble, all the trouble that you're going through, that's when you stop listening.

Bill informed me that next year, the whole team would be returning to London to film a new movie. I was being given the chance to meet up again and this time, meet all my celebrity heroes and inspirations, most importantly Cristina would be joining them too. This was perfect for me, as much as I wanted to come to some sort of deal there and then; I knew I was pushing myself too hard. I would return to Gibraltar, fix myself up and return again to London in a few months, life had other plans before that. Little did I know that when I returned to Gibraltar, I would soon be diagnosed as epileptic, luckily before I left London, I had one more person to meet.

Heidi was a friend of Cristina, who too was taking the opportunity to meet Bill, Steve, Debbie and the rest of the team, since they were there in London, where she had her practice. It was a delight to meet Heidi, especially her cheerful attitude, she had a very positive energy. Heidi and Bill were talking about her practice, she was an Upper Cervical specialist, I had no idea what that was all about, but I was very lucky I learnt about it that day. I'd be visiting Heidi's practice upon my next return to London, once I had been diagnosed as epileptic. Months of seizures would soon begin to ruin my life, I needed to find a way to stop them. During this dinner, I was being given the answer to a question I didn't even know I'd be asking myself in the near future.

Upper Cervical Care is a radically different approach to health care, it's a natural way of healing, still using science to do so. Upper Cervical Spinal Care is a strict, non-manipulative discipline of chiropractic that focuses on the upper most part of the spine (the cervical spine). This is where the brain and spinal cord meet to form the brainstem, just about every nerve in your body meets and travels through the brainstem. An upper cervical specialist is a chiropractor who specialises in the correction of spinal misalignments in the upper neck region. All chiropractors make spinal corrections in the neck, however, upper cervical specialist have a unique and precise way to analyse the neck through precise x-rays and the correction methods are done without twisting, cracking or pulling. Upper Cervical specialists take great care in determining exactly how the neck is misaligned and take great care in the delivery of the correction.

When we finished our dinner, this was the last time I was going to see my new friends for a few months. I couldn't believe this had happened but as we hugged each other and said our goodbyes. I realised, life could be good again, only if you don't stop looking for it. That night before going back to my hotel, I went for a quiet stroll through Kensington Gardens, I was using this, as I would use the Nipperish back home, hoping to be alone with my thoughts. As I was walking, I began passing various people, suddenly someone came up to me, this was random, people don't usually come up to others for no apparent reason, this had to be a hallucination. It was no hallucination, someone wanted me to take a picture of them; as stupid as it might sound, at this exact moment, I felt normal. My nerves being around my celebrity friends had vanished along with them; for the first time, I was enjoying what I had just experienced. At the same time, a stranger asked me to take a picture of them and it made me feel so normal, I felt happy, I was working my way back into a social society.

My flight wasn't for another few days, I worked on my screenplays in London, I looked over my photos with Bill, Steve, Debbie and the rest of the crew and I continued touring London. After three days of being mostly alone, with the occasional British hallucination now and again, I started to crave the need to speak to a familiar face. I was over the moon having achieved my childhood dream, I had spoken about it via computer with many of my family, but I needed someone actually present with me, who knew how much this meant to me.

Finally, I was able to speak 'llanito' when I went to London's train station to meet up with Germaine, who after twenty minutes had still not shown up; ten minutes later, I realised I was at the wrong train station. As I run up the steps, back out into the city, I found myself face to face with Germaine, it was so nice to see a familiar face, far from home, one I had not seen in many years. Germaine had lived in England for almost five years now and had become very familiar with London. Every night, I would walk twenty minutes to what I believed was the nearest Nando's, my favourite restaurant to visit whilst in London, we have none back home. Thanks to Germaine, I realised there was another Nando's much closer to where I was staying.

I wanted to tell Germaine about Ashby but did it make sense? Had I seen a ghost or was I just hallucinating about my friend because I missed him? Talking about having seen Ashby, seemed all so normal to me but the more I thought about it, after years of not seeing each other, this was probably not something I should share with her. Instead, we had a great time through London, especially when we entered the magical world of M&M's. Back home M&M's are nothing more than a bag of coloured chocolates but in London, they were running their own store. Walking through London with Germaine, I kept thinking about everything good I had experienced that week, life felt normal again, life felt worth living.

Germaine and I soon said our goodbyes and once again I found myself alone in London, soon enough voices began to keep me company. The last day of my holiday, I didn't want to go back, Abdul did not want to see me go home either, he suggested I get on a plane and disappear to America and follow my dreams. I wish I would have listened to Abdul; instead, I returned home, determined to save up enough money to come back to London next year but my old job wasn't done making life harder for me. The upside was that now returning back home, I had something I never had before, I had hope, life wasn't over for me yet, I knew I was going to go back there someday.

Chapter Thirteen
Resignation Day

I returned to Gibraltar and back to the shithole I called work; the reason I ever started working was not with the desire to save up and buy a car, a house, start a family but rather to travel to Hollywood. I always wanted to meet a nice American family, who would help me during my struggle to achieve my dream, and the American family I had met, were actually the franchise I hoped to work for. Everything seemed perfect, life was fixed, time to move on or so I thought. Soon after arriving back from London, I suffered my second grand mal seizure in front of my sister and nephew. At this stage, my hallucinations began getting much clearer, a lot stronger and I had still not shared this information with anyone. In November, I suffered another grand mal seizure, come December I suffered three of them in a row, this kept me from breathing, for a very long time. According to my parents, this was the day, they thought I would die… Merry Christmas to you too.

Suffering from a seizure every month or so, kept me hospitalised and out of work for two weeks each time, I was having a terrible end to 2012. Although I had gotten a taste of the life I wanted back in London, soon enough I was back into the same bullying routine, with the new addition of epilepsy. By this time, I had realised how faint my hallucinations once were, they had always seemed so real but now, they appeared as though I had upgraded to a higher definition. I would return back to work, hoping the voices I heard and illusions I saw would stay at home, I could not concentrate with them around me. My hallucinations had now been happening for a little over a year, although I knew it was strange, they had become normal to me by now.

As humans, we learn or rather are taught that there are certain things we cannot and are not supposed to be able to do. Living life surrounded by 'ghosts' had now become normal for me, it was part of life, we can adapt so easily, even to the strangest of beliefs. If aliens began to roam the planet, most of us would be in shock, even those of us who always suspected them to be real. However, in less than two months, seeing people posting pictures on social media with aliens they've come across on earth, would quickly become normal within our minds. How many of us think about robots and instantly think about the future? The reality is the future is now and robots are all around us, at the time of this writing, one has even been granted citizenship within our world. Robots living around us will soon become the norm just as video calling, which once seemed so futuristic, is now part of our daily lives. As the present becomes the future, we adapt to technology which we never thought possible, the same applies to our beliefs.

Since November, I had started taking different forms of medication to try and stop my seizures, nothing seemed to be working properly, this was all new to me, I still hadn't even researched what seizures were at the time, I had no idea what they did to you mentally. As I recovered in hospital, it was always bitter sweet, it was a break from work but at the same time, all I could do was worry about dealing with bullies and hallucinations when I got back. Finally, by December I had started taking Lamicital, which at first only made me feel drowsy and drugged the whole day long. I was slowly falling into a greater depression, I was losing my mind but during work, I tried so hard to be 'normal' that by the time I reached home, I no longer had the strength to concentrate on my mentality. My brain would run lose on me, I could no longer control my thoughts, I was practically daydreaming the entire day, I was lost within my mind.

At the end of December, everybody received their salary except me, I had just left hospital a few days earlier. I had not been at work when the pay slips had been handed to us but that shouldn't have stopped my salary from entering my account. Since it was the Christmas holiday I couldn't ring anybody to find out what had happened, I was forced to wait. I had no money for presents, food, bills and not even enough to buy my medication, I found myself suddenly without an income. Luckily, my parents lent me some money, mainly to pay off my bills through Christmas, with the understanding that I would pay them back the following month. For yet another year, I did not celebrate the New Year, instead I stayed at home, lying on my bed, listening to the voices around me.

I was hoping to find out why my salary had been stopped upon my return to work after the New Year. They had a valid reason, my position was no longer available, I had been replaced and my replacement was earning my salary. I did not understand how had I been replaced? Apparently, I had missed too much work in the last few months due to my seizures and because of that, my position had been given to someone else. Human Resources assured me I had not been fired, I should just wait around until they called with a new position available for me and my salary would then recommence. I had bills to pay, loans to keep up with and most importantly, I was trying to save up to travel to Hollywood and become a screenwriter, this did not work for me.

My seizures came from a stressful area in my brain, this was not helping my stress levels at all, I had recently learned I had developed a scar on the hippocampus region of my brain, I was now taking stress very seriously. Since I was technically still employed by the Gibraltar Developing Company, I couldn't request unemployment benefit. I had begun the New Year diagnosed as epileptic yet unable to stabilise my seizures. I now found myself a semi-unemployed-epileptic-unable to write-writer spending most days surrounded by hallucinations. I owed my parents money, I had new bills to pay each month, my dream of flying off to Hollywood didn't seem like it would become reality, only but another illusion in my thoughts. My life was quickly falling apart, much faster than it had the few years prior, I no longer worked for my bullies, at that point that didn't make any difference to me anymore. I felt like the world was passing me by, I truly hoped there was something better waiting for me.

I went to visit Human Resources as well as Unite the Union on many occasions, as the days went past, I began to realise, I wasn't going to be getting my job back; why they still kept me employed, I had no idea. I knew what they wanted me to do and finally they won, I did what they had wanted me to do for the last five years, I resigned from the Gibraltar Developing Company. Surprisingly enough, the next day I was informed, that my resignation letter had not been accepted. Were they not allowing me to resign? I had written a lengthy resignation letter detailing why I felt the need to resign, they did not approve of it. Apparently, my resignation letter was too long, I have no idea why but I wrote a second resignation letter, this time it was accepted, I was finally free.

I requested copies of my file from Human Resources, who in return provided me with only a handful of reports, I knew there were a lot more, again I requested all my reports. This time around, I was informed by Human Resources that my file had been misplaced, I no longer had a file within the Gibraltar Developing Company. I still had a bad work record, but it had now all been summarised into a few reports, where were all the examples that had me worried at least once a week for years? How could these not be on record anymore? I decided to send the Data Protection Act in the hopes that they could retrieve my file, I knew it hadn't been lost. I doubted very much that my employers would lie to the Data Protection Act but apparently they did. Luckily for me, I had been keeping report after report since as far back as five years earlier, when Shale provided me with one each week, I had already caught them in their first lie.

I was finally fully bully free, and everyone thought I would start feeling better for it but I didn't. I had never felt so broken in my life, after a few months back in the reality that I called my life, even meeting my idols couldn't keep me from hitting rock bottom. The only thing that was giving me strength in life was the fact that I hadn't given in to my bullies, as soon as I resigned, it meant I had, they won. I stood up for myself for five years, only to find myself worse off than when I first started. Don't get me wrong, I did put up a fight, I lasted for as long as I could, people will argue I should have left earlier but now that I was in a sense 'free' instead I hit rock bottom, as I knew would happen to me the day I resigned.

I had in a sense become immune to the bullying after so many years, what I most feared was giving into them. My bullies had already tampered with my health, I couldn't run away from them, I had to stay strong, resigning was the weakest thing I believed at the time that I had ever done in my life. Throughout the years, I requested transfers and even applied for other jobs but with my new record as worse employee in Gibraltar, I was having a hard time finding a place to start over. I did not want to resign without a backup plan, since I now suffered from epilepsy, even returning back as a cable car operator was out of the question, even if a job was available for me.

My life in 2013 did not look like it was getting better for me, my seizures were still not completely under control, I had no money to eat, let alone travel, the only bright side, I wasn't working for my bullies anymore. I began collecting unemployment benefit in the form of twenty pounds a week, I couldn't really do much with that, at least I could buy food for myself. I couldn't pay my parents back after Christmas, since I couldn't pay my bills either, my parents were forced to keep paying for my expenses. I had become more independent in the last few years, yet here I was again, eating my parent's food, needing their money and unable to pay for my share of the bills. At this time, I had also found myself without many friends, I had isolated myself from most of them and the few times

I did meet up with friends, I was very negative to be around. I was also very strange, I can only imagine, most times voices and hallucinations would join us, I'd appear insane whilst trying to ignore them and continuing our conversations.

I was no longer driving anymore, being epileptic meant that me behind the wheel was a danger to everybody. I had actually stopped driving when I returned back from London, I felt it was no longer safe for me to drive. Not being able to drive, I suddenly found myself more confined to my bedroom, now even if I did feel like socialising, I had no car to help me get anywhere too far and no money either. I used to enjoy driving to the beach, I'd sit on the sand and stare at the ocean but now having to walk to the beach, for a quick look at the ocean, didn't seem as appealing as it was quite a lengthy walk. I could no longer escape to the top of the Rock, only walk midway, I had lost all my independence by then. As the years began to pass, I became quite used to walking, Gibraltar is probably roughly the same size as Disney World, if you walk fast enough, you can enjoy every ride.

My days started to become so long, I would wake up each morning, without the need to leave my bed for any reason, no need to shave or get dressed, simply locked away in my bedroom, pretending I was sane. Since I was depressed and scared of having a seizure whilst on the move, I literally spent my whole day moving from my bed to the sofa, sometimes on occasions to the toilet. I would leave my curtains closed, blocking the sun from entering my dark bedroom as I lay in bed, waiting for the day to end. At the end, I would then get up, open my curtains to find the sun had gone and spending most of the night sitting at my computer. The worse part was I could not concentrate on my writing, I had just returned from meeting my idols, all I wanted to do was write, I was inspired but my mind wouldn't allow me to create stories.

Writing had always been my form of escaping life's problems, I would use this to relax but now because of my seizures, my brain was not allowing me to concentrate, let alone come up with stories. Sitting at my computer, I would spend the day listening to music, another very relaxing engaging activity when you're depressed but only if you make the effort to sing along. I'd spend the day marooning with Maroon5, watching people appear to be walking in and out of my bedroom, I couldn't handle it, I had to speak to someone about this. The hallucinations had always bothered me but to an extent I was fine keeping them to myself but now that I was experiencing seizures it was becoming more apparent to me that I was slowly losing my mind. I feared I would lose it all one day, especially after the time I had forgotten my parents' names, after one of my seizures.

On occasions, I had commented about ghosts, voices and hallucinations to some in my family but I would immediately stop the conversation and pretend I was joking. The reactions I was getting to my 'jokes' were not making me feel comfortable saying what I actually wanted to say. I usually tend to joke about difficult subjects, it seems to make it easier for me to confront them. I'd start by telling my sisters a scary ghost story, they always found them ridiculous and laughed at me; they thought I was jokingly trying to scare them, which led me to pretend I was just joking around.

I was sitting in the kitchen one night and my mum started walking down the stairs, at this point the stress I had brought into the house, was affecting her too, she was very worried about me all the time. I was terrified that my parents would think that I had totally lost my mind and placed me inside a mental hospital. I had to be very careful with my words, this is why I prefer writing, one gets to edit their mistakes. My mum was suffering so much because of me, could I seriously burden her now with having to think I had lost my mind by speaking of ghosts and worldly dreams? I felt I had no choice, I had to tell somebody, who better to tell you can see dead people than your mum? Maybe an exorcist but I didn't go down that route. It had been happening for over a year now, I needed to share this with somebody but I had to make sure this time, not to change the subject midway.

Joining me in the kitchen I asked my mum if she believed in ghosts, she looked at me knowing where I was going with my conversation. "Do you think you saw a ghost?" she asked and all I wanted to say was "yes, I've seen many of them, first in my dreams, then in reality, they even followed me to London and once I saw my dead body unconscious below me". Instead, I started with what she was familiar with, her dad, I told my mum I had seen Grandpa Arturo a few months earlier, sat in the patio, smoking a cigarette. I knew she didn't believe me but at the same time, she didn't make me feel crazy for sharing, I think she was more worried than anything. We discussed the fact that now that I knew I had epilepsy, they were probably simply hallucinations. Although I agreed with my mum that these were hallucinations, the fact that I lived with them for over a year made them still feel real for me. At this point, I began to realise I had not developed a sixth sense just a mental illness, however could they be one in the same? I still had hope that these hallucinations from my subconscious had meaning to my reality.

As the months progressed, I was becoming a real financial burden on my parents, though they never complained, I felt terrible for it. With the help of doctors, we were trying to find a way to stop my seizures but so far Lamicital was not doing the job, we upgraded my dosage and hoped for the best. I came to realise that taking Lamicital whilst I felt a seizure taking over actually stopped it from happening. I was on a strict routine to take two tablets in the morning and two tablets in the evening, it's dangerous to change your dosage without warning a doctor but if I felt a seizure coming, I now had a way to stop it. Taking Lamicital didn't mean my epilepsy was cured, I was just finally in control of my seizures; although at times, they would catch me by surprise but slowly things were getting better. Once again, I begun suffering seizures mainly at night, when I was unaware that they were happening but during the day, I now had control of them again.

It is important when depressed to try and help control your sleep pattern as much as possible. It's very easy to tell someone who is depressed not to go to sleep during the middle of the day but for someone with depression, sometimes that is not possible. My recommendation would be to at least spread yourself around the house, if you want to sleep, take a nap on the sofa. Always make sure only to lay in your bed at night, that is when your body needs to properly shut down. Try and get your body to associate your bed with a peaceful sleep and your sofa for simply napping. It is also important not to block yourself from the sunlight, open the curtains, turn on the light, this way at night, when it is truly meant to be dark, your body and sleeping patterns can adjust. If a person spends over seven days locked in a dark room, their body clock will break, our body's internal clock needs to be exposed to the sunlight. This allows our body clocks to function and set properly, feel tired at the right time and get certain hormones our body requires through sleeping.

One day whilst everyone was at work, I became tired of watching television, I had felt fine all morning, I needed a little bit of sunshine, I decided to be brave, leave my house and walk to the Nipperish. As soon as I left my house I realised, I had not stepped foot in the sun for a few days, I hadn't realised how much I missed its warmth against my skin, I was slowly feeling re-energised. I reached the Nipperish and as I always did, I sat and admired the view, it always helped me relax. It had been a while too since I had seen Ashby's memorial picture. I liked being there but since I had begun suffering grand mal seizures, I was scared to go up there, in case I experienced a seizure, one isolated from the rest of civilisation.

I think I began worrying myself so much over the fact that I might suffer a seizure alone in the Nipperish that I slowly started having a panic attack over it. The sun now felt hot instead of warm, I had to find shade, I felt very disoriented, my vision had begun fading inwards, allowing me only to focus on the bright sun at the centre of darkness. I lied down on the ground, back against the grass, knees bent, with my feet still firmly on the ground and I began practicing my breathing techniques. I started breathing in through my nose and out through my mouth, I continued repeating this until the moment past and slowly, although weak I started to feel better. I stayed lying on the grass, unable to sit up straight, I felt so tired, broken and angry, all at the same time. I still didn't know it but Unite the Union who I had put all my trust into, were not keeping their promises to me. I was hoping to take my government to court over unfair dismissal and personal injury but Unite seemed more eager to see me fail than succeed. All I had at that moment was hope that Unite would be able to fix this for me; instead, I soon realised I was paying them, to set me up for failure.

Chapter Fourteen
Workers United

Whilst still employed by the Gibraltar Developing Company, I had approached Unite the Union for help a few times along the way, specifically so after I returned from London and began suffering seizures. I never wanted to take anybody to court, that would take years, I did not have years to spare, I simply wanted my problems dealt with, my record refreshed but as Unite explained to me numerous times, there was nothing they could do, unless I resigned from my position. What was the point of fixing the problem for me if I had already resigned? Yes, that did seem strange to me but this is Unite we're talking about, I pay them a monthly fee for their assistance, there is no way they would accept my money and lie to me at the same time, the world is a nicer place than that?

Unite is supposedly dedicated to serving the best interests of its members. They are meant to protect workers' rights, negotiating with employers and government to improve the quality of working life for their members. As a primarily industry-based union, their structure means they can effectively represent our interests in the workplace, where we work or what sector we're from does not matter. Unite's community membership also means that those facing unemployment are welcomed into the union family, what's the point? Members are entitled to a large range of legal and member services. This includes help with personal injury claims, employment rights matters, conveyancing, wills and many other issues, relating both inside and outside the workplace.

This is all complete bullshit, at least it didn't apply when it came to me. I could share many stories, from others who have found themselves in similar situations by Unite, but I cannot back up those claims; however, I can share my story within Unite.

Unite was a complete waste of money for me, as a past member, I'm led to believe its members, those of us who pay for their service, are not getting our money's worth. Either because Unite have no proper knowledge of what they're doing or only help those whose cases does not involve government. I wanted to take my government to court and, for some reason or another, Unite gave me the impression, they didn't want me to achieve this. We pay for their help, even before we know if we need it or not, we pay them and at the same time provide them with the opportunity to allow us to fail, if it is not to their benefit. I got the impression that helping me take my government to court was not to their benefit, either that or they genuinely had no idea what they were doing; therefore, I have no idea why I ever paid for their services. Why do we even need a union when one works for a government department? Should our governments not provide us with a safe and reasonable environment to work in without having to pay for our rights to be defended in the process? I'm not saying a union is not needed but when it comes to working for government, their services should be included for free, via a government work based union.

When I had resigned from the Gibraltar Developing Company, a few months earlier, changes were made within Unite, most importantly to me was the fact that this new team promised to tackle bullying at work. By 2013, after I resigned, I met a man who promised to help me; I met Hector, our new regional manager. At this point, my only option was taking my employers, a government entity to court for unfair dismissal and personal injury. I had suffered five years of bullying and as much as I hated the thought of it, I was willing to go through it all again, even if it lasted another five years, I needed this fixed. I now had a record which painted me as the worse employee ever to work in Gibraltar, which was not going to help me with my future, this is the main thing I needed cleared and if it meant going to court so be it.

I was very relieved when I first met Hector, he seemed like a nice person who was not only invested in helping me but also concerned for my well-being. The worse kind of enemy is one who pretends to be your friend. I had explained to him how I had suffered from anxiety, depression and panic attacks for the last few years. I also explained how along the way, I suddenly developed epilepsy, I provided him with my medical records. I was at my lowest, I was losing my short-term memory due to the continuous seizures, I told him all of this. My life was a terrible mess at the time and Unite promised they would help. I was angry, I was hallucinating, I had lost my focus, nothing made me smile, I had no idea what to do next. I hoped Unite could take it from here and sort this out for me, something I learned from this experience, never put your trust in anyone but yourself.

Since I was no longer employed, I had no income and therefore if I wanted to keep being part of Unite, I needed to find a way to continue paying for their services, otherwise they could no longer help me. I had paid Unite a member's fee for five years and now that I most needed their help, I had lost my job, they could not help because I could not pay. At least, I was now receiving unemployment benefit in the form of twenty pounds a week, this is what helped me to buy food, pay bills, my medication and continue my Unite membership. I was desperate to remain being part of a union; without them, I had no idea how to handle the situation. Something I came to realise as a union member was the fact that they never seem to be able to help individuals, only groups; why pay for individual help, when as a group, you will be included too? Only one person from each department in reality needs to pay in order to get Unite to help all of them. What I began to realise here was how easily one will allow money to be removed from their salary for something we can simply start paying for, when assistance is needed.

I was throwing up every other night, shaking uncontrollably and all other symptoms that came with seizures; I was relieved when Hector promised he would help me fix my work situation and get better. Hector informed me that I should keep this all to myself until he could resolve my problem; he asked me to bring him my file with all the evidence I claimed to have collected throughout the years. I was never able to collect my file from Human Resources but luckily, I had built up my own file throughout the years, with all of Shale's reports. I made copies and delivered Hector my evidence, now we could finally get things moving, I thought, but things only kept getting delayed longer each time.

Hector explained to me that those in charge of Unite before him would spend their annual budget carelessly. Now everything had to be sent to Unite the Union's main branch in England for approval before any fees could be spent on a lawyer. As the weeks past, I would constantly try to get in contact with Hector, hoping he had sent all the evidence to Unite's main branch in England for their approval, months past and he never got around to doing this. During this time, I was still having seizures and went to London hoping to be cured. I asked Hector if I could take my evidence directly to Unite's office myself since I was travelling to England. Hector informed me that this was not the correct procedure and that it must be sent by him directly and that he would get to it soon.

So began the many weeks of my life where all I did was wait; people tell you to be patient but sometimes being patient means someone is fucking you over. I went to Unite and learned Hector had gone to London for meetings, he would be back in two weeks. I was not working anymore, all I did was wait for two weeks to pass by, I had nothing else to do. When I returned to Unite, I was told Hector was in a meeting inside his office. I eagerly sat outside Hector's office like a puppy, waiting for him to open his door and acknowledge me. I was sure that since he had gone to London, he had taken my evidence over with him for approval, when he finished his meeting, he informed me that he hadn't. Apparently after many weeks, I had not signed a specific paper, I signed and again continued to wait.

As the months continued to pass, I started becoming suspicious that Unite were in fact playing me, everything was taking too long. Sometimes after a seizure, I'd be hospitalised for a week. I always returned home thinking Unite would have an update for me, they never did. Another excuse Unite used to delay things for me was the fact that a new Anti-Bullying legislation would be coming into effect in the coming few months, and this would help my case massively. Once the Anti-Bullying law came into play, I was informed it did not apply to me as my situation had occurred before this law took effect.

A team from Unite joined by trades council members, had been working hard on drawing up an anti-bullying and harassment document, one to be presented to the Gibraltar government for final approval, to legalise the rights for workers to be free of bullying and harassment at work. Whilst I was being ignored and misguided by Unite, they were busy working with my government to campaign publicly about bullying at work. I was starting to open my eyes, as happy as I am that this law came into effect, it happened for all the wrong reasons. At least future Gibraltarians now have a fighting chance against bullying at work, this was a win, a small victory towards our evolution.

After six months of being unemployed, I finally received a letter from Unite, providing me with an appointment to meet with their lawyer in a month's time. Since Hector had informed me my case, including my evidence had to be approved by Unite's main branch in England before anything could be done, I can only assume they were aware of the situation. I asked Hector numerous times if he had sent my file to England, he would not give me a definite answer. A month later, I finally got to sit down with Unite's own appointed lawyer. I asked Phil if we could make a court claim, he told me he had to review my file first and would get back to me. Phil never got back to me, when I went to his office to make an appointment a few weeks later, I was told he had gone on a two-week holiday. Again, I waited like a desperate puppy for the help always promised to me to pull through and I was quickly getting used to never receiving it.

Two weeks later, I went to Phil's office hoping to talk to him but was told I needed to make an appointment; sadly, they were fully booked and would call me as soon as something became available. I contacted Hector and told him about my situation, Hector said there was nothing he could do anymore since I now had a lawyer, I had to work solely with him, who would then speak to Hector on my behalf. I realised Unite and my new lawyer were playing around with me, I went to the Ombudsman to seek advice. This is the one government department in Gibraltar which, in my opinion, actually get things done. They phoned Unite's lawyer on my behalf; as I walked out of the Ombudsman, I receive a call, from Phil's receptionist, I now had an appointment to meet with him the next day.

After weeks of waiting, I had finally received my second meeting with Unite's lawyer, it was time to get things started, it was time to stress out my bullies. I wanted my bullies to go into work every day, fearing what was waiting for them as they had done to me in the past. As I sat inside Phil's office, I could not believe I had finally made it here; it had taken months but here I was speaking to a lawyer about my case, one who had reviewed my file, what could he possibly have to say, for the first time in a long time, I felt excitement again. Apparently, I had waited too long to file a legal claim and had missed my deadline to take any legal action against my previous employers, sounds about right, it is my life after all. I wasn't extremely upset, I had approached Unite the very next day after I had resigned from the Gibraltar Developing Company, over six months ago, it had been in there hands ever since, I'm sure they knew what we had to do next.

I left Phil's office and quickly went searching for Hector, who refused to meet with me, I was told by his receptionist that they had already done their part and there was nothing else they could do for me. I told them I wanted to request a second opinion, she said that was not possible. I wanted to ask Unite's main branch in England myself directly what had happened, the receptionist told me they could not handle that for me. The worst part about this was that Hector was in his office the whole time; I remember begging him to come outside and talk to me, I needed closure. It couldn't end like this, I had put up almost six years of abuse only to have it end like this? Had I foolishly been waiting almost a year for Unite to help me, only to realise they had played me all that time in the hopes that I would not get my case to court?

Unite and their lawyer made me feel like I had no case, that I had missed my deadline, they made me feel like this could not be won and if I continued to try, I would only be disappointed. This was the final straw, I had not only put my trust in Unite but I had also paid them for their assistance, not only were they not able to help, they actually managed to close many doors for me, they helped my bullies instead. Now I truly was alone, how was I supposed to get legal assistance to take my government to court, especially considering the fact that since I had not taken any action sooner I had missed my deadline to file a legal claim, I had basically paid Unite to set me up to fail.

The sad part was Unite and their lawyer had misled me, with cases of unfair dismissal at work, a person has up to three years to file a legal claim against their employers. If the case relates to personal injury then they have six years in which to file a claim. Although Unite had played with me for months, I still took their lawyer's word; legally I had run out of time, it was over for me, even if I wanted to continue fighting, I had wasted my time waiting. The fight was over, my bullies had won and again I had been played, this time by Unite, this is what finally completely broke me, I felt truly defeated by life.

I wanted to start shouting, screaming, breaking down the door, throwing things around, yet I knew that would not work in my favour. Instead, my emotions were released through tears, embarrassing tears which forced me to leave Unite's office. This time I couldn't deal going home as I could not face my parents, I could not disappoint them anymore, they had also been suffering and were just as stressed as I was, they believed in me to stand up for myself but I had failed them. I had been bullied by people much older than me, both male and female; I had a bad reputation about myself and everybody else was secretly wondering if I was crazy. I began walking up the Rock of Gibraltar ready to do something I had been thinking about doing for a long time; luckily, I couldn't find the courage to do anything about it, and later on that night, I returned home.

That night I wrote directly to Unite's main branch in England, I shared my story with them too. I was hoping they would help me fix my problem, I needed to believe they hadn't fucked me over whilst taking my money in the process. They never replied to my emails, never even acknowledged they had received them, I sent multiple emails to various addresses and never received a single reply from anyone. What are you going to do when the times get tough and the world is treating you unkind? You've got to hang onto your optimistic outlook and keep possession of your positive state of mind.

I had now been out of work for nine months, I had lived without an income for that long, I did not socialise, I had no life. All I would do was sit in my bedroom wondering how nine months had passed by and I had achieved nothing. I felt as though I would spend years hoping to make progress only to realise I had been wasting my life away that whole time. By this point in life, I had managed to cure my epilepsy, thanks to various natural remedies. It was time to move on; it was time to put all this behind me and start my life afresh. The thing was, I had spent years dedicated to this life, I didn't want to start a new one, I wanted to build from what I had learned these past few years in life.

I began applying for various jobs, nothing that truly excited me, what I was unaware of at the moment, or at least didn't want to admit to myself, I had phobia of going back to work. I was terrified that my new job would follow the same pattern of bullying as my previous employment. I had convinced myself that bullying and work were one in the same. I missed my first interview; I remember my mum called me and asked if I was ready for my interview, I said yes but the reality was I had broken down in tears upon opening my front door to leave the house. I never went to that interview, I did manage to go to the second, third, fourth and so on but nobody was interested in hiring me. I was broken, you could easily tell the moment I began a conversation with someone. I had no confidence, my voice was usually trembling and on top of that, I had a bad working record attached to me everywhere I went.

Before I knew it, 2014 had almost arrived, the days appeared to pass by so slowly but the years seemed to fly by very quickly. I was stuck, I couldn't find work, I had no income, I owed a lot of money and the only emotions I could feel were sadness and anger. I'd spend most days being sad and non-productive, but on the occasions that the anger took over, I welcomed it, as it was the only time I had strength to try and fix my life. Being angry at my bullies meant my attention was completely focused on them, they weren't even in my life anymore but yet I couldn't stop thinking about them. Love, money, friends, none of this mattered to me, this wouldn't make me feel better, justice was the only thing that would cure me, otherwise I would have to continue living the rest of my life bitter and angry.

I was not going to let my government get away with bullying me and trying to cover it up, I was going to make sure, I found justice…does anybody know what I need to do next? I had no idea how to handle the situation, never in my life did I ever think I'd find myself in a state where I would be taking my government to court, since I had no income who was going to pay for this, government? I approached various law firms, hoping one of them would be able to take my case on a no-win, no-fee basis, but understandably, nobody wanted to go to court against their government for free. I was informed that so much money would be needed simply for medical exams that there was no way this could be done without a budget, I needed to request legal assistance that would be my only fighting chance. How is one supposed to get their own government to grant them legal assistance to take them to court for something they've had Unite stop you from trying to achieve for the last year?

Chapter Fifteen
Humpty-Dumpty

Humpty-Dumpty sat on a wall, Humpty-Dumpty had a great fall, all the king's horses and all the king's men, couldn't be bothered to put Humpty together again. Politics tells you how a society must be set up and how one should act within a society. Politics is the term used for activities associated with the governance of a country or other area, especially the debate or conflict among individuals or parties having or hoping to achieve power. The requirement for a political system is that the individuals within that system are allowed to fully function according to their nature. If that's not the case, they will either rebel, or the system will eventually collapse. This has happened many times in our past, it will only continue to get worse in the future, and right now, we are witnessing the fall of many great countries, by those who are meant to be leading them.

Following the system, working hard, obeying our leaders and never questioning the truth, this is why the education system is important to our government. The main purpose of going to school isn't so much to learn how to be a good and clever student but rather how to be an obedient and loyal citizen. Who in their right minds would start living their life trapped inside a box into adulthood, when all they've ever known in childhood is freedom? Our governments need us to attend school as children to function properly in their society as adults. As humans, we are not being taught how to become self-aware but rather how to follow instructions accordingly, intelligent people cannot find happiness because we live in a dumbed down world. At this point in my life, I had come to realise that the legal system in Gibraltar and probably the rest of the world is a joke, nobody in power plays by the rules and those who do are known as law-abiding citizens.

Why are we not taught how to grow our own food in school? We are not allowed to grow our own food in society, why teach us such a necessary skill? If humans grew their own food, not only would we eat healthier, save money, we would become more independent. There is great ecological benefit to our earth as a whole, by regenerative growing methods such as permaculture and natural farming, the process of growing food, flowers, shrubs and trees alongside is also a process of regenerating land and wildlife in our cities, and a process of reducing the need for destructive industrial agriculture. Why are we not taught about natural remedies and healthy eating? We are meant to take whatever is prescribed to us or available in our local supermarkets. Our governments have no need to teach us how to build up our immune systems, discovering cheap alternatives for expensive products, we would all feel much better for it but when humans thrive, health profits plummet.

Why are we not taught survival skills? We are not meant to need them, it is better if we do not have any, this way we are forced to reform to being part of society. Although it is important to be prepared for disasters by having the right supplies, many preppers overlook the importance of having the right skills. They are not adequately 'trained' to handle the disaster situations in which they find themselves. Having the proper skills and training will provide an individual with a well-diversified knowledge base to help them survive during and after a disaster. Why should our education system teach us how to survive without a government? This way we need to rely on them for something as basic as drinking water.

Who chose the lessons we learn in history classes? Why didn't they teach us the truth about other ancient civilisations? True history is meant to be kept from us, wars and battles, that is what they want us to learn, to be ready for future battles we might be needed to fight in. Our leaders keep secrets from us, they say it's for our own good, but this is not the case, they don't want us to advance, once we do and we are able to think for ourselves, we will realise that we need no government controlling us, all we need is to be responsible. If people are happy, if people are comfortable with the life they are leading, they will not rebel yet humanity as a whole is a long way from being responsible, even our leaders can't handle it at times. If we knew everything there was to know, our minds would be open to a whole new world of living, being mentally ill should not get you thrown away into a mental hospital, meditating should not be shrugged at, all this should be studied.

When I'd complain about going to school, my grandparents would always tell me how lucky I was, when they were younger, if they misbehaved, teachers had permission to smack them with a ruler. If any teacher ever smacked me with a ruler, I'd jab them in the eye with a pencil, then use a rubber to erase any evidence left behind. How was this allowed? Were parents not affected or angry when their children arrived home from school, claiming their teacher had used a paddle on them? If it was legal, I guess there was nothing wrong with that. This form of cruel punishment is not lost back in our history, this behaviour was widely accepted until around the 1970s and worse part of all, in many places, this educational punishment is still being enforced today. Luckily, as we progressed, this way of teaching soon became illegal, it is no longer accepted yet if it were ever legalised again, would parents allow it? The system has failed us before, not only with education but race, religion, beliefs, sexuality, barriers, walls and most importantly priorities.

Taxes are special kinds of fees or charges that the government requires people to pay in order to live and work in their state or country. The government needs money to operate, and taxes is our way of paying rent to live in our country. This money goes to fund many different types of programmes, it may be used to fix roads, pay for the military and even further our children's education. We elect our leaders, we pay them taxes, then we learn money has gone missing, this is our money they cannot account for. If our governments learned how to prioritise money, there would be no need for taxes; imagine a world, where you didn't have to pay to be part of it, this is the world I hope we get to live in one day. Money is an illusion, we all work hard for it, thinking that we need it and we do but that is only because we play by our governments rules. A world without money, build your shelter, grow your food, produce your electricity, live your own life. We think money makes us powerful, we live our life fighting for it, in order to forget the trap that is money, the whole world needs to ignore it, sadly that won't be happening in this life time.

When our governments are not able to provide everyone with a healthy form of living, no matter what they are capable of, then that government has failed. The homeless, the prisoners, the financial worries, not being able to keep up with the system, these are all signs, that those in power have failed us. They always will because truth be told, we would all live healthier and happier lives if nobody told us how to live ours. They take advantage of the loyal and just ignore the needy, they specialize is causing stress, spreading fear and doubt.

This is how I now view political parties, it's certainly not a party I want to dance at. The world is slowly waking up, protests are taking place in all parts of the world, people are voicing their concerns, people are questioning the system. It has reached a point, that our leaders have become such embarrassments to our countries, that we have no option but to finally realise, that those in charge, don't necessarily have our best interests at heart.

My Grandpa Alberto was an electrician in his younger years, he was responsible for making sure people had power in their homes. During his time working at the generating station, Grandpa Alberto was approached various times by government officials; they instructed him to shut off everyone's power after seven o'clock. Why? I have no idea, it was a political move I suppose, showing people who was in charge, making us worship the light they give us. Grandpa Alberto would not act on their demands, he did not intend to switch off anyone's electricity and so he too was a subject of bullying at work, the only difference from me was, he knew how to handle his bullies. Grandpa Arturo's father was from Sevilla, he was a writer, living in the days of Franco, a ruthless Spanish military leader, who ruled as dictator of Spain from 1939 until his death. My great grandfather wrote an article condemning Franco for his actions in the local paper and for this, found himself separated from his family and sentenced to a life in prison.

A politician must be stern, must be fearless, must be willing to take risks, which can affect many and then live with those consequences, this is why good-hearted people are not cut out for politics. Being a politician in power means you no longer need to follow the rules, you can fill your pockets and get away with it, who would not be tempted to do that, if they were in power? People who reach these positions of power are no different than you or me, in fact they are worse, they are even greedier. These were the people I was now dealing with; I had moved away from my work bullies and realised my whole government was out to get me. After being forced to resign from work, I not only got in contact with Unite, Data Protection, Citizens Advice Bureau and the Ombudsman but I also began reaching out to many government officials including my own Chief Minister.

I contacted everyone who had the power to help me; sadly, I realised they all knew I was right. They all knew I had a case but nobody could do anything about it because then they would be admitting that all this was government's fault. The reason I was being stopped at every turn was because they did not want this becoming public knowledge, if I got to court, not only would they be in the wrong, everyone would find out about it. I found this very unfair as every time I read the Gibraltar papers, any minor offence a young person in a community of thirty-thousand might commit is exposed for the whole country to read. Most of the time the crime is so petty, there is no need to name and shame the citizen but when it came to government, none of the Gibraltar publications were interested in sharing my story.

I had now spent a year out of work, and by 2014, I had found myself left with no other option but to give into my bullies and move on with my life. As much as I tried, I couldn't get over what had happened to me over the last few years. I found this very unfair, I couldn't move on and if I did, I'd never be happy with myself, I couldn't live my life running away from bullies. Unite had fucked me over, I could not get my case to court on a no-win, no-fee basis, and after six months of trying, nobody would employ me, I had given up. I had been depressed for too long but I always had hope, that is what kept me going but now, no matter how much I tried, I couldn't help but give up hoping. I should have gone abroad to university to study, I should have stayed in London, I should have never left the cable car, I had begun regretting my whole life.

One day whilst sitting at the Nipperish, no longer surrounded by hallucinations, I was able to think with a clear mind. The best advice I ever received was at a diner, by a man named Pete. "Hey! I tell you what is, big city, hmm? Live, work, huh? But is not city open, only peoples. Peoples is peoples, no is buildings, is tomatoes, is peoples, is dancing, is music, is potatoes. So, peoples is peoples, okay?" We are us, we are not who they want us to be, we are who we want to be. I wasn't ready to give up, I was not going to be just another citizen my government could play around with. I hadn't gone looking for this problem, they had created it and now here I was, unemployed and lost in life, all because I decided to be part of the system.

I had tackled all my legal options so far and none of them were working, I was ready to give up, not just because I was broken but because I had nothing else to try; every time I tried to open a legal door, another would be shut in my face. I knew it was hopeless, at the same time, I wasn't ready to give up and had only one more chance to make this work for me. I should at least try requesting for legal assistance, I had nothing to lose. I was convinced I would not be granted legal assistance, it seemed like another obstacle to waste my time with but yet I decided to apply and hope for the best. I applied for legal assistance explaining why I had not taken any legal action beforehand, I explained how Unite had led me to believe otherwise and how I thought they shared a connection with the government. I wasn't expecting much, after all I was basically asking a government department to help me take them to court. My requests were submitted in writing, hopefully that would at least get me a response, I did receive one, legal assistance pending further revision on both claims, I was used to this by now, the waiting game.

In order to receive legal assistance, one must have no money, none at all, preferably not even a bank account. The more bills you have to pay the better, only if you cannot afford them, you have to have nothing, that's our justice system for you; luckily for me, at that point I was that pathetic. I spent months waiting for my legal assistance request to be granted, it was not being granted, although it wasn't being denied either. Some people were just trying really hard to stop me from receiving legal assistance, finally allowing me to get to court without any further hurdles from government being thrown my way. How could they now accomplish this, without crossing any lines, which might get them in trouble? Whilst I waited patiently for my request to be granted, government granted legal assistance to benefit some very powerful people. These people had money yet were offered legal assistance immediately simply because they're important and I'm just your average citizen.

Justice is a privilege the rich can fight for in court, the poor don't have a fighting chance, many cases never reach court, simply because the defendant cannot pay such fees. Even if I were to have taken on two jobs at a time, there would have been no way for me to afford my legal fees. If I wanted a chance at getting my case to court, I would be better off remaining unemployed and hoping for legal assistance, in the long run, this way I would lose less money. Unfortunately for me, this meant I had no case against Unite, technically since Unite (Gibraltar) is simply a branch of Unite the Union, which is officially based in England, I could not be granted legal assistance for this. At this point, I had also come to realise what a strong connection my government and Unite had recently made together. Not only were they appearing side by side, backing each other on many endeavours but when it came time for elections again, Unite very publicly showed their support for this same government.

As I waited for my legal assistance to be granted, it was advertised everywhere that the new anti-bullying legislation had been passed in Gibraltar. The faces associated with this were everyone from government and Unite that had fucked me over. There they were, my political leaders, my union representatives, parading their faces through the media as though they were huge supporters of anti-bullying. The reality was they were the biggest bullies in all of Gibraltar, they control all the power and therefore they are the most dangerous. This had me fuming, it had taken me months to accept I was being bullied at work but it took me even longer to realise, my government, were also my bullies. I couldn't stop thinking of all the times I had approached my government, waited for meetings, filed reports, all against my employers and they didn't plan on doing anything about it. I was not a priority to my government, I was not even a concern, I was just a number, attached to a problem they had created, one they wished to simply sweep under the rug.

All over the world today, most people mistrust most politicians; I had now become one of those people. Political scandals, conspiracies and corruption occur daily in every country and in every political party, hence most politicians are mistrusted even by their supporters. Many believe that politics necessarily breeds corruption and I believe they are correct as power corrupts. No wonder many people mistrust not only politicians but politics itself, many refuse to vote, they no longer believe elections can make a significant change. Often people disgusted by most politicians' deception seek trustworthy politicians, if they find some, those too eventually disappoint them. Some people believe a dictator should replace parliament, whilst others rejecting dictators but seeing no alternative, give up and leave politics to politicians. This makes matters worse as politicians concerned more with their power than with the interests of society are left to run society. I could have been a bully, I like breaking things apart, I could have been a union but I just had too much heart, I could have been in politics, because I've always been a big spender or I could have just given up.

People of the world unite! Stand up for your human rights! Don't let your government stop you from collecting rain, just stand up and complain. Let this be the people's cause, point out every leader's flaws! Something is wrong with all of them, we're tired of so much pain, just stand up and complain.

Democracy and dictatorship show difference between them in terms of their methodology and concept. Democracy and dictatorship are two types of rule over a country. The person, who has complete power over a country, is called a dictator. A dictator enjoys an absolute rule over a country or a state. On the other hand, in a democracy, the choice to create laws is with the people. In other words, we can say a democracy is taking decisions by discussing it with all. That means people have the say in deciding what to do…it's time to turn the world around.

Chapter Sixteen
Reality Check, Please!

At the beginning of 2013 whilst starting to deal with Unite and my government, I was still dealing with hallucinations and seizures. I couldn't go on living like this, I had to concentrate on my life but my mental illness was holding me back, for many reasons. The biggest being not only that I did not want to socialise but I couldn't, I was having a hard time balancing the voices in my head with those being spoken to me by real people, I could no longer ignore my hallucinations. My doctors were trying to figure out a way to cure my seizures but I had nobody helping me find a cure for my insanity. At this point, my hallucinations were becoming ridiculously consistent, people of all ages, dressed in very different style clothing and of many different nationalities would approach me at all times of the day. Most times, I'd know if they were real or not but sometimes I could not tell the difference, worst-case scenario was always when out in public.

My mum was now aware of what I was going through, but I had still not gone into much detail about it with her. I was experiencing it and I couldn't believe it myself; I had to share this carefully, I couldn't tell my mum everything at once. I began researching epilepsy, sleeping patterns, dreaming, hallucinations and slowly I was able to piece the puzzle together. It was starting to make sense to me, every time I experienced a seizure at night, I would remain unconscious, I'd immediately reach a deep sleep soon after. This allowed me to dream lucidly as my subconscious mind was still dealing with my conscious mind. As my illness progressed, the damage or rather rewiring caused to my brain was now making me hallucinate. Seeing someone who was not actually there had now become so normal to me, after over a year of living with ghosts, no science was going to get me to immediately ignore their existence. I still believed there was a chance I had experienced a spiritual awakening and was dealing with actual spirits rather than simple hallucinations, against my better judgment, I decided to visit a spiritualist.

Spiritualism is the belief that the spirits of the dead can communicate with the living. The spirit world, is seen by spiritualists, not as a motionless existence, but as one in which spirits continue to evolve. Spiritualists believe that spirit mediums are 'gifted' to carry on such communication, but that anyone may become a medium through study and practice. Spiritualists will speak of a concept which they refer to as spirit guides, specific spirits, who are relied upon for spiritual guidance. Spirit guides are incorporeal beings that are assigned to us in life, as well as on a rotational basis, they help nudge and guide us through our journey on earth. They're responsible for helping us fulfil our spiritual obligation, spirits are capable of providing useful knowledge about moral and ethical issues as well as teaching stuff our governments keep hidden from us.

Spiritual guides will stay with you throughout your entire life, and others might appear every now and again to help you with specific areas of your life or goals you are trying to achieve. Spirit guides are at varying levels of consciousness themselves, when we pass on to the next phase, one must also learn and adjust as we do here on earth. There may be spirits who have had physical incarnations, such as we're experiencing now, or they might be spirits who have never taken corporeal form. Some may be highly ascended masters such as our religious leaders and others might be your average spirit who after death has figured out how to communicate through energy. Spirits may appear to have a male or female form and at times can even appear to be bears, though in reality they are just energy.

Our spirit guides are meant to guide us without intervention, specifically so because most of us are unaware of their existence, coincidences are their speciality. Fortunately for some, through hard work, persistence, perseverance and sometimes mental illnesses, we're able to communicate with them. Our spirit guide is not necessarily guiding a single person, they might be guiding many, hoping to achieve a goal, always pure. Spirit guides can see what's going on in our lives, and when it's time for them to actually intervene, they have several ways through which they can accomplish this. Signs are all around us, many times we mistake them for coincidences, spirit guides can arrange synchronicities to help alert you to something you need to see or know about. One must pay attention to those when they happen, you never know what, who or where the next place of your life will lead you to.

Cristina grew up in Spain, I live in Gibraltar, at one time we were country neighbours but then she moved away to America. Through our shared interest in entertainment, we connected online and eventually we met in London, for many reasons this meeting changed my life. On my last trip to London, I met Heidi who explained to me what Upper Cervical Care was all about. A few weeks later, I was diagnosed with epilepsy; a few months after I returned to London, I remembered having met Heidi, which again changed my life. At age three, alongside my dad, I rented a VHS tape which would begin my life-long obsession with Hollywood. Had I never picked up that VHS tape, twenty-three years later, I would have never met any of these people; spirits tend to like arranging and nudging us on the right path.

One's spirit guide sometimes gets together with other people's spirit guides and together they try to create a meeting between their charges. Have you ever bumped into someone you haven't seen in years just whilst or soon after you had been thinking about them? How long has it been since you last spoke to a good friend? And how long after did they call you over the phone? If it feels like a coincidence, consider that it might be more of a set up. Have you ever walked to work and on the same route seen the same person each morning as they too made their way to work? Has it become so normal for both of you to see each other, that without ever having spoken, you both greet each other goodbye? This person is meant to be in your life, there's no such thing as strangers; when a stranger says hello, everyone is family, we should be having so much fun together.

Have your ever missed out on a job opportunity? Perhaps had you got that job, you'd never know where you could be working next. In my case, had I got the job as a screenwriter the first time around, I never would have taken my government to court. Had I then got any job back in Gibraltar thereafter, I would have never been legible for legal assistance even though without it, I could not afford any legal fees. Have you ever bumped into someone you hold a grudge against? For me many years later, I bumped into Shale, I felt nothing, no fear, no anger, no hate, I felt good, until that moment, I hadn't realised, how unaffected I now was by her bullying in the past. Everything happens for a reason and most times what seems like a missed opportunity, if you are truly working hard for it, consider it more a stepping-stone for your next opportunity.

Ashby's mother Mati believes feathers that appear in her life, are sent to her by Ashby. One could argue that feathers are everywhere but it is when one believes they have meaning, that they are truly seen. If a spirit wants to communicate with us and we believe feathers are the answer, they will make themselves heard. Many of us always expect signs but never truly stop to consider, what sign we're waiting for; if we made ourselves heard, our spirit guides will listen. If we wish to communicate with spirit guides in the real world, we must learn to be aware of our surroundings and not shrug of coincidences as simply a chance encounter. Ask your spirit guides for what you want and then watch for signs that you've been heard. Would it not be great if you could just speak to your spirit guide via telephone or video chat? It's actually very similar to communicate with spirits as it is with humans, it just takes time and practice to be able to hear, see and feel your spirit guides.

That little voice in the back of your mind that says 'don't trust them', 'don't go out tonight', 'this is a good idea', 'go for it' isn't just a passing subconscious. Following your gut instinct and trusting your heart is something we all experience, not all of us listen to our intuition, not to be mistaken with ego. One might believe it's nothing more than a passing thought, it is in fact your subconscious mind communicating with your body. Your body is reacting to what you're feeling, even if your conscious mind is not aware that this is how you should be feeling at that moment. I've learned this is one of our most valuable tools when trying to make a decision in life, always go with your gut instinct. Spirit guides can poke, jab and if need be, punch you in the gut, this is when you're experiencing something they want you to pay attention to. 'Gut' feelings are generally regarded as not modulated by conscious thought, and as a reflection of intuition rather than rationality. Most of us are unable to communicate with our spirit guides simply because our subconscious mind only works whilst we're sleeping. However, our subconscious mind and our body can still communicate whilst the conscious mind is alert without our knowledge.

When the voice in your mind speaks to you, it is nothing more than a passing thought, when you think, you are not hearing anything, you're merely thinking it. The closer you get to controlling your subconscious, the clearer these voices become, to a point where you will start hearing them in your head with sound. Eventually, these passing thoughts will sound so real, you're led to believe someone is standing next to you as they speak; in reality, you're hearing your brain literally speaking to you. If you repeat a

134

word in your mind, the longer you concentrate on the word, the clearer the thought will become, until it eventually becomes a sound. A person can also achieve this by working on their visual thinking, don't view a picture in your head as a slide show, imagine it as a portrait. Add colours, add detail and slowly you'll realise, the image in your head is becoming much clearer. At this point in my life, my intuitions were not simply passing thoughts but rather voices telling me what to do. I was lucky, this was all a very slow process for me. I had time to understand my new 'illness', and therefore, I didn't lose control of my mind. I did not allow my conscious mind to freak out when the subconscious mind began working alongside of it.

I hoped someone who knew about all this stuff better than me might help guide me in figuring out what it all meant. I basically wanted someone to reassure me that even though I was mentally ill, spiritualism was in fact a real thing and I was experiencing it. I hoped I'd find what I was looking for, I kept thinking to myself as I made my way towards the spiritualist's house. I had my money for our session that alone already made me doubtful. If someone truly has this gift, you feel such a sensation of giving, that there is no way you will accept money for it. I understand people need to make a living but using this ability to do so, feels wrong, let this be your hobby, one we can all master if we took the time. I reached the house and was greeted by the spiritualist, there was incense all throughout the rooms, in all honesty, I felt very relaxed when I arrived.

The first thing I realised, somebody else had joined us in the room; the second thing I realised, was the fact that my spiritualist was not aware this person was there. I was asked to lay down on a bed and concentrate on my breathing, whilst the spiritualist's hands hovered above my body. We had a ghost in the room and my spiritualist had not noticed it was there. The longer I laid in bed, the clearer it became to me, this spiritualist was not going to be able to help me. A true spiritualist would have realised there was a spirit in the room with us, or would they? Does a spiritualist have the ability to see and communicate with all spirits or only those that reach out to them? Perhaps, I wasn't spiritually awoken and was simply hallucinating, therefore my spiritualist had nothing to see. As much as I wanted help figuring out if ghosts and hallucinations were one in the same, I eventually got up and left. This particular spiritualist could not help me, we were not on the same page, either we weren't seeing the same ghost or I was just mentally ill and needed my doctors instead.

I got home that night very disappointed with the whole experience, I thought I'd have answers, instead I only found myself more confused. I kept having lucid dreams and in them I kept experiencing different places but now mostly recognised everyone from my dreams, those who were once strangers, had now become my friends. I was starting to confuse reality with illusion, I began making deeper connections with those who shared my hallucinations and dreams than actual living, breathing people all around me. I now preferred being in the company of monkeys and ghosts as opposed to humans, I wanted to live my life through my dreams. In my dreams, I was always happy, relaxed, the conversations I had were much more interesting to me than the gossip being spoken in the real world. Part heaven, part space, or had I found my place? I didn't want to just visit, I planned to stay. I was living in an illusion but the truth was I was happy, I wanted to stay dreaming forever, I didn't want to leave the magic. One of the best ways to meet and connect with your spirit guides is to meet them halfway, open up your dreams to them.

I had only ever experienced this once, yet here I was again, looking down on my unconscious body as I hovered above myself. What most worried me this time around was not the fact that I believed I was in a lucid dream but rather, I had not gone to bed, my body was laying on the floor below me. I immediately gathered, I had experienced a seizure. There was blood pouring out my mouth; I could only imagine how painful those bite-marks must feel in reality. Every time I had a lucid dream or had an encounter with an illusion, I was never scared, I felt so at peace, I felt so calm but when this happened, I was nervous. This time I was especially nervous thinking to myself, perhaps this was not a dream as I had thought the first time around, perhaps I had died. All I wanted to do was rush into the next room and tell my parents or my sisters, anyone, to come check on my body.

I kept trying to look at my hands but I could not see anything in front of me, all I could see was my body below. I started hovering around my bedroom like a drunken fly, and suddenly the window caught my attention. At this moment, not only did I remember this had happened to me before, I was also aware that last time it happened, I was eager to fly out of my bedroom. Last time, I felt relaxed, I thought it was a dream; this time, I was convinced I had died, I wasn't eager to leave my body out of my sight. I did recall that last time it had happened, the next morning I had placed a playing card faced upright, on top of my DVD collection on my highest shelf. This meant I had no idea which card I had placed out, it had been so long I had forgotten all about it but in that moment, I remembered. I hovered towards my DVD collection and on the top shelf, I found the seven of spades. I immediately experienced every emotion of shock one's body would feel, even though I was nowhere near mine. I couldn't believe the card was up there, I was now truly convinced this wasn't a dream, I was dead.

One would think that realising you were dead would make you feel sad, I was very nervous and confused but once I accepted the fact that I was dead, I felt normal. I still felt alive, I just couldn't comprehend how I could see my body resting below me and have no flesh surrounding my thoughts. I literally began looking around me, trying to find a bright light, I was very confused, I wasn't scared, I just didn't know what to do. I wanted to explore my house, I wanted to see my family but all I kept looking at was the closed window. How I wished that window was open, all I wanted to do was experience this, whilst exploring the outside world. As I reached the window I realised, there was no need for it to be open; I past right through it and before I knew it, I was no longer looking at my body inside my bedroom, I was looking down on my house. The whole world was still there, people were walking, cars were driving, noises were heard, I couldn't get over the fact, not that this was happening but rather how I was viewing it. I now had a bird's eye view of all of Gibraltar, and as I continued to move, I eventually found myself staring down on the Rock of Gibraltar, this was unreal. There comes a moment in your life, like a vibration you can feel your future there before you, a perfect life to live, but reality calls with unknown voices, pulling you away.

Is this death? Flying around like an invisible Superman with no place to go to? Should I not see a bright light? Should I not be guided by an angel? Should I not feel at peace? All I wanted to do was continue flying up; I wanted to reach the stars but even with all those possibilities before me, all I truly felt like doing was visiting my family and properly say goodbye to my body. Suddenly, the next thing I know, I'm lying on my bedroom floor and my tongue is in great agony. This time around my muscles had not locked up on me, but as I tried to get up, I realised I had no strength to do so. I yelled out for my parents, who came running to my bedroom, finally I was not alone. After a seizure, my short-term memory usually failed me but this time, I was able to remember everything perfectly. What worried me most was I had not dreamt about the fact that I had suffered an epileptic attack, it had actually happened; somehow, I had been experiencing reality as though I were an illusion as opposed to the other way around.

An out of body experience, also known as astral projection, is supposed to be the phenomenon when a person's consciousness is detached from the physical body and travels or exists outside of the body. During these experiences, the person is aware of their surroundings and is often aware of what is being said around them. The experience can be extremely vivid and therefore feel very real. Neuroscientists and psychologists regard an outer body experience as a detachment caused by different psychological and neurological factors. As much as I enjoyed lucid dreaming and to an extent even communicating with my illusions, it was after this experience, that I was finally determined to cure my epilepsy.

The thought of dying whilst depressed and becoming mentally ill at the hands of my bullies terrified me. This was not the legacy I wanted to leave behind, if I were going to die, I was going to make sure I made a difference in this world before I did so. I was ready, to find a way, not to control my seizures but rather to cure my epilepsy, even if it meant I could no longer explore my dreams or interact with my illusions, I hoped they weren't one in the same, but I was doubtful. When I found my strength to stand up again, there was only one thing on my mind, the seven of spades. I reached out towards my DVDs on the top shelf and my fingers began to tremble. I knew the playing card was up there but as soon as my fingertips touched the card, goose pimples rushed up and down my body. If these dreams and hallucinations were all in my mind, then how could my mind give me the answer to something I did not know yet? I picked up the playing card, suddenly nothing made sense again, I was holding the seven of spades.

Chapter Seventeen
London... Again

My doctors couldn't seem to find the right dosage of medication to control my seizures permanently and were not sure at the time what exactly triggered them. The medical system is slightly better now but back when I needed it, Gibraltar had no permanent neurologist working in our country. When this happens in Gibraltar, they usually send us to the United Kingdom to undergo treatment there. Since a neurologist visited Gibraltar every six months, I was not given this option, I had to wait. I was losing my mind every single day, I couldn't wait months until the neurologist was due to return again, my parents agreed. At the expense of selling my car and motorcycle, I was able to return to London again, this time around I went accompanied by my mum and Stacey. I was too ill to travel alone, this was not a business trip, it was a medical one.

Luckily for me during my last trip to London, I had already met the person who would end up curing my epilepsy and I arranged an appointment to visit Heidi, amongst other specialists. I was excited for this trip, it had been four months since I had resigned from work, I was leading a very boring life at home always, I needed an adventure, I needed a holiday but was too ill to do so alone. Seeing as I had not worked in four months, meant I owed my parents a lot of money, they kept paying my bills for me throughout. Selling my vehicles was not nearly enough for a trip to London and helping my parents with my finances. Stacey did me a huge favour, she took out a loan under her name for me, I hoped that I could use this money wisely to pay my bills, pay my parents and find the right specialist. Coincidentally, my Hollywood friends had already returned to London and had started filming their new movie, I wanted to meet up with them too. There was nothing left for me in Gibraltar, but London held so many possibilities, if only I could get better first.

When we arrived at London, I felt much calmer than I had the first time around, it's always easier to travel with company. My mum, Stacey and myself were staying in a big apartment compared to the small hotel room I had stayed in last time. The next day consisted of visits to many neurological specialists who I hoped would help. Truth be told that other than reviewing my medical records and advising me to keep taking Lamicital, they didn't offer much alternatives. I was beginning to realise that epilepsy was something I would have to live with for the rest of my life, the best I could hope for, was to control my seizures. Controlling my seizures meant I'd still have epilepsy, and I had concluded that whilst I was epileptic, I'd continue to hallucinate. I feared I would spend the rest of my life living in a fantasy world, one I was trying to escape too, as much as I enjoyed my dreams, I knew I had to stop this.

That night after eating at Bella Italia the three of us were making our way back to our apartment, when in the distance we saw a body lying in the middle of the road. Another person was standing next to the body, the three of us looked at each other in disbelief. We had no idea what was happening, had this been a hit and run or had the person standing up knocked the other one out? As we began approaching the two figures, we realised it was two teenaged girls, Lizanne was lying on the ground unconscious and Nadine was worriedly pacing around her. We asked what had happened and apparently Lizanne had suffered a seizure; luckily, she had been in the company of her friend. A man on the side of the road called an ambulance, whilst my mum, Stacey and I stood around an unconscious Lizanne pretending to be traffic cones. It was very dark, we feared cars driving along might not realise there was a girl lying unconscious in the middle of the road.

The ambulance arrived and soon Lizanne and Nadine were on their way to hospital and the three of us, in shock, back to our apartment. I think I was the one most shocked out of all three of us, this was my first time at the other end of an epileptic attack, the first time I got a glimpse of what my family must go through when this happened to me. It had all happened so fast, when we got back to the apartment we were still in shock and suddenly my mum burst into tears. My mum repeatedly kept telling me how glad she was that I had not come alone on this trip. At the same time, she felt sad, knowing I had experienced something similar last time I came to London alone.

We had spent two days in London and so far, I had not experienced any jolly good old hallucinations. I knew they were part of my subconscious. This time I wasn't hoping my illusions had remained in Gibraltar, I knew they'd eventually show up, they were

140

probably busy sightseeing these first few days. That night whilst sleeping on the sofa, I felt somebody touching my hair, I immediately woke up but realised I was paralysed, my muscles had locked up on me. I was used to this by now, normally all I'd have to do is wait a few seconds and I would regain my movement but this time, I was experiencing something different. Somebody was touching my hair, but nobody was there, for the first time I felt a little scared. I wanted to move, I wanted to get up, but I was frozen, then I began to feel somebody touching me from my shoulder, all the way down to my foot. Although I could feel someone touching me, it didn't necessarily feel like a hand. My hallucinations had never touched me before, I had never felt them, when I reached out to them, my hand would pass right through them, how was it possible for this to be happening now?

As I began panicking, I suddenly heard the most soothing female voice I had ever heard, "Don't worry Nicholas, everything is going to be alright." Although I only heard one voice, I had a sense that three spirits were around me. People usually say that they've sensed a spirit walk into a room, I never understood that, until that night. I simply felt as though three female spirits were standing around me but after hearing that gentle voice confirm everything would be alright, I felt a sense of calmness throughout my body and suddenly I could move again. As soon as I got up, I peeked into the bedroom where my mum and Stacey were sound asleep. I wanted to walk into the room, wake up my mum and tell her what had happened, although I was not scared, for the first time I was nervous to be alone. Feeling as though my hallucinations had physically been able to touch me once again, had me believing the possibility that, although in my head, these were very real illusions.

I went back to bed and that same night I woke up feeling someone playing with my hair again, and as last time, I couldn't move. This time around I was not as nervous as the first time, all I could do was stay laying on the sofa, waiting to hear the voice again or at least gain movement. After what seemed like minutes, but probably only seconds, I felt nobody touching me and was able to move. I wasn't sure what was happening anymore, might I be dreaming? I always enjoyed knowing when I was in a dream but hated when in real life I wasn't sure if I was in reality or not. There was a piece of paper and a pen on the table in front of me, I decided to scribble on the paper and go back to bed. If the next time I woke up, I found the paper had been scribbled, then I had in fact woken up earlier and it wasn't a dream. I went back to sleep and for a third time in a row, I felt someone touching me again. The same calming voice spoke to me as I remained paralysed on the sofa, "Nicholas, don't worry, everything is going to be alright."

This time upon being able to move, I quickly looked at the piece of paper on the table, it had been scribbled on. I still wasn't sure if I was dreaming or in fact awake, I needed confirmation, I approached my mum in the bedroom and woke her up. The two of us walked back out to the sitting room quietly, hoping not to wake up Stacey and there I explained what was happening. She confirmed I was awake and proved it to me by pinching me, I was awake because that hurt a lot. Whilst I was explaining to my mum what was happening to me, we heard a creek coming from the floorboards just outside the bedroom. What made us both nervous about this was the fact that we had become aware, that every time we walked into the bedroom, the floorboards creaked right outside. My mum suddenly went white, I found that strange but doubted a ghost would cause the floor to creak, yet my mum looked so scared that for the first time I was feeling scared too.

"We have to get Stacey out of the bedroom," my mum said to me, I knew there was no danger, but still I honestly felt more at ease knowing Stacey was with us in the sitting room. My mum and me looked at each other and began laughing, we were nervous and although I was used to it, I knew my mum felt ridiculous for feeling scared. I'm not sure if my mum being scared was also starting to scare me but for some reason we were both walking towards the bedroom very slowly. As we got nearer to the door, the floor creaked again a few steps in front of us, my mum jumped up in a panic and rushed into the bedroom. I followed my mum, who was now bringing a half-asleep Stacey out of bed. Stacey began waking up and had no idea what was happening, all she knew was me and my mum had woken her up in the middle of the night to join us in the sitting room. My mum told Stacey to lay down on the sofa and go back to sleep, she was so sleepy that she did not even question my mum and went straight to sleep.

My mum and I continued talking, whilst we were discussing what had happened, the doorbell rang, it was 4:30 am who was knocking at this hour? I was terrified, if it were a person I'd still be worried but if it turned out nobody was there, for the first time, I feared ghosts. My mum quickly woke up Stacey and as I approached the door she told me not to open. I looked through the keyhole and a man stood outside, I had to make sure he was real, I asked my mum to look too. We asked the man through the door what he wanted, and apparently, he wanted sex, he thought we were prostitutes. We learned that the apartment next to us was a brothel, our new neighbours were prostitutes, no wonder they didn't bring a pie over and welcome us to the neighbourhood. That next morning, we checked out of the apartment, there was no way we were staying there for the remainder of our time in London. My mum hoped our new hotel room was not haunted, I only hoped I was not the one haunted but rather the apartment. Unknown to me at the time, this would be my last experience with illusions, I was about to get cured.

The three of us had been invited by Bill to the set of their new film, which was currently being shot on location in London, including additional scenes at Pinewood Studios. I had been so caught up with my epilepsy, hallucinations, ghosts, specialists, I had not excited myself over the fact that I was about to meet everyone that had inspired me to become a screenwriter. The best part about this experience was that I was getting to share it with my mum and Stacey. They were also fans of the franchise because all their lives, they had been forced to watch me grow up watching the same movies and shows repeatedly for years, it's not easy being related to me. Cristina had made all this possible for me, ever since we met online almost a year earlier, I was very excited to meet her, who was this mysterious woman?

Before I reunited with my friends, I had an appointment with Heidi; I hoped Upper Cervical Care was indeed the answer I needed. Many doctors just wanted to control my seizures with medication, Heidi wanted to use a more natural method to hopefully completely cure me from my epilepsy. As the three of us waited in the waiting room, unbeknown to us, the next hour was about to fix everything. We were not the only ones in the waiting room, joining us was a woman, grinning at us as we walked in. Michelle introduced herself and asked which of the three of us had an appointment, I told her it was me and she asked why, so I explained. Michelle also had her own story to share, she was a dancer who a few years earlier had caught a disease, which affected the nerves throughout her body. She was left unable to move, forced to live her life in a wheelchair but as I looked around me, I saw no wheelchair anywhere.

Michelle expressed how sad she had been for many years, how she had given up ever walking again, let alone dance. Last year, her brother, hoping to find a way to cure his sister, suggested she try Upper Cervical Care. At the time, she had no idea what this was all about, granted I wasn't that sure either at the time. Upper Cervical Care is a relatively new form of treatment, one that today is still not as well-known as it should be. After visiting Heidi the first time around, she felt much better yet was still unable to walk, she continued returning for treatment every now and again and she felt much better for it. Michelle was glowing, she could not speak without a smile on her face, she had so much energy and then suddenly she got up from her seat and began to twirl around the room. What an amazing woman, she was determined to dance again, and here she was doing just that, I had never felt so inspired in my life.

Heidi then entered the room and greeted us, it was lovely to see her again, the first familiar face I recognised from my previous trip to London. I introduced Heidi to my family and soon enough she left back to her clinic, joined by Michelle, who happily skipped behind Heidi whilst looking back and smiling at us. Another woman then entered the waiting room, I wondered what her story was? We both said hello to each other, as she picked up a magazine and sat next to us, whilst I waited to be called in next. After finishing with her first patient, Heidi came back out and greeted the woman sat in the room with us; her name was Cristina. We had both been sitting in the same room as each other and we hadn't even realised who we were. I couldn't believe it, I was finally meeting the woman that saved me from death, I had no words to express my gratitude, and she's amazing.

Before my family and I joined Cristina for an unforgettable British-Hollywood experience through London, I had my appointment. I had no idea what to expect but thankfully Michelle gave me hope, that I was in the right place. Heidi performed some tests, the standard medical stuff and after analysing x-rays of my brain, she asked me to lie down, on what appeared to be a massage table. Heidi began adjusting my spinal cord, which hopefully might rewire my brain, it honestly seemed too simple to work. After we were finished, I didn't feel much different, besides the fact that as odd as it might sound, my head felt lighter. I felt as though a pressure inside my head had been released, I had been so used to this, that until that moment, I had no idea how 'heavy' my head felt. I felt like I was walking on air, something had changed inside me, specifically inside my head.

One of the world's best-kept secrets, the key to enjoying a better quality of life and living pain free without the use of drugs is within your reach. The secret is a relatively unknown yet simple scientific procedure that maintains head and neck alignment which in turn, allows the brain to communicate efficiently with all parts of the body without interference. The secret is best known as Upper Cervical Corrective Health Care. The human body is a complex creation with a phenomenal ability to heal itself, given the right conditions. The brain, like a powerful computer system, controls and monitors all bodily functions. Brain messages, signals from the brain to the body, are the medium used to communicate instructions from the brain to the different body parts. These brain messages move in a vast network of connections, our nervous system, which allows the brain to communicate with even the most remote part of the body.

The spinal cord extends through hollow openings in each vertebra in your back. It contains various nerve cell bodies (grey matter) and nerve processes or axons (white matter) that run to and from the brain and outward to the body. The peripheral nerves enter and exit through openings in each vertebra. Within the vertebra, each nerve separates into dorsal roots (sensory nerve cell processes and cell bodies) and ventral roots (motor nerve cell processes). The autonomic nerve cell bodies lie along a chain that runs parallel with the spinal cord and inside the vertebrae, while their axons exit in the spinal nerve sheaths. The brain, spinal cord and nerves consist of more than 100 billion nerve cells, called neurons. Neurons gather and transmit electrochemical signals. They have the same characteristics and parts as other cells, but the electrochemical aspect lets them transmit signals over long distances (up to several feet or a few meters) and pass messages to each other.

I left the clinic that day in the company of my mum, Stacey, Cristina and, unknown to me at the time, epilepsy free. The four of us ended up spending the day together; finally, I was getting to know the woman who replied to my email, when I was at my worst. Cristina was just as kind and positive as I had imagined her to be through her emails; she didn't just introduce me to my idols and to Upper Cervical Care, she also introduced me to healthy eating. We visited an organic food store, healthy eating is very important but usually very bland, this place made me realise eating healthy can be very delicious. Instead of using artificial chemical fertilizers or pesticides to boost yields, organic farming uses traditional, mostly natural methods to achieve the same ends.

Together again, it was good to be together again, the next day I reunited with Bill, Steve, Debbie and finally got to meet the rest of the team. What most excited me of all was the fact, that unlike last time, I was starting to believe this was happening. My mum and Stacey were starstruck, not only were they meeting my idols but this movie consisted of many celebrities, most of whom appeared in television shows that they both liked watching. I really enjoyed being able to share this experience with them, when you're from Gibraltar being on a set of any movie is ridiculous to us, we're not used to any of this. After two weeks of being behind the scenes, I was never readier to see a movie in my entire life. I really wanted to stay behind, sneak into my friends' luggage and wake up in Hollywood but the reality of life was starting to hit me.

I've always been a dreamer, I've always believed if you want something bad enough, it'll magically work out for the best, I still believe that but to wish for magic, you must put in the effort to become a magician first. I had unfinished business back home, which I wanted to deal with first, I had started something in Gibraltar, I was going to see it through, I needed my bullies accountable for their actions. It was not my time to start something new in Hollywood, it was time to finish something old in Gibraltar. Who said that every wish would be heard and answered when wished on the brightest star.

Chapter Eighteen
Young at Mind

When I returned to Gibraltar, I felt as though I had been reborn, it was time to start living again, time to start relearning everything I ever thought I knew about life. School's out forever, I was a blank slate, ready to be filled with truths, not lies. As the days turned into weeks, I began to realise, I was no longer hallucinating, I was no longer hearing voices and if I were having dreams, I was no longer remembering them anymore. Nobody was suddenly walking into my bedroom, nobody was approaching me randomly in the streets and nobody was around to talk with anymore. The sad thing was, I realised I had become better friends with my hallucinations rather than people in the real world. I was left with no friends, nobody was there for me, when the rain started to pour. Was I cured? Did I no longer have epilepsy? At the time, I was taking four Lamicital tablets a day, I reduced it to two, eventually one a day, now I'll take one once a week, simply to be better off safe than sorry.

Usually a two-week gap between hallucinations was normal for me, but after two months, I realised they were gone. What was most odd was the fact that I missed my illusions, I missed exploring the dreaming world, I missed the connection. I was happy to be cured, I could continue living a 'normal' life now, but I felt as though my friends of two years had all just suddenly left without even saying goodbye. Hallucinating goodbye, why is it sad? Makes me remember the insane times we've had, much more to say, crazy to try, it was time for hallucinating goodbye. I didn't want them to leave, but we all knew, sometimes it's better to go. Hopefully, we'll meet again, not sure quite where, when or how, they're in my mind, so for now, want to smile, want to cry, hallucinating goodbye.

I knew there was a whole new world to explore, now that I was free from epilepsy didn't mean I was locked out, I just didn't have a short cut anymore. I was going to have to put in the work, to go back there someday. School had brought me up thinking a certain way, life got me thinking differently, come live with me in an upside-down world, everything is not as it seems. It's frustrating to be in an upside-down world, there's upside-down everything, everywhere I go. Nothing was as I was meant to believe, everything I always believed to be magic was nothing more than science yet to be understood. My teachers, my homework, my government, my union, they had all lied to me but I soon realised, my brain always told me the truth. I just didn't understand at the time, I thought I was crazy and maybe I am, but in an upside-down world, crazies what you need to be. I was now open to spirituality and life after death, it might have all happened inside my head, but to me, I was able to reunite with both my grandfathers, my friends and mentors after they had passed away. Death doesn't mean goodbye, people don't die, people evolve; once you've evolved too, you'll be reconnected, our energy never disappears. If you wish to evolve sooner, one does not need to face death, one just needs to unlock their subconscious minds. Everything we've ever experienced, all our knowledge, it's all stored away inside our subconscious, our memories live on forever. Have you not seen a picture, which has brought back a memory from your childhood? Perhaps, twenty years had passed since you had that last experience and suddenly you remember it? It might have taken you twenty years, but you remembered, even though you were unaware, this information, was locked away inside your mind this whole time.

Mama Angela evolved a few weeks after the three of us returned from London, she was finally at peace. I missed my grandmother and for the first time, resented the fact that I had already been cured from epilepsy. I wanted to have a lucid dream where Grandpa Arturo showed up holding Mama Angela's hand. I wanted to hallucinate about seeing her sitting in our patio too, just as I had with Grandpa Arturo. In my dreams, Grandpa Arturo and I talked about Mama Angela. Many years before he died, they both moved into a retirement home, where round the clock nurses were able to keep Mama Angela stable with her medication, a job that had always belonged to him. I missed them both but I knew, they continued to live, in a world, I could no longer reach anymore. Mama Angela is one of the most caring, good-hearted people I've ever known, she was not one to gossip or hate, all she did was bring joy to everyone around her, she was always making people laugh.

When your heart stops pumping blood to the rest of your body, the brain ceases to function. The lack of blood circulation causes your temperature to drop, and worse, your breathing to stop. Without blood flow or oxygen to your brain, it begins the process of dying along with the rest of your body. If your brain is the control centre for your life, the heart is the core component that feeds the brain to keep it operating. When the heart stops pumping blood and breathing stops, clinical death has occurred. However, our consciousness and awareness linger on after our heart stops pumping blood to our brains; once our bodies die, our brain continues to function for a short while after, your subconscious mind begins to take over. We like to associate life with an interactive exchange between ourselves and our environments. However, if we continue to be aware, even though we can't interact, that means we're not dead, we're in a fucking coma.

A life review is a phenomenon widely reported as occurring during near-death experiences, in which a person rapidly sees much or the totality of their life history in chronological sequence and in extreme detail. It is often referred to by people having experienced this phenomenon as having their life 'flash before their eyes'. Our body has shut down, yet our brain is still functioning at a slower speed, our brain is beginning to reach a meditated state and therefore our subconscious takes over, whilst our conscious mind begins to fade. This allows a person to experience their life flash before their eyes vividly for the short time whilst their conscious and subconscious minds interact together. The person is basically dreaming, they are having a lucid dream about their pasts. Then when the conscious mind ceases to exist, our subconscious takes over and slowly releases itself from our decaying corps in the form of energy, we live on in a dream world until we experience a rebirth.

In school I was taught that when a person dies, they go up to heaven and live on forever, this didn't make sense to me? Where was heaven? Was it in the sky or somewhere far away across the universe? Why was death considered freedom of the soul? Where did the soul spend eternity? Jumping from cloud to cloud? Heaven, or the heavens, is a common religious, cosmological or transcendent place where beings such as Gods, angels and saints are said to originate, be enthroned or live. According to the beliefs of some religions, heavenly beings can descend to earth or incarnate, and earthly beings can ascend to heaven in the afterlife or in exceptional cases enter heaven alive.

Heaven is often described as a 'higher place', the holiest place, a paradise, in contrast to hell or the underworld or the 'low places'. In school I was also taught about hell, this is where my religion lost me as a child. I didn't believe in heaven and so hell didn't exist either, I supported my religion wanting everyone to be kind and generous to one another. Scaring us to believe we'd spend eternity in hell if we did not follow these rules that I could not support. The reality is, they were right, hell is very real, maybe not a devil surrounded by fire but living the afterlife stuck in a nightmare was not as rewarding as a dream. There is a theory that consciousness creates universe and not vice-versa, this theory holds that whatever it is which keeps us aware and alive is so important that reality could not exist without it.

Reincarnation is the philosophical or religious concept that an aspect of a living being starts a new life in a different physical body or form after each biological death. Almost every religion in the world believes in rebirth, it is said our body is new but our soul (energy) is very old. Believing in rebirths can be very rewarding for you are accepting that you have lived hundreds, maybe even thousands of lives already. If this is true, how can one tolerate living a depressing life this time around? We may have infinite number of lives waiting for us in the future, imagine each life considered only as a single year for our souls. What proof do we have of this? How can we know if we've lived before in a different form?

Have you ever found yourself with a special talent you had never even practised before? Perhaps, you're a great footballer, artist, writer, pianist, mathematician etc…without having ever practised or studied? The thing is nobody is good at anything, without some form of relation to it in the past. Why do some people suddenly find themselves inheriting a rare disease, one that does not run in known family history? Do you have a phobia of dogs, clowns, locks, fire, without any reason to fear them? Do you hold a special attachment with certain people or places you might never have any recollection ever meeting or visiting? This might be because in our subconscious minds we might have memories stored, which we do not remember.

This is one way to view it or maybe it's something much simpler, perhaps your ancestors experienced some great trauma, diseases or connection in their lives, then there is a chance this is hardcoded into your DNA. When a brutal event takes place then changes are made to the chemical tags attached to our DNA and these amendments are passed through generations. Could this also apply to our memories? Might we inherit memories from our ancestors, memories that if unlocked, will help us fully understand our lineage? If this were so then how are we able to accomplish 'magic' with people not within our bloodlines? When it comes to our subconscious, our DNA does not play a factor yet our subconscious is able to alter our DNA. Just as someone can fall in and out of love, your chemical reaction can also be easily changed.

Many people believe that your DNA is what it is and cannot be modified; your genes remain the same throughout your life. However, DNA alteration is possible and that our perception of the world around us changes our DNA. One can create over 30,000 variations from the same DNA structure. Your belief about the world you live in has a major influence, it matters immensely if you have positive expectations or if you live in constant disappointment and fear. This information is slowly processed by the body through mind and begins affecting your genes. The human brain is remarkable and what you can do with your mind is exceptional. All one must do is believe, positive thoughts and emotions are extremely powerful and if you learn how to focus and use them, you can access your subconscious and make changes within your DNA structure. This basically means your mind can influence your body, all the way down to the cells in your genes. The power of your mind and your belief system, what you think is powerful enough to heal our physical symptoms.

One must also be very careful, as the opposite is also true; if a person lives in constant fear, anger, frustration and other negative thoughts and feelings, this can damage their health. Your body gets sick and your performance level drops. When you often allow yourself to be in a stressed situation, constant anxiety or deep anger, you are hurting yourself physically. These emotions damage your body at all levels including the cells in your DNA. Deoxyribonucleic acid (DNA) is a molecule that contains the instructions an organism needs to develop, live and reproduce. These instructions are found inside every cell and are passed down from parents to their children.

Perhaps when we die, the white light we see, is the beginning of our new life, our soul, our energy, entering the next body becoming available at that very moment in time. Maybe our consciousness has simply reached enlightenment. Our DNA structure is formed whilst we're a foetus, but there is a special process during birth where personality and memory is transferred to us; a baby gains their consciousness at their point of birth. Imagine perhaps as babies, we're aware of who we once were, that we had just died. Since our conscious minds have not fully developed yet our subconscious mind is in control. Once our conscious mind takes over, everything we once knew begins storing away within our subconscious. As we grow older, we begin adapting to our new life and unless unlocked, our past lives become nothing more than weird dreams, until we reach death again. It is important to keep in touch with the innocent child within you, for it is this child like mentality, which will allow you to open your mind, to the true world around us.

In this cycle of rebirth followed immediately by death, when does one experience the dreaming realm? We do not necessarily have to visit this place upon death, if you can visit the dreamt-up world of heaven during your current life, you are more than ready to start over upon death. There is no time limit for one's rebirth, if your energy lives on forever, taking human form, is not a priority. It is scary to begin a rebirth for many reasons, if you are not in control of your mind, upon being reborn you will lose all memories from your past, including those you've most loved. Being reborn is as intimidating as facing death, although in this case, you have a choice as to when you're ready to restart over.

Many of us take years to meet our soul mates, myself included, I'm still looking; once we finally find that person who makes us feel complete, why would we ever want to separate ourselves from them? Life is short but only because we don't take care of our bodily vessels, our information lives on forever. How many computers have you bought in your life? Those who take the time to install anti-viruses and clean up their hard drive on a regular basis, can keep their current information in the same computer longer than those who download illegal porn on theirs. If you can maintain a healthy body, not only will you retain a healthy mind, but you can keep sharing them for a longer period of time. If we had relaxing lives, the right mentality, the right atmosphere, the right nutritions, the right diet, the right amount of rest, then we could remain young, well into what is considered old age nowadays.

There is no need to say goodbye to those we love so soon, there is no need to wrinkle and crease as we become older. We assume that looking older is the same as getting old, they are both completely different. A tree can last hundreds of years, but if one begins to rot away after only ten years, is it as old as the tallest and healthiest tree in the forest standing tall for over 200 years? No, the tree has simply began rotting away earlier than it should have. Turtles and tortoises are some of the most long-lived members of the reptile family. Even small species that are typically kept as pets, like box turtles and terrapins, live between 30 and 40 years if they're kept healthy. Larger species such as sea turtles are estimated to live about 80 years. The giant tortoise, the largest of all land turtles, typically lives at least a century, some of them have even been known to live for more than 250 years!

The longest-lived of all the turtle species, the Galapagos giant tortoise, eats a strict vegetarian diet that's full of greens and free of fat and cholesterol, therefore developing a very slow metabolism. These slow-moving gentle giants are extremely docile and peace-loving creatures that generally live stress-free lives. This combination of calm and healthy living is probably one explanation for their extreme longevity as well as having a very slow metabolism. In other words, don't be a fast hogging fat pig, be a slow, calm, healthy turtle in life and live longer, with a beautiful shell to protect you from danger.

The idea of living forever might seem like one that's impossible and perhaps it is, but extending our relative life span for a longer period is not far out of our reach. In the 1800s, the average life expectancy was approximately 40 years but since then it has increased, consider all the advances made within humanity since then. Nowadays, men have a life expectancy of 75 years whilst women have an expectancy of 80 years. If life expectancy can double in two hundred years, then could we not continue to double it again following the right methods to do so? Although these are rare examples it is not uncommon to find someone living to reach over 120 years in life. Our bodies are capable of living on well past our current expectancy. Some have already added an extra 80 years, to what was once considered the average in the 1800s. How many people consider the age of 60 to now be the new 40-year-old back in the day?

In the future, with the proper diet, proper environment, proper way of living, one could begin to take on the aging process at a far later date. We could all keep our youthful looks well past the age of forty. We could in fact begin developing our first white hairs, our first wrinkles, our first signs of old age, at the time that we reach 80 years as opposed to how rapidly most of us age these days. People blessed with youthful faces are more likely to live to a ripe old age than those who look more than their years. People who look young for their age are actually aging slower than what is considered the norm. Key pieces of DNA called telomeres, which indicate the ability of cells to replicate, are also linked to how young a person looks. A telomere of shorter length is thought to signify faster ageing and has been linked with a number of diseases. People who look younger have longer telomeres, the secret to staying young forever is keeping a long telomere.

The mind if used properly, can heal your body and even change your DNA structure, allowing you to alter the aging process within your DNA. In order to achieve this, we must all live like turtles, positive thoughts, healthy eating and avoiding the fast-paced rat race of life. Then we could not only remain looking youthful for longer, we can also live longer too. Early life forms on earth, starting at least 3.7 billion years ago, were single-celled organisms. Such organisms (prokaryotes, protozoans, algae) do not age and are innately immortal, this is how all life on earth began, we are created by immortal organisms.

I was no longer going to take life for granted, I realised it was far more special to be alive than I had ever believed. I was going to make sure to make the most out of mine, I wanted to live a long life yet at the same time, I wanted to continue exploring the world hidden within my subconscious, all my friends were there. The advice my illusions provided resonated with me, it felt like it was coming from them and not me. Their advice always made sense and when I listened, I saw results. I'll never lose my dreams, no matter how hard it seems, I'm such a long way from any illusions that might keep my dreams from fading.

When we are faced with the reality of spiritual progression, we need to be prepared for rapid expansion and to let go of all beliefs and notions we hold about the laws of reality. As only when we unlearn the lie can we glimpse at the truth, and only we can provide ourselves with these means of breaking down the barriers blocking our consciousness. If you think I've completely lost my marbles at this point, here's a spoiler alert, in the next four chapters, I end up in a mental hospital.

Chapter Nineteen
Naturally Non-Manufactured

The secret to living a healthy life style is not by consuming or medicating with what is available at your local supermarket or pharmacy. Sometimes one must think outside the box and consider how our ancestors did things back in the day. Mama June, as I imagine many grandmothers are known to do, always had a special way to cure an illness, without having to go to the pharmacy. As a child, I just assumed this was an old person's way of thinking; they hadn't adapted to the times of modern medicine. After everything I had experienced through life, I was beginning to question if our new expensive methods don't fall short when compared with older cheaper methods handed down throughout the generations. Every bite you take is either fighting disease or feeding it, be careful what you consume. Think carefully about what you're putting into your body, as one would do when downloading a new programme onto their computers. There are many natural remedies out there, for all kind of causes, these are examples of the ones I've began introducing into my life.

Fruits and vegetables have been in the human diet over the entirety of human history. We eat them raw, cooked, chilled, frozen, and in ever creative combinations with other fruits and vegetables. We drink them in juices and in some cases even use them to make us beautiful. Fruits and vegetables, in actuality anything that grows within nature, even including plants are an important part of a healthy diet, and variety is as important as quantity. A diet rich in vegetables and fruits can lower blood pressure, reduce risk of heart disease and stroke, prevent some types of cancer, lower risk of eye and digestive problems and have a positive effect upon blood sugar which can help keep appetite in check. I never ate fruit or vegetables at all, not until I was around twenty-eight years old; once I added them to my diet, I realised, how wrongly I had been eating all these years. Suddenly, I began feeling healthy, but the most surprising thing was that all these years, I thought the way I felt was normal. I now realised my diet of pasta, meat and chicken was not giving me all the nutrients my body needed.

Eat a variety of types and colours of produce to give your body the mix of nutrients it needs. It might sound silly, but nature's natural foods also come with instructions themselves. Each coloured fruit or vegetable comes with their own benefits to help protect various parts of our body. Fruit and vegetable of white colour helps protect our immune system, greens help with detoxification, yellows with beauty, reds with heart health, purples with longevity and orange with cancer prevention. The colour is not the only instruction, weirdly enough, each fruit and vegetable resemble the shape of the body parts both inside and out, that it helps. If you peel your fruits and vegetables before you eat them, you may be making a nutritional mistake. On many fruits and vegetables such as carrots, apples and cucumbers, a good percentage of the nutrition is stored in the skin. That means when you peel them, you're peeling away nutritious benefit. The skins also contain a lot of fibre but thanks to pesticide, we don't really have that option, so unless you've grown your own food, start peeling.

As humans, we can live without meat but we cannot live for very long without plants. Plants contain all the essential vitamins and minerals our bodies need as well as carbohydrates, fats and proteins. The only exception to this is vitamin B, which cannot be obtained directly from plants but can easily be found in foods such as fish, eggs, cheese and meat. Weight for weight plants are more nutrient dense than many other foods and can displace less healthy foods from the diet. Each plant has their own special ability within our bodies too and many hold a lot of healing powers, but all this sounds ridiculous, I mean who do I think we are, animals?

When my sisters and I were younger, Mama June always used to boil gooey bananas with cream for us when we stayed over to sleep at her house. Apparently, this helped us fall asleep easier, when I was young, sleeping wasn't really a problem. Whilst I was suffering from insomnia, I was so desperate to fall asleep, that I got up one night, and started boiling bananas. Bananas, especially the peels (if not loaded with pesticides) are loaded with potassium and magnesium. While magnesium helps prevent sleep disturbances, both magnesium and potassium work together to help relax muscles. In fact, magnesium is the most powerful relaxation mineral known to humanity. This only takes five minutes to prepare and can be enjoyed every night before bed instead of taking sleeping pills and counting your sheep. All you need to do is cut off both ends of the banana and place it, peel and all, into boiling water. Boil it for around ten minutes, using a colander, pour the water into a mug, and I personally always sprinkle cinnamon into the tea.

Everybody needs to sleep, even trees do it too; finally, I was slowly finding a way to fall asleep much easier. As the days past I realised, I was not only sleeping better but because of it, I felt less anxious too, granted not being around my bullies any longer was probably also helping, can't give bananas all the credit. Bananas have similar effects as to a pharmaceutical drug class called beta-adrenergic blockers. Beta blockers are prescribed to treat anxiety, reduce blood pressure or heart conditions. Beta blockers prevent adrenaline from binding to beta receptors which results in lower blood pressure and pulse rate, which normally skyrocket when experiencing anxiety and under stress. Bananas also contain tryptophan, a protein which can be converted into serotonin, found in most pharmaceutical drugs. They also contain a high amount of B vitamins which can aid in calming the nervous system.

I was spending most of my time going from my house to work and then immediately back home again, I was not spending enough time in the sun. In London I realised, how important sunlight is to our wellbeing, it provides us with energy. Having enough vitamin D is important for a number of reasons, including maintaining healthy bones and teeth and supporting the health of our immune system, brain and nervous system. As well as supports lung function and cardiovascular health and influences the expression of genes involved in cancer development. Vitamin D comes from your skin when exposed to sunlight, if you are exposed to plenty of sunshine, you should not need vitamin D supplements. As soon as I made it a priority, to walk through nature, absorbing the sun's warmth, I began feeling better for it, I began to find my energy again.

I was slowly becoming a walking skeleton during my days hoping for Unite's help, I had lost my appetite thanks to depression and anxiety. I wanted to get rid of them, since I could not get rid of the mental effects, I hoped to perhaps rid myself of the physical ones. When it comes to fat, there's one type you don't want to cut back on, omega-3 fatty acids. Two crucial ones, EPA and DHA, are primarily found in certain fish. ALA (alpha-linolenic acid), another omega-3 fatty acid, is found in plant sources such as nuts and seeds. Not only does your body need these fatty acids to function, but also deliver some big health benefits. We cannot produce Omega 3 fatty acids on our own, we need to get this into our system through outside sources. Aim to eat fish high in omega-3 fatty acids including

Anchovies, Bluefish, Herring, Mackerel, Salmon, Sardines, Sturgeon, Tuna and whatever other fish you can think of.

So far, I had figured out how to reduce anxiety with warm bananas, gain energy, pretending to be a flower in the sunlight, fight depression with fish and eating healthily during my walks through the garden. Mama June also introduced me to honey, why? I had no idea. It is very unlikely for honey to go bad, properly stored, honey can last many years without even any degradation of flavour, let alone spoiling. In the extreme, honey can last centuries, though the flavour and colour will be affected the longer it is stored. Raw honey is a common natural healing agent that has been used for centuries as a topical antibiotic on wounds and acne. It can also be used for sore throats, colds and other common ailments due to these properties.

Despite being used throughout recorded history, only recently have honey's medicinal effects been studied in a scientific manner. One of the most important attributes of raw honey in this context is that it possesses inherent antibacterial properties. This makes it particularly useful in treating burns, peptic ulcers, gastroenteritis and infections. I was starting to realise there's always a cheap, natural remedy for most illnesses, I just had to think for myself as opposed to following. I had suffered almost two years with epilepsy, a slight adjustment to my spinal cord cured me; perhaps life is in fact, that simple. Our ancestors didn't have all this medication we have today, yet they still cured themselves throughout history, I was going to change my way of thinking…honey I'm home.

Life can be so simple and all we must do is learn from those who know how to eat healthily, eat as the animals do. Monkeys eat bananas, bears eat fish, bees protect their honey and giraffes enjoy gardening. I was starting to think and eat like an animal, not a supermarket, I was even considering peeing outside my bullies' door. Some believe in the possibility of a heaven on earth in a world to come, I would like to believe that but unless animals take over from us, I do not see that happening. People believe we are the civilised ones, we're not; we're just the most advanced, the civilised are those who do not spend money. Animals kill out of necessity to survive, the food chain, they do not kill out of habit, they do not pollute the earth, they are not slowly killing us all, they do not hunt us for fun, they do not go into politics. Fruits, vegetables, plants, honey and everything healthy grow everywhere; nature provides what we need. If we had grown up in a society where eating plants was normal, one would never go hungry. Food would be free and available to all, we'd be helping the environment and in the process slowing down our metabolisms, thinking like a turtle.

This was all very interesting and beneficial for a healthy future but at the time, I had still not been cured from my epilepsy. If I couldn't at least control my seizures, I believed I had no future to look forward to. The first natural product I ever experimented with was coconut oil and I soon became obsessed. I use it now for everything, but at the beginning, I hoped to use it to cure my epilepsy. Coconut oil is the fatty oil obtained from the coconut, the large, oval, brown seed of a tropical palm. Coconut oil is an amazing source of fatty acids, when you consume it, you're also giving yourself a healthy boost of fatty acids. Coconut oil consumption raises the blood ketone levels to safe therapeutic levels to treat epilepsy. Coconut oil is known to reduce the incidence and intensity of seizures in patients. It is also seen that epileptic patients become seizure free after receiving a ketogenic diet and a reduction in seizure up to 90%.

The 'ketogenic diet' is a high-fat, adequate-protein, low-carbohydrate diet that is used primarily to treat epilepsy. The diet forces the body to burn fats rather than carbohydrates. The medium chain fatty acids in coconut oil are transported to the liver, which are then turned into ketone bodies. Any brain degenerative disorder can benefit from a high-fat diet. Alzheimer's patients have a diminished ability to use glucose in some parts of the brain. The ketone bodies supply energy to the brain, and this release of energy replaces the glucose in the damaged brain cells. Basically, the fatty acids contained in coconut oil transforms into ketones which helps reduce seizures. The more functioning ketones available within the body, helps control further epileptic seizures from developing.

As much coconut oil as I consumed, I was still experiencing seizures; at this point, I wasn't trying to cure my epilepsy, just control my seizures and so far, my Lamicital tablets had not started doing its job. Luckily, coconut oil also helps reduce high blood pressure; as a result of saturated fats, it increases the amount of good cholesterol in your body. Our heart benefits greatly when you increase the amount of good cholesterol in your body, lowering the risk of developing heart disease and even reducing your chances of developing high blood pressure. Coconut oil also fights against diabetes, it helps ensure that cells react to the insulin created by the body. It achieves this by balancing insulin reactions and ensuring that the reactors within the cells work properly. A healthy digestive system is also promoted by the oil, allowing the pancreas to work at a normal, healthy rate. Over time, this ensures a proper, working digestive system and helps your body gain the energy it needs from the food that you eat.

Coconut oil has many other spectacular health benefits such as healing many skin diseases, providing us with energy, helping with hypothyroidism and killing bacteria, viruses and fungus. Coconut oil helps with bone strength, weight loss, stress relief and even relieves one from kidney problems. It can also be used to condition and strengthen hair, penetrate roots and kill lice, helps with skin care, stops wrinkles from appearing, helps nails grow faster and can be used for healthy teeth. I once tried mixing coconut oil and baking soda to create a tooth whitening paste but it didn't really work, for natural teeth whitening, I'd recommend activated carbon. Incorporate more coconut or coconut oil into your diet and make sure that you eat a balanced diet of meat, fish, fruit and vegetables, and you'll be on your way to staying healthy and your reward, you'll live longer.

Since coconut oil was not necessarily working for me, I tried to find another natural remedy. I needed something to help control my seizures; I decided to call Dr Marijuana. Unfortunately, when growing marijuana has a longer sentence than raping someone, we are facing a national crisis, we are not evolving properly. This was going to be difficult to experiment with, I was used to using cannabis recreationally but to use it medically, I was going to need a lot more, I couldn't afford it or risk it. Cannabis oil is a thick, sticky, substance made up of cannabinoids such as THC and CBD, that is extracted from the cannabis plant. Cannabis oil is the most potent of three main cannabis products, which are the actual cannabis flower (marijuana), resin (hashish) and oil (cannabis oil). Cannabis oil is the most concentrated form of the three main cannabis products. That is what makes cannabis oil the most potent, it can be digested or applied to the skin.

Cannabis oil contains anticonvulsant properties and is a natural muscle relaxant; these properties come from a chemical in the plant called cannabidiol (CBD). Cannabis oil is a healthily non-conventional alternative to prescribed medication usually available. Cannabis oil exhibits little to no side effects and it gives the patient almost instant results. The active ingredients in marijuana dissolve readily in alcohol, you will get the most out of this process if your cannabis is grounded as finely as possible. Place the marijuana in a blender and let it run until the material is thoroughly pulverised. Put the marijuana in a jar that can be sealed tightly and pour the alcohol over it. Put enough alcohol in so there is enough to cover the marijuana completely, and let it sit for about 24 hours.

The alcohol will turn distinctly green after at least a 24-hour period. Pour the liquid through a coffee filter into another jar. This will remove the plant fibre and give you a green alcohol mixture that contains alcohol and the active ingredients from the marijuana. Then simply wait for the alcohol to evaporate, you can also heat the mixture on the stove to evaporate the alcohol faster, be careful when doing this, remember alcohol is involved. The result will be a thick green tar, it can be difficult to work with or smoke, just because it is so concentrated and sticky, but it is useable at this point.

I was now going to go a step further, I was going to create cannabis coconut oil, depending on the amount of cannabis oil you have available, heat up your coconut oil and then slowly add it to your green mixture. At the start of 2013, I finally found a way to control my seizures, just as effectively as Lamicital would soon become, they both worked just as well. Every time I began having an epileptic seizure, Nurse Mary-Jane would make sure I consumed cannabis coconut oil during my seizures. I was never aware but according to Nurse Mary-Jane every time she fed me this, my seizures would begin to pass. This began working so well, that now each time I had a seizure I did not feel the need to visit a doctor, as it had been controlled before doing much damage to me. My favourite part about this, I no longer bit my tongue to shreds, the seizures would stop or at least slow down where I'd never reach the point of tongue shredding.

One of the most important aspects of human physiology is homeostasis, which is the drive to keep the internal makeup of the body in a stable balanced state. Part of this involves controlling the relative amounts of acidic and alkaline chemicals in the body. Maintaining the right balance of acids and balances in the body is critical for cells and proteins to function properly. Another health beneficial nutritional plan is the acid/alkaline balance diet. The idea behind this eating plan is that most people have chronic acidosis because of consuming too much acid-producing food. Although the body is able to counteract the effects of this acid, the acid-generating foods can stress the body and reduce some of its minerals. We're meant to be an alkaline organism and eating poor foods likely mean we're also eating too many acidic foods, which can change our blood pH from a normal alkaline level to harmful acidic levels. That, in turn, affects our immune system and makes us more susceptible to disease.

Cancer is the name given to a collection of related diseases, in all types of cancer, some of the body's cells begin to divide without stopping and spread into surrounding tissues. Cancer can start almost anywhere in the human body, which is made up of trillions of cells. Normally, human cells grow and divide to form new cells as the body needs them. When cells grow old or become damaged, they die and new cells take their place. When cancer develops, however, this orderly process breaks down. As cells become more and more abnormal, old or damaged cells survive when they should die, and new cells form when they are not needed. These extra cells can divide without stopping and may form growths called tumours. Cancer has always been believed to be caused by genetic cell mutations, in reality it can be caused by infections from viruses, bacteria and fungi.

'Cancer' cells thrive in an 'acidic' (low pH) environment, but cannot survive in 'alkaline' (high pH) surroundings. Cannabidiol (CBD) oil targets and reduces cancer cells and tetrahydrocannabinol (THC) is very high in alkaline properties. Even acidic 'fruits', like oranges and lemons, become 'alkaline' after they have been digested and absorbed by the body. Fruits that are high in alkalinity include pineapple, berries, avocado, papaya, plums, kiwifruit, apricots, passion fruit, pears, raisins, apples, guavas, mangos and grapes. When aiming for an alkaline diet, dark 'leafy greens' and most green vegetables are great choices. Kale, collards, chard, lettuce, spinach, arugula and all other leafy greens qualify. Other alkaline green vegetable choices include broccoli, green peppers, zucchini, celery, artichokes and cucumbers.

A potent alkaline, baking soda mixed with water into a soluble drink can help reduce heartburn, indigestion and kill fungus. Raw, organic, virgin coconut oil is considered a superfood because it helps increase cardiovascular function, heals damaged cells that can lead to cancer and other disease, and cleanses the body. Cancer cells can form due to oxidants rampaging through the body. Pure honey is full of bioflavonoids (antioxidants) that have a powerful influence in decreasing the capillary weakness and fragility that abundance oxidants can create. I was trying to understand how life works from scratch but in the process I realised, I had completely forgotten how life works in a society, I no longer belonged to one.

Chapter Twenty
Life Outside Civilisation

While the rest of the world is thinking about paying loans and settling on Mars, there exist some tribes who still map their way by studying the stars. For decades, these native tribes have shunned all contact with the outside world, the life we lead is not one that is as rewarding as one might think. They even react violently when people from the outside try to contact them and most times probably with reason. Since they live in voluntary isolation, they are usually believed to be in a constant danger of disappearance. The truth is our civilisation will probably be the one, who will end theirs, it's been done to animals, why not people? If you're not part of modern society, you won't just be left behind, you'll be unable to survive, this is completely immoral, because it is unnecessary.

The world, as we know it today, is built on the ruins of thousands of years of advanced cultures yet many of us believe ours knows best. Humanity is not currently at the peak of modern age advancements in technology and weaponry, not at all, we've been here before. This information is lost to our history, and so we make the same mistakes over and over again, humans erase themselves from existence every couple of thousand years. Adam and Eve have lived many times over, in the forms of humanity repopulating and restarting our civilisation, time and time again. In the bible, God allows Adam and Eve to live happily in his garden, all he asks is that they obey his one rule; they were warned not to take a bite from the forbidden apple. As a kid none of this made sense to me, first of all what about evolution? Secondly, why would God be so stingy with his apples?

The snake tempts Adam and Eve into taking a bite from the forbidden apple, humanity only have to fight temptation, in the hopes of living in a beautiful, peaceful garden. When one is tempted to eat the apple and falls into temptation, then the garden is lost, humanity's greatest fall is temptation. Nuclear warfare is nothing more than recent repeat in a series of nuclear blunders that have come, gone and returned with the passing of time and with the rise and fall of different civilisations. Nuclear warfare is a military conflict or political strategy in which nuclear weaponry is used to inflict damage on the enemy. Nuclear weapons are weapons of mass destruction, which can produce destruction in a much shorter time frame and can have a long-lasting radiological warfare dimension. A major nuclear exchange would have long-term effects, primarily from the fallout released, and could also lead to a 'nuclear winter' that could last for decades, centuries or even millennia after the initial attack.

Our chosen leaders have too much power over us; we sit back too easily and allow them to control our world for us, a world which can only work if we're all in control of it together. We made the world a promise, there's nothing we won't do, we're here to make life easier for each and every one, our goal should be pure, we should all be making sure, that humanity gets its mail. We are born with many talents, we are creative geniuses, but through school, through society, through modern life, we slowly get dumbed down. We believe what is normal to be magic and what we consider normal is actually poison for both our bodies and minds. Work, money, television, supermarkets, pharmaceutical drugs, Pokémon Go, psychologists, doctors, lawyers, rules, society, I was done with all that. I broke out of the system, one that had not been working towards my benefit for years. I felt like an outsider amongst Gibraltarians, I felt like a monkey running around the Rock, I didn't belong to society anymore.

I no longer had epilepsy, therefore, was no longer losing my mind but I was still anxious, depressed and broken. I had no direction in life, I had nothing to get me out of bed in the morning, not even my illusions were there to greet me anymore. I woke up each day and wondered what for, it seemed to me, there must be something more. Something more than feeling sorry and hating where I was in this pathetic life. I looked around me and I wanted to cry, I felt like the world was passing me by. I just couldn't help but wonder, was I doomed to sadness and resent? I hoped there was something better waiting for me out there. The truth is, when you give up, you'll never find something better, you always have to keep on trying, keep on looking, you can't take no for an answer.

When I found out through Unite's lawyer that I had missed my legal deadline, I gave up; even applying for legal assistance myself didn't bring me hope. All I could do was remain unemployed and hope for the best, but I knew I wouldn't be granted legal assistance for one case, let alone two. I wasn't just wasting my time, I was wasting my life, I was wasting working for an income. To the strain of my parent's bank account and relationship, they maintained me throughout my illness. The thing was, I was now a twenty-seven-year-old man, still living at home with mummy and daddy, whilst being supported by them. Gibraltar is a very small country, houses become available as they are built; therefore, many Gibraltarian families live together for longer than they would like. At this point in life, I had spent nine years on the housing list; finally after nine years, I was offered a house. Sadly, I had to turn it down, I couldn't even afford bread at the time, how was I going to buy a house?

Money, we all have to work for it, even if we don't desire it, I was fine living without it, I didn't want to buy anything for me personally but in the world I live in, I needed cash to survive, not skills. Stacey had taken out a loan for me, one I used for medical expenses, travelling expenses, food, medication and any surprises that might have arisen. That money had disappeared long ago, and now I was left searching my sofa cushions for 40p, hoping to buy a plain warm bread roll from the grocery store. Stacey was also paying the monthly instalments on my behalf, this had been going on for longer than I had anticipated, I had to find a way to start paying her back soon. Stacey had also joined the housing list a year after I had, and she too had been offered a house. Having a stable job and income, she was able to take out a mortgage and buy a house next to the beach, the same area I had also been offered a house, one I could not afford. Kaylie was now living with Nicky and Aiden in their own flat and had started her family. I was the eldest of the three, yet I could see I was going to be the last one to leave the nest, I was scared to jump, I didn't know how I was going to fly.

I wasn't epileptic anymore or joined by an entourage of hallucinations either, I wanted to try and go out and mingle, it had been so long since I had gone on a date, I could have mistaken it for dried fruit. I had no money to spend out and about, hoping to socialise; I began to realise that to keep up with others, I needed money. My friends would at times ask me to join them for a drink at the square, knowing I had no money, they would always remind me that the drinks were on them. This was humiliating, I had to start saying no, I had no money, and I could not be the one, everybody always had to pay for, since I had no money I was forced to isolate myself even further.

Thanks to my parents I was not starving but I was constantly hungry, I was embarrassed to eat too much of their food, because of this I was not eating as much as I should. Had I not been so lazy and started growing my own fruits and vegetables in my patio, perhaps I could have somewhat avoided this problem. I could no longer afford to even have hobbies, I used to enjoy collecting memorabilia from the franchise I had grown up watching but now all I could afford was to develop my photos of our time together in London. Family, I wanted one of my own but not only was I too broken to start one, I soon realised in today's modern society, one must even have money to start a family.

Imagine a world without money, no banks, no cash, no wages, no bills and no money of any kind whatsoever. Would we revert back to a more primitive life style? Living a meagre existence, growing crops and livestock as peasants would? We've spoiled ourselves that is why most of us would be too lazy to grow our own food and would probably start stealing and even killing each other to survive. There would be a complete breakdown in society, no laws to follow or social order, no iPhones, no movies, no stylish clothing, life doesn't have to be like this. We do not need to give up our perks in life and our civility, all we have to do is forget about money, stop using it, yet live life as we still do, if not better than we are now.

How free are you? Do you owe money to anyone, a bank with credit card debt or a mortgage? Are you still paying off your car or that holiday you went on five years ago? You can't ignore these things, if you don't pay them, you might lose your home or go to jail. Most people only work because they have to, you have to work to pay your bills, if you don't work the lights go out, water is turned off, phones get disconnected, you can't buy food and can't continue your subscription with Netflix. We are not free, most people think this is a fact of life, you have to work to make money to live, as our parents did. This is not a fact of life, we don't need money, we need the things it buys for us, food, clothing, home, electricity, phone, computer and flashy cars.

Money itself is a middleman, by itself it's useless, just causes misery for those who don't have enough of it. With today's technology, everything we produce for ourselves is done by machines and computers; a huge reason why many can't find employment anymore is because machines took our jobs. This is a good thing if we did not live in a world controlled by money, technology has completely freed us from hard labour, we should be celebrating that. If we don't need people to produce this stuff, it means producing things is easy; if producing stuff is easy, there is

166

no reason why it shouldn't be done for everyone, not only the ones who can pay for it. Our economy is about moving money around, not giving us what we need, the only constraint to producing what we need, is what is not available, not what is not affordable.

Our planet has plenty of resources to provide for everyone, the only thing we're short of is money. Why not make everything free, forget about money, it's our world, we can make our own rules, the only thing money creates is inequality, a scoring system for humanity that decides who gets what and who doesn't. For the first time in history, our technology allows us to get rid of this motion of rich and poor. This is only the beginning, making a free world unleashes a full technical potential, allows us to tap into clean energy sources, bring meaning, prosperity and knowledge all across the world. End to war and injustice forever, food produced to the highest standards in plentiful supply, bigger and better hospitals and schools with no budget problems and a free iPhone for everyone.

Take away cost and the only limit is our imagination and the raw materials needed to make whatever we want. Remember there is another way, a new way, a free world without money, where everything is free, you are free, we can provide for everyone. Put an end to starvation and poverty, society can become as fair as it possibly can be. Technology unhindered by costs so advanced we could not recognise ourselves; it is all possible now if we choose it. Just imagine what if everyone in our world lived together in one big house, sharing the same income between all. You know what the big secret we have yet to realise? We all do live in one big house together.

Life did not seem like it was getting any better for me, no matter how much I tried to improve it, I was in a terrible rut, one I could not get myself out of. At this time, my parents also separated, they were also very stressed in life; they hoped that by not being together, they'd feel less stressed out. It was actually a good decision on their part, they were much happier and calmer for it, marriage is a sham, something new for me to learn. Eileen and Stanley had gone their separate ways; I was now a twenty-seven-year-old child of divorce, and truth be told, I still found it difficult to cope with. When I was younger, I remember I felt so lucky, most of my friends' parents were separated but mine weren't. I felt sad for my friends, I had no idea how they handled the pain, how did they get used to their new arrangements? Divorce seemed very scary to me back then, love is supposed to be real and it is, but knowing you're in love with someone, in my case at least, is never something I'm fully sure about.

Many people confuse love as self-developing and love does in fact help us grow, but it is not part of who we are. In life, many of us are lost, we take on partners hoping to share our life with another person, this is all very well and good but only if done so for the right reasons. If a person does not know who they are or what it is they want in life, it is a scary thought, having someone by your side makes the journey less scary. This is the problem, when one gets married we stop growing, we fall into a pattern of maintaining for our family, that we stop developing as individuals and then resent the other person for this. When a person breaks up with someone and claims that a piece of them is missing, it just goes to show they have no idea who they are; they are lost in life without a partner, being lost in life is what life is all about. Having a partner is beneficial but only if you don't forget to help keep each other growing as individuals. Once a person is married, they become more comfortable with who they are, and they forget that the test of life does not end upon marriage, it ends upon death.

When I was ten years old, I remember thinking people who were in their twenties who were not married yet were rebels. If you reached your thirties and didn't have a child by then, you had completely fucked up in life. At this point in life, I find myself a thirty-one-year-old single male, who has never been married and still intends to have children one day, I consider this normal now. As I was beginning to reach my thirties, I began to worry about this but soon realised, many people who were in school with me, although in long-term relationships, are still not married and half of them still don't have children. I've come to realise my generation is split into two categories, those who have remained old school and make me feel old beyond my years, and those who are breaking away from the average lifestyle.

I have friends who are my age and have kids who are already fifteen years old, I fear sometimes that my friends might become grandparents before I have my own children. Then I have friends who have children under the age of eight, these are the same friends who would tell me I was staying behind. I had to have children, so they can grow up, whilst I'm still young and able to continue enjoying my life. I seriously do not see the point of that statement, once I have a family, I don't need my children to grow up to continue enjoying life, I just have to understand who I am in the process. Many families struggle financially, because of this they don't live a happy life; I did not want to start a family if I could not provide for them properly. Many of these friends, when I ask them, inform me that looking back now, if they had the chance, they would have waited longer to have their children. As much as I want a family, I see where they're coming from, the way I've always seen it, once you start a family, if you are truly dedicated to them, you have no time to dedicate yourself to anything else.

Once I start a family I intend to be all in, I can't afford not to work in order to write a book, I can't move around the world taking them away from their friends and surroundings. I have to live a rather stable lifestyle once I start a family, and for now that's just not me; why start something I might not be able to finish properly, the way I found myself at that moment. In today's society, it is not uncommon for both males and females to marry and start a family in their thirties. As humans begin to slowly increase their life span, we will realise, there is no real rush to start a family, at least not until you're ready.

After my parent's separation, my dad moved in with Mama June temporarily for a few months. Kaylie no longer lived with us and Stacey would spend most of her time preparing her new house, which was almost ready for her to move into. Stacey was having a hard time getting her house ready seeing as she was paying off my loan, this was not fair, I needed to start doing something about this right away. My mum and I found ourselves alone in a very big house; my parents were having a hard time financially, it would still take time but unfortunately, they had to put our house up for sale. They needed money and this house was too big for just two people, money was now more important to me than ever. If I couldn't find some soon, I'd be forced to continue living with my mum in a small apartment or joining my dad at Mama June's house. My life's problem was not only affecting me, it had started to affect everyone around me and that was what most encouraged me to find a way to end all this, the sooner the better.

The movie I had watched being filmed in London almost a year ago was soon about to hit theatres worldwide, what had I accomplished in that time? I managed to make my life worse, I had spent over a year unemployed and my legal assistance was still pending further review. To make matters worse, a case concerning a law firm run by four sisters in Gibraltar, accused of committing fraud on their clients, had immediately been granted legal assistance. I did my research and I was furious. It was clear that these four sisters were still wealthy enough that they should have not been granted legal assistance, but for one reason or another, they immediately were. Meanwhile, I had been waiting over four months for my legal assistance to be revised and had not heard back since. After the longest criminal trial in Gibraltar's history, meaning taxpayers shelled out a lot of money for this case, the four sisters were found guilty. Since then legal assistance has been discontinued from Gibraltar, this is no longer a privilege. If you want to go to court for any reason, the financial burden is now on every single Gibraltarian, or so I believe, this might have changed again by now.

I was worried I was being played as a fool again, just as Unite had done with me earlier the year before. I felt stupid for a very long time after that, whilst waiting patiently I had been fucked over, I wasn't going to let that happen again. I thought they might argue that I was now fit for work but refused to do so in the hopes of being granted legal assistance. I had to cover all my tracks just in case, without legal assistance, I would finally have to give up. I had been quiet for too long, I was going to start making noise; I needed a plan to get things started, and I did, things were about to get legally political. This is where my story gets exciting; slowly I had come to realise, the whole system had not only failed me but played me too, this is where I decided to play back. Loopholes, probably the favourite word in the government law books, I was tired of this, as a citizen I tried to solve the problem using the right methods but all I was doing was simply helping my enemies set me up to fail. I needed to make sure I followed the rules enough so that I wouldn't get in trouble, but at the same time, finding my own loopholes along the way.

You know the expression 'I have nothing else to lose', that was exactly my train of thought as I lay in bed, in my dark bedroom. Curtains blocking the light from entering my room, penniless, jobless, no respect, pathetic, broken, what did I have to lose? At this point in my life, I had realised I wasn't going to get the help I needed, how is a person supposed to get legal assistance from the government to take them to court for something they've had Unite try to put you off from doing for over a year? Apparently, my case was not important enough, I was a mistake disposed of by my government, nobody wanted to listen to me, in fact not only did nobody want to listen to me, they wanted me to keep quiet too.

Chapter Twenty-One
Freedom of Social Media

"Today, social networks are mostly about sharing moments, in the next decade, they'll also help us answer questions and solve complex problems."

—Mark Zuckerberg

Only a few technology-loving, mind-stimulating and idea-generating individuals out there are still unplugged with social media. I am sure those too will join soon as well, since social media is not just a platform for easy and simple advanced online marketing, it is also the revolution of our century. Social media allows us to communicate with each other, all over the world, with the touch of a button. These days most of us use social media to keep in touch with our friends, most of whom we can actually meet up with on a daily basis. Many of us now also have many more friends around the world, who we could not as easily keep in contact with, if it were not for this overlooked miracle, which is the age of internet.

Autobiographies are wonderful, some are inspiring, some are overlooked but almost all of them are always entertaining and full of worldly information. Most times, a person's life story can be much more rewarding to read than any history book based from those who were not present. I could never get anyone to publish my story within Gibraltar, and I did not necessarily want to take my dirty laundry anywhere else. I decided it was time to publish myself with the help of Facebook and a little entertainment borrowed from YouTube, hoping to reach a worldwide audience around the web. Gibraltar is a small community and because of this, I knew that posting my message on various Gibraltar social media groups would get me heard by most of the country. Facebook is a popular free social networking website that allows registered users to create profiles, upload photos and videos, send messages and keep in touch with friends, family and colleagues. Facebook is available in thirty-seven different languages, helping bridge the gap of communication between people all over the world. YouTube was the first large-scale video sharing site on the web, it is available in nearly every country and over fifty different languages. Anyone can upload content on YouTube, which makes for an utterly astonishing array of watchable content.

Before I did this, I had to be very careful; for starters, members of the government have taken legal action against others who have accused them of crimes online before, all at the taxpayers' expense. Secondly, I was still waiting for my legal assistance to be granted, if I were arrested or shared my story and evidence, I would not be liable to qualify for legal assistance. Throughout the years, I had prepared a testimony, during my time with epilepsy, in case I ever forgot anything that had happened to me, since I began working for the Gibraltar Developing Company. This testimony was accompanied by dates and evidence to prove each accusation, I wanted to share this but how could I do that without breaking any rules?

I was going to go all out crazy; if I got in trouble, I could simply blame it on my mentality; hopefully, I'd be able to reopen any doors which my social media outburst might have closed for me. My testimony became my diary, and I rearranged the whole thing as if it were my own personal diary entries, which I had shared online, how could I get in trouble for sharing my diary? In between, I added segments using video clips, pictures, and at times, I even pretended to be a professor, as I conducted an experiment through bullying, using actual bullies to gain results. As the days past by without sleep, I slowly started to lose control of my mind, what had not happened during my time with illusions was about to happen after five sleepless nights. The first night, I prepared my popcorn, sat in front of my computer and began sharing everything online that had happened to me the last six years.

After six years of trying to get the right people to listen to what I had to say, I finally gave up. I decided that the only way to get my voice heard was to go public, that is exactly what I did at the start of 2014. I made my story available all around the Rock of Gibraltar via Facebook. When I first made Gibraltar aware of my problems, I tried to keep my posts funny, light hearted and cleverly worded, even though this particular story was somewhat sad, depressing and at times horrifying. Honestly, if I would have just complained about my life and the injustice I had suffered, no bullies would have paid much attention to me, and I probably would have got myself in trouble. If I began to blabber on about third-eyes, brainpower, spirits, lucid dreaming, boiled bananas etc...people would have undoubtedly labelled me crazy. It was going to be a difficult journey in writing, especially since I was foolish enough to post my chapters as I was writing them. This was stressful if I'm honest, but I didn't want to lose my bullies or my audience, I should have taken more time with my story.

My story, although it might seem interesting, in actuality is very depressing and very long to explain; if I wanted to catch people's attention, I had to make it entertaining. Lots of people share their story online and many times as much as I want to read them, after a few sentences I get bored. I had to make sure not to simply complain about the situation but make it entertaining as well. In this case, even funny by adding references only Gibraltarians would pick up on, as they were my target audience. I ended up writing an online book in the course of a few days. I had people following what I had to say throughout; most importantly, I had my bullies as well as other Gibraltarian bullies finally listening to me, every single word I wrote, no matter how bizarre or foolish it might have sounded.

The aim was not only to reveal my story but also to break all the bullies in Gibraltar along the way, gathering extra evidence, exposing cyber-bullying and keeping my bullies' attention for as long as possible. I hoped that in the process, I'd be able to figure how to sort out my life, which was falling apart before my very eyes. I hoped my bullies and all other bullies in Gibraltar would remain participating throughout the whole experiment, even if they did not want to, simply because they feared they needed to. At first, my intention was to play around with my bullies, I had them worried for two nights that I was going to upload a video catching one of them in the act of bullying but which one? I got so many phone calls, messages and emails leading up to that moment and then I delayed it, just as government had delayed all my appointments with them in the past. Eventually, I shared the mysterious video, all my bullies learnt was that the response to 'Mahna-Mahna' is 'Doo-Do-Doo-Do'.

I had shared many videos and by calculating the views on each one, I more or less had an idea of how many people were still following my story. Into the late hours of the night, across three separate Facebook groups, all dealing with Gibraltar politics. The main challenge I was facing was how does someone write something, spread a message, getting everyone to read it but then if need be deny the blame later on? I planned to argue that I had gone insane, ironically in the process I did. After I finally shared my story, names and all, I received so much support and all those I accused did not make a sound, all except for Shale. My bully finally spoke out, did she apologise? No, instead she accused me of cyberbullying her.

Along with Shale, I came across a few other haters, some of who recommended I go kill myself and stop complaining. Government will always have their blind followers, who will stand behind their political leaders no matter what; luckily for me, these were the minority. Sadly, I came to realise those who agree usually tend to keep quiet, whilst those who disagree are more prone to make noise. This is why many times we're led to believe there exists more negativity in our world than positivity. That is not the case, negative people just like to complain more, whilst positive people don't always express their support. A few days later, I learned that a group of accused bullies had in fact approached the police, hoping that I would be arrested for sharing my story or at least have me stop sharing. My bullies were informed that this was not a police matter, if they had a problem with what I was doing, they had to file a lawsuit against me. They didn't go through with it, why? I presume they knew they would lose, and so I kept sharing until the point where I had nothing else to say…at that moment. I wanted to smack them all like the bad, bad cyber donkeys they were being.

My approach to that story was not the same approach I've taken with this one, this time I've had time to write; last time, I was sharing each 'chapter' upon being written. I understood what I was trying to say but to my fellow Gibraltarians, I was just coming across as someone having a mental breakdown online. I gave simple instructions on how to deal with a bully, hoping to keep it light hearted, this is a sample of what I wrote:

"Welcome to bullying for dummies. I am Professor Napoli; I've spent the last six years getting my degree in Bullyism 101, and today I would like to share my knowledge with everyone who wishes to take it. It has taken me six years to master this art yet it was worth it; now I am trained well enough, that I can deal with any bully in no less than six minutes. The advantage to this long hard six-year training is that you can then live your life bully free forever once you graduate. You will now have the skill to stop your bully within six minutes. The advantage to this is that, by dealing with a bully in six minutes, it does not harm your health, self-esteem and most importantly does not begin to affect your daily life. This is how I deal with bullies, in time we shall all develop this skill, please stand away from your screens whilst I demonstrate.

Step 1: Recognise that you are being bullied; if it does not feel right, don't doubt yourself, try to handle the situation immediately.

Step 2: Approach your bully with caution; try to reason with them, tell them how you feel, why you feel the way you do, reach out to them as one fellow human being to another and ask them to stop. Hopefully, a Level 1 Bully will usually move on and forget about you; on rare occasions, it has been documented that a Level 1 Bully might even go as far as apologising for their actions. If this is not the case don't worry, there's still four more steps yet, get ready because you are now dealing with a Level 2 Bully.

Step 3: If your bully continues to bully you, remember if they're the bully (especially at Level 2) that means you are the smarter one of the two. Eventually, all bullies get exposed, caught up in their own lies and exaggerations that it all blows up on them. Your bully will now begin to bully and pick on you more for having tried to reason with them, the way they see it, you are disrespecting them but they do not see the disrespect they themselves are showing towards you. At this point, begin collecting as much evidence as you can because if not, it soon gets removed, edited, shredded, eaten or whatever way people get rid of evidence these days.

Step 4: Outsmart your bully, not only to shame them but to get rid of them, you've already wasted four minutes of your life, why waste anymore? Prepare for the bullying to get much worse very quickly as your bully will become aggressive and makes it their own personal mission to have the last word. Make sure to try and reason with your bully one last time, if that fails do not waste any more time and move on to Step 5.

Step 5: Catch your bully off guard with the element of surprise…surprise evidence! (I posted some evidence in different, creative fashions, which I hoped would not affect me in court, if I ever did get my chance). Even though you have proven your point, do not gloat, you are better than them, you just need the truth to be revealed and you will feel better, they need the power to feel better, that's much harder to keep forever. If this fails and your bully does not apologise or disappear, then you're fucked, cause you're dealing with a Level 3 Bully, so be very careful how you approach Step 6.

You will usually notice that after Step 5, a consistency which all Level 3 Bullies share in common comes into play. They remain silent for a while; do they go into hiding? Do they go looking for a new victim? Do they try figuring out a way to keep this madness going? Perhaps, they begin building up an army of more bullies as now it is not as easy to handle one on one, as they always preferred. So many theories but sadly I am not trained in that area. Usually, you do not come across a Level 4 Bully but in my life, I did.

Step 6: You've already exposed the truth, sit back and watch a new episode of *The Big Bang Theory*. This has been a lesson in how to handle a bully and what defines actual cyber bullying. If you want to learn more on Bullyism please join our group: Gibraltarians Against Bullying, feel free to share this useful advice with whoever you feel might benefit from this knowledge."

This was a fun experience, people were commenting; finally, I was hearing from Gibraltarians who had nothing to hide and most of them were on my side. It might sound petty but I was very excited knowing I had pissed off my bullies, they always had to have the last word, would they now in public? Nobody said a thing (apart from Shale) and believe it or not that also pissed me off, what else did I have to do? Yes, my fellow Gibraltarians were on my side and their support, believe it or not, saved my life; yet, those who had actually wronged me, those who could fix the situation ignored me. Government will always have those who like to make noise with no facts, once they have the facts, they go quiet.

For so long, I had been censored by so many that I feared Facebook might do the same to me; luckily, they were one of my biggest supporters. It reached a point where videos I posted would not show up for an hour as they were under review; eventually, they would all appear and in HD quality. The next working day, all internet access to most government departments had been disabled, in my mind, this happened so people could not continue following the story at work. I spent almost five days awake writing away on Facebook, attempting to psychologically stress and to a point bully my own bullies. I had nothing to lose, I wanted to go to court to share my story. Hopefully government, Unite, anyone I had accused would take legal action against me, which in return would speed up my court proceedings, which hopefully I had not fucked up in the process.

The methods one must use today to get their message across is completely insane compared to how our ancestors were able to communicate so well with each other in the past, even before the age of social media. Nobody contacted me, again everyone involved hoped this would quietly be forgotten, I wasn't even asked to remove any of my accusations. Some admins removed it from their groups, others left it up, the important thing was it was being read and discussed by Gibraltar. This fuelled me, for the first time my bullies didn't try to shut me up; they knew I had a strong case and the fact that they knew this confirmed what I had thought for the longest time. I might not be a lawyer but I knew I could win regardless of what Unite had me believe. I had finally made noise, I had finally spoken out over what had been consuming me for six years; for the first time in a very long time, I felt relaxed, even though I had not slept for five days.

I wasn't sleeping, I couldn't stop thinking about my problems; when I began telling my story and actually getting my bullies to listen to me and provide me with extra evidence, I couldn't look away. At first, I was happy having my bullies join me watching inspirational and funny videos online, whilst I dealt with my insomnia but that is exactly where I made my mistake. Everywhere I looked, I could find false accusations being posted, public information being removed, my bullies watching music videos instead of trying to help me, before I completely hit rock bottom. The experiment backfired for the simple reason that I was already broken, I was already weak, I was already tired whilst my bullies were fixed, strong and well rested. I allowed their bullying and negligence to continue fucking up my mind, they finally broke me with everything they said, did, didn't say and didn't do.

Before going public, I had not slept for five whole days, I was suffering from extreme insomnia for even when I did 'sleep' for an hour or two, I would wake up remembering exactly everything I had thought about whilst I 'slept'. Going to bed to rest your body is very easily said and very easily done but trying to rest your mind is a totally different matter and from my own experience, resting the mind is just as important as resting the body. I had shared my whole story, I had come across as completely crazy, I didn't want to leave my house, I didn't want to see anybody. All I wanted was for one of my bullies to reach out and either apologise or take me to court. Nothing happened, after all this I found myself with only one option, go to bed and pretend this never happened. To make matters worse on the fifth day, my government and Unite had gotten together to take photos, promoting their new anti-bullying law which had recently taken effect.

I was ready to go to bed, I couldn't think clearly anymore, my vision was blurry, I had not eaten for almost just as long and suddenly Ashby appeared sitting next to me on the sofa. What was happening to me? Had my epilepsy come back? Was I about to have another seizure? Was I losing my mind all over again? All I can imagine is that after five days of not resting properly, being sleep deprived for so long, I was what some would call delusional. To be more precise, my sleeping pattern had allowed my subconscious and conscious minds to interact together again, whilst I was in a state of insomnia. As happy as I was to have at least one of my illusions back with me, this was not the time for me to start losing my mind again.

Ashby never spoke much when he appeared to me last time, and this time around was no different, all he had to say to me, was that I continue making noise. I had always associated Ashby with computers, he was a wiz when it came to handling any electronic device, he hacked my computer many times. If anyone was going to show up at that moment, whilst I was using a computer to stand up for myself against government, I was not surprised it was him. It was time to make more noise, but this time, I was nervous as I had to leave the comfort of my own house to start yelling outside my government's headquarters, I really hoped I had thought this through properly.

Chapter Twenty-Two
Breaking Crazy

As I reached the government building where my chief minister and other government officials were located, I was ready to walk inside and make a scene. As I reached the door, they closed it and I was locked outside, that wasn't part of the plan. I hadn't gone all the way down there not to make noise, I needed to make a big enough impact, so my story would not be quickly forgotten. I didn't want to hurt anyone, I just wanted to make a scene, the rest of my movie relied on me getting results that day. Hey a movie! They'll be crooks and cops, they'll be villainy, but with my insanity standing on call, I might get out of this perfectly, starring every politician in Gibraltar and me. I proceeded to kick down the door but on my first kick, I twisted my ankle, I ended up punching the shutters on the windows instead. My plan at that point wasn't even to get inside, I just needed to get their attention but after a few minutes of going crazy, I was starting to feel stupid, how come nothing was happening? I had no idea what else to say or do, should I start twerking? Luckily in the distance, I heard police sirens arriving, I was so grateful, they listened to me, I was important enough where they had to act instead of ignore.

The police were coming, I was dreading this encounter, since I was very young I always felt targeted by them, until I was finally old enough to stand up for myself legally; unfortunately, this encounter had to happen. The first police officer patrolling nearby arrived on foot; embarrassingly it was someone I knew. The police officer was trying to calm me down but that wasn't part of my movie, I didn't need a co-director, I needed actors and suddenly the sirens came to a stop, my actors had arrived.

Two other police officers showed up, in their police van, Action! The first thing the police officers did was search me for drugs aggressively. I told them I wasn't on drugs, I was having a break down but they would not listen. I was a person having a mental breakdown but was being treated as a criminal for it, granted maybe I shouldn't have punched my government's windows. I was handcuffed and placed inside the police van, on my way to the police station. If I got arrested and charged, I could kiss my hopes for being granted legal assistance goodbye, it was time for a miraculous well-timed seizure. It had been almost a year since my last seizure and even then, I was always unconscious during my seizures, I had no idea how to imitate them but I was going to try. It was time for my big finale, makeup ready, scenery ready, sound was ready, camera rolling, I looked around, took a deep breath and began my big acting scene in the back of the police van.

After five sleepless nights, I was practically losing my mind but finally having to toss myself onto the floor of the police van and pretend to have a seizure, made me consider my sanity. Luckily at that moment, I did have a semi-seizure or explosive panic attack if you will and fell off my seat and began shaking uncontrollably at the back of the police van. This seizure was somehow different, I was aware of everything that was happening to me; suddenly, I heard one of the police officer's in the front seat tell the other one to change direction and drive us to hospital, time for my big closing musical finale. As we made our way to hospital, I was left in the back of the police van, my head being bumped from side to side as I rolled on the floor. Had this been a grand mal seizure, I probably would have died at the back of that police van on the way to the hospital.

When we arrived at hospital, I unexpectedly woke up from my seizure; once I was in the presence of doctors and nurses, I began to mumble and slur. I began informing them about my third-eye, dreams and hallucinations, by that time they had stopped. People always looked at me as though I were crazy when I spoke about this, so I decided to play that card, knowing it would work. As I continued blabbering inside a room full of doctors, I could see the two police officers still standing in the room with us. My goodness what does a person have to do to get himself locked up in the looney bin? I either needed to find a way to pass out and remain in hospital or I had to go all out bonkers, but I was not going to jail, that was for sure.

"Arghhh!" I got up from my stretcher and began running out the door, I looked behind me and the two police officers had begun chasing after me. I pretended they were bears and managed to out run them, all the way out of the hospital. The three of us began to play catch outside the hospital. I didn't necessarily want to run away from them. I just wanted to be labelled momentarily 'crazy'; I began running back into the hospital. Doctors stood by the entrance, police officers were chasing behind me, I got caught, I gave up, was I crazy enough for them? I couldn't keep this up, my brain was about to shut down on me, either that or I was going to have another seizure, I had to lower my stress levels. I was given a tablet to relax; next thing I know, I was falling asleep and as much as I tried, I couldn't keep myself awake.

I woke up the next day in a small room with only me and a bed inside, sitting on a chair by the door was a woman looking right at me, were my hallucinations back full time? I asked her who she was and she replied, "I'm Nurse Janet." I wasn't sure if this new Nurse Janet in my life was real or not, I asked her to hand me a glass of water, I wasn't even thirsty, I just wanted to figure out if she was a hallucination or not, she wasn't. Nurse Janet was actually helpful, she tried to help me realise that I had to let go of everything my bullies had put me through, time to start fresh. This was all very easily said but to get it done, I needed a clean work record and to do that, I had to continue fighting. I wasn't arrested, I was admitted into a mental hospital where for the first time in years, I was able to relax; for the first time ever, I was locked away, I had no power to control my life, sounds terrible but after six years I welcomed the break from my life.

That first morning, I went to breakfast where I was introduced to the rest of the staff and became familiar with most of the patients. We all sat down around one giant table, just outside the kitchen area, and one by one we'd be served an English breakfast, having not eaten much the last few days, it was like dining at a restaurant for me. As the day progressed, I began to realise, what I considered to be an hour, was only twenty minutes, time was moving very slowly, there was nothing much to do, other than watch television, read magazines or play board games. Luckily, my mum had brought me a copy of a book I was reading back home at the time, *The Lost Book of Enki*, a fascinating read. As much as I enjoyed my book, I soon hoped for something else to help me pass the time. Smoking was something most patients eagerly anticipated every hour, when they were allowed a cigarette in the smoking room. I had stopped smoking at that time but having nothing else to look forward to all day, I took it up again.

Finally, nighttime came around and all patients were instructed to go to the medication room, where everyone was given their medication just before bed. There was no need for me to go, I wasn't taking any medication; on occasions, I'd take a Lamicital tablet every now and again, but besides that, I needed no medication, at least not today. Soon Nurse Janet came looking for me, I needed to take my medication, what medication did I need? Apparently, I had to take my Lamicital tablet and Valium. I understood why they wanted me to take Lamicital but why Valium? They considered me suicidal and believed Valium would help control my mood, I knew my body, I declined to take it. Sadly, I was tricked into taking a very high dosage of Valium because the next thing I knew, I was stumbling my way towards the pay phone. I had been drugged, I had no control of my thoughts, I could sense the 'euphoria' kicking in. I needed my head firm on my shoulders, if I wanted to get out of here, I couldn't afford to be dancing in La-La Land in the meantime.

I phoned my house, as I held the phone to my ear, whilst sitting on the ground, back against the wall, in a very long, dark corridor, I finally broke. My mum picked up the phone and I was a sobbing mess, I asked her why she hadn't come to visit me that day, was she angry at me? Apparently, the doctors at the mental hospital had recommended my family to stay away from me for a while, they believed they were helping, I see no logic in that. After a mental breakdown, one feels most comfortable and at ease speaking to their family, not to strangers who wouldn't even let me poke my head out the window for fresh air. My mum was trying to be strong on the other side of the phone, she said she would come visit me soon but they were not allowing her to see me today. This wasn't what I had signed up for; I expected to spend a day in the mental hospital, they'd realise I was not crazy and by the end of the day, I'd be out. Instead I was hanging up the phone on my mother, as I dazedly tried to make my way back to my room, I fell asleep immediately upon reaching my bed.

Being isolated inside a mental hospital, allowed or rather forced my body and brain to rest. I had come to the realisation that whilst I was in the mental hospital, my life was on pause. My problems hadn't gone away, my problems hadn't started solving themselves but for the first time in six years, I was literally not able to do anything about anything, I was able to let go. The next day, I had realised I wasn't going anywhere, anytime soon, it was time to start making friends. I made friendships with seventeen of the most interesting people in the world to me, those considered to be mentally ill or broken to be part of society. These friends were the first people I had interacted with socially in a long time, I could not have been luckier to meet them all in one go, best part, they were all real.

Matt was quiet yet when he spoke, was very wise; strangely for some reason, he wanted everyone to call him uncle, Harry was the craziest of us all and Guy was always all smiles. Ludo was big and strong but had the mentality of a ten-year-old, this could at times be very scary, he was unfamiliar with his own strength. Walter was a friend of mine back in school, I hadn't seen him in years, as unfortunate as our circumstances were, it was somewhat nice catching up with him again. Rowlf was a musician, one who thought there was a conspiracy against him, to steal his songs and make millions from it. Sam was always angry, he wanted nothing to do with anybody but truth be told, I could tell he was very lonely and broken. Madam Janice was a special person, she could communicate with spirits, voices in her head, she was considered insane even by the patients, I on the other hand, could relate to her very much. Oscar, Junior, Earl, Lew, Yolanda, Rosita, Marjory, Kira and especially my hip wheelchair bound good friend Floyd were all there to keep me company.

Floyd immediately became my new best friend, why was he there? I have no idea, he needed special injections, three times at different intervals throughout a twenty-four-hour period. Since Floyd was wheelchair bound and apparently nobody could go to his house to provide the necessary injections, he was forced to spend most of his days at the mental hospital. Floyd was very knowledgeable, we talked about Buddhism, medical cannabis, the collapse of society and the universe in general. Walter and I knew each other from school, but the first time I saw him at the mental hospital, was when he surprised me naked in the shower. Walter was trying to force me to brush my teeth with his new toothbrush, this wasn't the same guy I knew from school anymore. Kira and I enjoyed playing scrabble and many other mind challenging games. Lew was forever trying to escape, he didn't want to be there, less so than I did.

Junior had an interesting past, he had learnt a few years ago that his parents were actually his foster parents, who had accidentally killed his parents in a car crash when he was young. They kept Junior and raised him as their own, once his foster mother past away, his foster father told him the truth. Junior searched out his birth family and when he discovered his grandparents, members of his new family, murdered his foster father. Junior's foster father still held a very dear place in his heart, regardless of the consequences of their meeting, this had broken Junior to the point where he would not speak to anyone. Rosita was a lovely old lady, we became very good friends very early on, as she only spoke Spanish and most of the staff was English, at times I became her translator. I had lots of nice, pleasant, normal conversations with Rosita, the only problem was, she was forever complaining, she was very sad, very depressed. For the last few days, Rosita didn't even get out of bed, she missed her daughter Abby, who had not come to visit her in over three months.

Yolanda suffered from a nerve disorder, she could not control her shaking hands but how was she supposed to get better, surrounded by a bunch of energetic, maddening people? Marjory was not mentally ill at all, she simply suffered from severe depression, having mentally ill people, in the same surroundings as someone with depression, is not at all helpful. Marjory and I enjoyed our late-night chats, whilst watching television alongside Earl, Oscar and Sam. We could never agree on what to watch, we usually always ended up watching South Park, we all enjoyed it, laughing with this group of people, sometimes made me forget, I was locked up in a mental hospital.

Gibraltar has always reminded me of South Park, we're a small community, where most of us know each other, everybody always finds out everything the moment it happens. South Park is like a dream to me, there is so much interesting, important and even knowledgeable information to pick up on but it's muddled up amongst nonsense, it is then up to you to decide what is real and what is fantasy. Many people will probably disagree with me and claim that South Park is simply a ridiculous show, maybe it is but something I've learned through my years is that the more ridiculous something is, the more attention it gets. South Park might be over the top ridiculous sometimes but they always use this to their advantage.

The patients were great, the staff was good but sometimes I felt trapped, prisoned and at times worried because something happened to me in the mental hospital that really annoys me to this day. Halfway during my stay, I was forced to go quiet, I was forced to concentrate on my breathing and nothing else, I could already feel what was coming. When I get anxious, angry and most importantly stressed, I begin to get very strong headaches to the point, where trying to concentrate becomes the most difficult thing in the world for me. That day I realised that listening to other people's problems, which had been what I had been doing for the last few days seemed impossible. Not only could I not concentrate but the more they kept talking and the more I forced myself to listen, the worse I began to feel.

I began moving away from the patients but being trapped in such a small area, it is very difficult to find yourself with even five minutes of alone time before somebody interrupts you. I couldn't handle it anymore, the pain inside my head, the pressure, the pulsation, it was too much, and for the first time, I locked myself away from everyone inside my room. Since you can't actually lock the doors, people kept coming in to talk to me, luckily none of them were hallucinations. That night I realised, there was no way I could read my book with that mindset, it was painful on my eyes and my mind. I could officially not concentrate any longer, for if I did, I feared I would be welcoming back my seizures after a whole year away from them. I went to bed that night and spent the whole time sweating, shaking, dreaming and waking up gasping for air.

The next morning when I woke up, I felt just as I did the night before and having not slept properly, only made me feel worse. I sat down and ate breakfast quietly, when my friends asked me how I was feeling, I'd reply by telling them I was not feeling well, they left me alone, which is exactly what I wanted. Thinking about anything was driving me crazy because the night before my brain had been on extreme overdrive, I really needed to recover. I spent most of the day trying to get away from everybody and eventually found myself isolated in my room again. The next few hours were terrible because as much as I tried to fight the strange sensation of déjà vu returning, it would not go away, and suddenly I began to feel sick, I made my way to the bathroom and threw up.

I knew what was coming, I was going to have a seizure soon, I had spent so long trying to find a cure, and now I was about to experience it all again. The only way to make sure that didn't happen was to reduce my stress levels, I did this by attempting meditation in my room. I had come to learn by now that when a person is stressed and anxious, meditation doesn't work, it might help relax others, but at that moment, it wasn't helping me. I made my way to the staff room and informed the nurses present that I was not feeling well, I asked if they could take my blood pressure. This was the first and only time I approached the nurses complaining about my health, they simply looked at me and told me they could not do anything about this until medication time. I didn't have the strength to complain nor argue, I simply asked if I could use the telephone and call my mum, I knew she would do something to help me. I used the staff telephone and called my mum, I told her I wasn't feeling well,

I asked if she would mind coming down to the mental hospital. My mum immediately recognised the trembling sound in my voice, she too knew what was coming.

As the nurses continued talking, I got up and made my way to the sitting room and just allowed my body to fall onto the sofa, as I closed my eyes and simply tried relaxing my body. Next thing, I knew everything begun going black, when I regained my sight, my mouth was completely dry and my memory, slowly returning to me. I tried to get up from the sofa but that was not going to happen, I had no energy left inside me anymore. A few minutes later, I heard my mum's voice, I forced myself to get up to greet her, when she approached me, I finally stopped fighting and just gave in collapsing at her feet. It had been a week since I had first been sanctioned into the mental hospital; all this time, I had not been allowed out for fresh air or sunlight, I was losing my energy. I had also still not been seen by a doctor, after what had happened the night before, I finally met Dr Roseblack.

"Do you consume cannabis, Nicholas?" I was asked by Dr Roseblack. I did on occasions, I mostly did this now, as it helped me feel safe from recurring seizures, not so much recreationally as I had in the past. His medical expertise came to the conclusion that my breakdown was due to cannabis consumption. What the hell was he talking about? Had he ever smoked a joint in his life? After smoking marijuana, the last thing a person feels like doing is going out of their house, hoping to get arrested or sanctioned into a mental hospital, one just wants to watch *Game of Thrones*, chill and eat some munchies. I had not taken any other drugs the night of my break down, my body, my mind, simply lost it out of stress, anger and tiredness, this had nothing to do with drugs. Dr Roseblack was not listening to me, he just continued repeating that cannabis was to blame, he hadn't even looked at my medical records, he was unaware I was epileptic until I told him.

Dr Roseblack suggested, I stop pursuing my case against government as it would only make me worse, and if I got worse, I'd have to keep going back there. Damn it! What had I done, I was seriously worried I might never get to leave; what made it worse was that every afternoon, they offered me numerous tablets as part of my medication. I only needed Lamicital to control my seizures, what was the reasoning behind trying to drug me, to the point where I could not think? What had I got myself into? I started to realise I wasn't leaving the following week, I was going to be here for a long time.

Chapter Twenty-Three
Mental Advancements

I needed to get back to social media and let all my readers know what had happened, I didn't want them thinking I had simply abandoned my story, my mission of exposing bullying within Gibraltar. Self-esteem also played a huge role in my mental recovery, even though I was isolated away from my problems, the fact that I had actually started to speak out about them, made all the difference in the world to me, even though my problems had only become worse. During my time at the mental hospital, I became very close with the patients; I got a real insight on how the human mind works. People who cannot control or make sense of their thoughts are considered mentally ill, my seventeen friends and I were no exception. Truth be told, being forced to interact with nobody else but a group of insane minds helped me realise, if you take the time to understand and listen, in their own ways, mentally ill people make a lot of sense, if you're open minded.

Madam Janice never spoke with anyone, she was always speaking to herself, whilst looking upwards, anywhere she was at. The staff mostly left her alone and the patients, even they felt she was too crazy to be approached. I had experience with voices in my head, I knew what she was going through, I had gone through the same thing, and honestly, I was still somewhat sceptical that she was in fact totally crazy. Still I had been where she was, and had nobody to properly talk to about the voices I heard, I hoped I could be that somebody for her. The difference between Madam Janice and myself was that I never spoke to the voices inside my head in public, I did speak to my hallucinations though, which to others is just the same. As I stood next to Madam Janice, she continued having a conversation with the voices in her mind. When I asked Madam Janice about the voices, she confirmed that she heard them all inside her head, no hallucinations were around us. For the first time, I was realising how I came across, when I talked about my voices, even though I could relate, it still felt crazy to believe.

I told Madam Janice that a year before being sanctioned into the mental hospital, I too heard voices in my head, I never knew if they were real or not. Madam Janice confirmed that she did believe they were real, she proved this by having very deep conversations with her voices out loud. I hoped I had been able to hide my insanity better than Madam Janice, but at the same time, respected her for fully taking control of her situation and accepting it, unlike I did. I tried to continue a conversation with Madam Janice but she was busy having other conversations, to continue with mine. I could not blame her, when I was surrounded by my voices, all I wished at times were that the people actually around me would shut up, so I could continue with my more interesting conversations. If I could go back and hear my voices, see my hallucinations again, I would, only if they didn't come with the addition of epilepsy, which in my case, was how they'd normally arrive.

I began playing with a deck of cards, I could hear Madam Janice speaking to herself in the background, but had mostly lost myself building a house of cards. Looking through the deck of cards, specifically at the seven of spades, I began to wonder what had happened to me in the past. At one point, it all seemed so real but now after a year back in 'reality', I was starting to think, all that had happened, I had lost my mind temporarily, I had just never accepted it. Suddenly, Madam Janice went quiet; I looked back at her and found her looking straight towards me. "Are you a writer?" she asked, how did she know that? Had she heard this was the reason for my arrival at the mental hospital? I was not sure but was very intrigued. Madam Janice informed me that she was now hearing different voices, calling out my name, ones telling her to tell me to keep writing.

I was both confused and intrigued but as I tried to continue our conversation, Madam Janice soon began ignoring me again and continued speaking amongst herself. I already missed my family, especially my nephew Aiden, but now I was also starting to miss all my illusions. If I still had them around me, I probably wouldn't have felt as lonely as I did. Luckily for me, I had returned back to society, somewhat, and now although I had no spiritual friends around me, I had real ones who now kept me company. However, I still started reminiscing about my hallucinated friends, family and mentors, I missed them all very much. I more or less had an idea of what I could try and do to get back to them, but in today's crazy world who has time for meditation? I was still eager to reunite with my spiritual friends once again, I was going to start trying, if it's weird and wild, try and find it, the crazier, the better I say. I believed that when a person meditates, they are simply reaching a state of REM sleep, whilst their conscious mind is still awake and in control, therefore lucidly dreaming in a state of trance.

I had no time to search for my hallucinations, as my new friends kept me plenty busy, even to attempt such a challenge. Later on, that day Ludo went on a rampage, he had asked for water, over an hour ago and none of the nurses had provided him with water yet. As Ludo began destroying everything in his path, the nurses locked themselves in their office, leaving the patients alone outside to deal with Ludo themselves. Luckily, I had a spare bottle of water in my room, I gave it to Ludo, and he settled down and was his friendly self again. There was no need for such a violent rampage; luckily Earl and Oscar were also there to calm him down. I did understand Ludo's frustration though, an hour inside a mental hospital, feels more like five. Uncle Matt was soon released from the mental hospital, we all wished him well, we were all going to miss him very much, at the same time this gave us hope, there was a chance to become sane enough for society again. A few days later, we were all sent to our rooms; Lew had managed to escape again, this time Harry had gone with him.

I enjoyed being mixed with all these different characters but at the same time, when one is trying to recover from anxiety and depression, this was not always the best place to accomplish such goals. Guy did not know how to be quiet, as much as I enjoyed his company, I could not handle his fast-paced speech. Rowlf was convinced there was a conspiracy centred around his music, either he made sense or I was losing it, but I believed his story. As the days continued to pass, locked inside a mental hospital, without having felt fresh air and sunlight in so long, was causing me to go crazy all over again. I had mental hospital fever, it was burning in my ears, we all had mental hospital fever, it was driving us insane. We were flipping our own nurses, we'd been stuck in there for so long, that we were simply going bananas. We had mental hospital fever, we'd lost what sense we had, we were all going mad, our sanity was hanging by a thread, since we were going nowhere, we were fucked out of our heads. Junior even started speaking, he didn't want to be there anymore, Rosita stopped complaining, when she saw Abby standing by her door and Kira stopped playing board games, they had finally become a bore.

'Mental illnesses' can occur when the process in our brain does not work correctly or rather when we cannot understand its signals properly; this is how I developed epilepsy. Communication between neurons can be electrical, such as in areas of the 'brain' that control movement. When electrical signals are abnormal, they can cause tremors or symptoms found associated with mental illnesses. Mental health includes our emotional, psychological and social well-being, it affects how we think, feel and act. It also helps determine how we handle stress, relate to others and make choices. Mental health is important at every stage of life, from childhood and adolescence through adulthood. Over the course of your life, if you experience mental health problems your thinking, mood and behaviour could be affected. Many factors contribute to mental health problems, including biological factors, such as genes or brain chemistry, life experiences, such as trauma or abuse and family history of mental health problems.

Mental illness does not discriminate, it can affect anyone regardless of age, gender, income, social status, ethnicity, religion, spirituality, sexual orientation, background or other aspect of cultural identity. While mental illness can occur at any age, most of all mental illness begin once in our twenties, when one begins to spiritually awaken, this happened to me at age twenty-five. Our brain begins processing and acting on things we have not allowed it to comprehend beforehand, we have not wired ourselves properly. The human brain is an amazing organ, it controls memory and learning, the senses (hearing, sight, smell, taste and touch) and emotion; this is how we've programmed our brain to respond to our body since rebirth.

The brain also controls other parts of the body, including muscles, organs and blood vessels; this is why the power of the mind is very important, positive thinking and negative thinking have a big impact on our health. The brain also is a very complex structure, it contains billions of nerve cells called neurons that must communicate and work together for the body to function normally, we are our own computers. The neurons communicate through electrical signals, special chemicals, neurotransmitters help move these electrical messages from neuron to neuron. Information is fed into the brain through the senses, what is heard, felt, tasted, seen or smelled is detected by receptors in or on the body and sent to the brain through sensory neurons. When these senses do not conform to what we're familiar with, our brain cannot translate to us, what is happening?

The brain decides what to do with the information from the senses and tells the body how to respond by sending out messages via motor neurons. For example, if a person puts their hand near fire, the sense of touch tells the brain about the heat and the brain sends a message to the muscles of the arm to move the hand away. What happens when we begin feeling sensations our brain is not familiar with, therefore it has no command for our bodies to react upon. Another type of neuron called interneurons, connects various neurons within the brain and spinal cord, which together make up the central nervous system. My central nervous system had a roadblock, one that did not let the appropriate neurons travel properly throughout my brain, once this was adjusted by Upper Cervical Care, my neuron flow was back to normal.

Just as there are different types of neurons, there are also different types of chemical neurotransmitters. The abnormalities in how particular brain circuits function contribute to the development of many mental illnesses. Connections between nerve cells along certain pathways or circuits in the brain can lead to problems with how the brain processes information and may result in an abnormal mood, thinking, perception or behaviour. Mental illness is no more than traffic flowing the unconventional way through our bodies, since we do not understand this new route, our body fails us. Changes in size or shape of different parts of the brain may be responsible for causing some mental illnesses, this is how my central nervous system first got messed up to begin with. It was all very complicated to try and make sense of, whilst locked away in a mental hospital, there were just too many options to tackle on the subject.

As the days past, I slowly began to feel better, I was relaxing again, although not seeing Dr Roseblack again was stressful, I wanted answers, when were they planning on letting me out of there? The patients and even the staff had commented that I did not belong there, they could see I was back to normal again, all I experienced was a simple break down, which had occurred almost two weeks ago already. When patient's family members came to visit, they sometimes confused me for a member of staff, I knew I was not a crazy person, these interactions only further confirmed it for me. Days after my first medical examination, I once again found myself in the presence of Dr Roseblack, who I hoped would at least let me out into the garden, I couldn't stand being locked inside any longer. Again, Dr Roseblack seemed more interested in my case against my government, than my actual health. One of Dr Roseblack's suggestions was to forget about all my past problems and start a new chapter in my life. I'd been trying to do that for six years, yet the problem continued to affect my life; I couldn't let it go, I had to clear my work record.

Every time I took a Lamicital tablet, reminded me I was ill, that I had fallen victim to bullying, it reminded me of all the people who got me to that point. If I needed to think about this problem for the rest of my life, I want to know I came out winning in the end. According to Dr Roseblack, cannabis had apparently led me to this point, not my bullies. It was all in my head, I was being paranoid, the only way to get better was to increase my dosage of Lamicital and remove myself from cannabis. Only then would I stop suffering seizures and get my life back together, was this what I was supposed to believe or what he wanted me to believe?

If occasionally consuming coconut cannabis oil and the occasional Lamicital tablet kept me reassured that I'd remain stable and seizure free without feeling completely drugged, who was he to take this away from me? I informed Dr Roseblack that marijuana was in fact medically beneficial towards reducing seizures whilst Lamicital, if I took too much, left me drowsy and unable to control my thoughts properly. Seeing as I had spent two weeks without cannabis in my system, whilst permanently observed within the mental hospital, and hadn't shown any signs of withdrawal, proved my point, in my opinion, that cannabis was not the problem. I felt like one of the only solutions that worked for me, was being taken away, without offering me another alternative that worked just as well. If we're honest, cannabis is less dangerous than alcohol, unfortunately for Nurse Mary-Jane, she's a wanted fugitive.

Besides cannabis was not the reason for my breakdown, my bullying, my life, my government, that was who were to blame, but Dr Roseblack insisted it was all down to drug consumption. Dr Roseblack continued ignoring me, this was frustrating; as I got angrier, I began getting aggravated. Dr Roseblack was quick to point out, that being away from cannabis was making me lose my temper, I was getting angry because of it. What the hell was he talking about? I had been locked inside the mental hospital for two weeks, it was not until this moment, speaking to him that I was getting angry. I could see Dr Roseblack writing notes in his notepad; I soon realised he was playing the same game as Shale, he was hoping to get me to snap, probably so I'd have to remain in their care even longer. I realised what was being hoped from me, I breathed in deeply, remembered how to handle anyone I thought might be bullying me, I did not allow them to affect me.

Dr Roseblack then proceeded to ask me questions, regarding third-eyes, spirits, lucid dreaming, as if I were going to bother trying to explain that to him, I simply told him that I didn't remember.

What Dr Roseblack was unaware about, was the subjects he assumed he could help me with were out of his comprehension. If anyone could help me figure this out, it wasn't the doctor, it was the patient; Madam Janice could provide me with much more knowledge than Dr Roseblack ever could. I asked if I could be granted access into the garden, I needed fresh air and sunlight, it was denied. Dr Roseblack came to the conclusion that my epilepsy stemmed from consuming marijuana on an occasional basis, I sensed my bullies might have been trying to get ready for court and cannabis was going to be their defence.

I left Dr Roseblack's office disappointed that day, not only had I figured out I wouldn't be leaving anytime soon, I also realised my bullies were getting ready to fight back against me. As I wondered around the mental hospital, I realised Yolanda's husband had brought her a new gossip magazine that day, I was so bored, I asked if I could read it. As I flipped through the pages, ready to lose my mind and give up on myself, I came upon a familiar face, one smiling right back at me on page seven. There was a picture promoting the release of the new movie, the one I had seen being filmed in London the year before. That day was the worldwide theatrical premiere of my Hollywood friends' movie, I had completely forgotten about it. A picture of a character which my friend Steve performed helped promote the movie, finally a familiar face, locked away with me inside the mental hospital. I cut out the picture and used it as motivation to keep going, I was not ready to give up, I was going to get out of here and continue with my ridiculous movie.

I found out a long time ago, you've got to learn to say 'yes' when life says 'no', don't dwell on the bad times, once they're past, that kind of thinking gets you nowhere fast. I had spent six years feeling bullied, now that I had finally stood up for myself, I was being kept away from my audience, from those willing to listen and perhaps even help. I needed to get out, I needed to find internet access, I needed to continue writing my story online. There is no mountain you can't climb, if you hang on tight and just make up your mind, once you set your thoughts to moving on, there is no road too long. I wasn't done writing, just because I didn't have access to Wi-Fi or even a computer for that matter, did not mean I wasn't going to keep on writing. That day, I called my mum and asked her to bring me a notebook and pencil, I had a story to write.

The staff at the mental hospital were overworked and understaffed and because of this, there were many flaws to be found, flaws which I began jotting down. Something the staff had come to realise was I did not belong there, they might get away with not doing their job properly when it came to those who were a little more gone, but I was all there and they knew it, this forced them to pull up their socks so to speak. I realised this and began to make them regret having me locked up in there; every time a staff member saw me writing in my booklet, they would ask what I was writing about. I'd make sure to explain to them, that this was a follow up to my social media rant, I was going to share with Gibraltar my experience locked up inside a mental hospital.

Gibraltar is a very small country; by now, most knew I had gone crazy outside our government headquarters and was locked up in a mental hospital on suicide watch. I knew they would be eager to hear what I had to say, if and when I got out, the staff knew that too. I wasn't going to stop writing just because I was locked inside a mental hospital, and the longer I was there, the more material I'd have upon my return to social media. I made sure the staff was aware of my story, I even interviewed various patients, who were also eager to share their story with those who would listen. Three days after I began writing about my experience at the mental hospital, I was once again asked to visit Dr Roseblack's office for a third and final time. Don't look back, don't you turn around, just keep your eye on where you're bound, and you're bound to get from here to there, a dream can take you anywhere.

Chapter Twenty-Four
One Mouth, Two Ears, Three Eyes

Dr Roseblack asked to see my notebook, as he looked through the pages, he asked why so many had been torn out. I had been giving my mum pages of my story to take home with her, I was not going to allow them to read it, or take it away from me. Dr Roseblack wasn't getting the information he wanted from me, again he began blaming cannabis for my mental breakdown and even my epileptic seizures. Dr Roseblack soon tried a new tactic, he was going to prove I was crazy, he hoped to prove I was making this all up. Dr Roseblack hoped I would let loose and give him the crazy he was hoping for, I was not about to give him any further ammunition to use against me. Dr Roseblack asked me to help him understand the power of the third-eye, what did that have to do with me he wondered. I informed him I once suffered from a mental illness, which affected my third-eye, a specific part of the brain. I was going to attempt to give him the scientific explanation on how to understand the power of your third-eye, aka the brain, the mind's eye, the pineal gland, the eye into the soul, the eye of spirituality, the sixth sense.

In our world, reality is subjective, the third-eye, depicted as being in the middle of the forehead about an inch above the eyebrows, is an invisible, mystical eye associated with powerful energy. The third-eye is located inside the skull, it is part of our brain, known as the pineal gland. It's commonly said that we humans only use ten percent of our brains capacity. There are sections in the brain, when activated, can even control our strength, simply put this is how a mother can find the strength to suddenly lift a car to save her child. One of these non-activated parts of our brain, is the pineal gland, which when activated, allows us the ability to control the tremendous power contained within the third-eye, which is able to transport us to whole new worlds, people and beliefs. You've got to see it in your mind, you know it's quick and easy to find, use it if you feel it, don't forget to fuel it, can you picture that?

The third-eye is the sixth primary chakra or energy centre, in the body and is often referenced as 'the soul's gate'. When activated, it grants greatly enhanced perception of other realms, bringing alongside knowledge and wisdom without reliance upon the material world. This is what I believed had happened to me, when I first began experiencing sensations of déjà vu, my third-eye was opening, my pineal gland was activating. Additionally, it is said that once opened, the third-eye grants the ability to communicate telepathically with other awakened individuals, to see the spirits of the dead and even receive messages directly from higher beings. There's really nothing to it, anyone can do it, it's easy and we all know how, now begins the changing, mental rearranging, nothing is really where it's at.

The seven chakras are the centres in our bodies in which energy flows through, blocked energy in our chakras can often lead to illness. It's important to understand what each chakra represents and what we can do to keep this energy flowing freely. Root Chakra represents our foundation and feeling of being grounded. Sacral Chakra represents our connection and ability to accept others and new experiences. Solar Plexus Chakra represents our ability to be confident and in control of our lives. Heart Chakra represents our ability to love, find joy and inner peace. Throat Chakra represents our ability to communicate with others. Third-Eye Chakra represents our ability to focus on and see the bigger picture of life. Crown Chakra is the highest chakra and represents our ability to be fully connected spiritually to our whole universe, a halo of enlightenment.

Interestingly enough the chakras are located on the surface of our etheric body, each of the seven chakras is in a different location (in order) upwards along the spinal cord, connecting to our brains. Each chakra influences a different endocrine gland and nerve plexus within our bodies. The openness and flow of energy through our chakras determines our state of health and balance. Knowledge of our subtler energy system empowers us to maintain balance and harmony on the physical, mental and spiritual level. All meditation and yoga systems seek to balance out the energy of the chakras by purifying the lower energies and guiding them upwards. Through the use of grounding, and living consciously with an awareness of how we acquire and spend our energy, we become capable of balancing our life force with our mental, physical and spiritual selves.

In order for us to become fully self-realised and in harmony with our physical and spiritual nature, our denser lower energies need to be harmonised with the lighter energies of the upper centres. Each centre has an integral function in creating our energetic balance. It is through the study of our energetic and physical being that we can create health, emotional stability and spiritual bliss. It is important for the energy in your chakras to flow accordingly; mine was not flowing as it should, upon the sudden opening of my third-eye. Upper Cervical Care cured my epilepsy by properly aligning the energy flow through my chakras along my spinal cord. Having opened my third-eye rapidly had been sending mixed signals throughout my body. Signals which once corrected, by Upper Cervical spinal readjusting, cured me from my seizures, which unfortunately meant my third-eye had to be closed again. This time, if I wished to open it again, I could not jump from first gear into fifth. I had to follow the steps accordingly, hoping to once again activate my pineal gland, yet this time controlling the effects, hoping not to suffer another mental illness in the process.

Located in the centre of the brain, the pineal gland is a very small organ, shaped like a pinecone. Pineal cells and neuroglial cells (which support the pineal cells) mainly comprise the gland. The pineal gland often appears calcified in x-rays, which is usually due to fluoride, calcium and phosphorus deposits that build up with age, blocking it from view and activation. How you think and feel every day depends on the pineal gland, as the producer of the hormone melatonin, the quality and duration of your sleep relies on how well it produces this hormone. This tiny organ regulates your daily and seasonal circadian rhythms, the sleep-wake patterns that determine your hormone levels, stress levels and physical performance. Melatonin is a special hormone because its emission is dictated only by light. Daylight and darkness help dictate your circadian rhythm, light exposure stops the release of melatonin, and in turn, this helps control your circadian rhythms. Melatonin emission is low during the daylight hours and high during dark periods. At night, the pineal gland increases production of melatonin, a hormone that synchronises the body's rhythms with the cycle of light and dark. Sunlight, complete darkness and meditation, all forms of helping activate the pineal gland.

The spontaneous, automatic opening of the third-eye is accompanied by certain symptoms, which one always hopes to avoid. These include loss of memory, convulsions, blackouts, heart attacks, seizures and even brain damage. It is possible to open the third-eye in a healthy way without negative symptoms through the mindful and deliberate practice of certain techniques. The pineal gland is believed to be the gate between the spiritual and physical world, this part can be activated through yoga, meditation and other ancient methods. Once you activate your third-eye, a portal for the soul, you can travel across the universe and interact with energy throughout it. A blocked third-eye can cause excessive dreaming, a diminished sense of intuition and emotional instability. This is why opening your third-eye is so beneficial, it allows for a greater understanding of life, it will lead you on a path to self-awareness. You will become finely tuned into your own life and the way your life interacts with the world around you. Decision making becomes easy for you, and you will let go of many of the stresses and anxieties that people who are chained to their physical 'self' struggle with, isn't this what we're all searching for in life?

Most of us are out of touch with reality, in this fantasy that is created we are in control, we call the shots, at least we think we do. Every person on this planet is part of a growing network, dark matter, that is our invisible connection to the universe. When physicists use the term 'dark', they are simply referring to forces and 'matter' that cannot currently be observed or properly understood. 'Dark matter' is an unobserved form of mass that exerts a gravitational force on the observable universe. With it we can do some incredible things, people of ancient civilisations knew more than we do today, it is known we have abilities, psychic abilities. 'Dark matter' is an invisible, nonluminous form of material that exists throughout the universe and can take any of several forms, including weakly interacting particles (cold dark matter) or high-energy randomly moving particles.

The average human body gets hit by a particle of 'dark matter' about once a minute. Dark matter being absorbed through the tissues of our skin is introduced into our bodies and can even take shelter inside our brains, within the area known to control our sleeping cycles. The connection between dark matter alongside the chemical melatonin in the brain connects us to the universe, as it is the key to unlocking our subconscious minds, activating the pineal gland. Energy from the past, present and future, flows through our universe and through dark matter, this energy is able to be transferred right to our brains. All creatures of earth share one common ability amongst each other, we are all able to communicate with the universe, far easier than that of a computer. The universe consists of matter which can be divided into energy and mass, energy is a part of matter. Matter in the universe is a conserved property, while energy is only conserved in closed systems where no mass change is possible. Our brain structure is similar to that of the universe, why? Because we are part of the universe, now and forever.

The third-eye, despite its unique properties, is still an eye and when it opens, it represents the addition of a sixth sense, and this has an impact on all of the other senses. Colours may seem brighter and illusions may manifest, scents become intensified, food becomes more delicious, sensations become stronger and new sounds can be heard, mistaken as voices in our head. This experience can seem hallucinogenic to those whose third-eye has opened automatically and can be quite disturbing, one might even believe they are going crazy. Dreams become more vivid, intense and understandable as we are able to guide ourselves within our lucid dreams. When the third-eye has opened, the dream state becomes one of the most receptive times for receiving communication from higher planes. The first law of thermodynamics states that energy cannot be destroyed, it merely changes in its nature. This rule is often used to explain matters that appear to happen of a different plane to the one we see here on earth.

It is not uncommon for someone experiencing this to seek medication in an attempt to force a more restful sleep, which can promote atrophy in the third-eye, possibly causing it to close again. In those whose third-eye has opened spontaneously, it is common to experience headaches and a feeling that the body has grown heavier without actually increasing in mass. This can be attributed to a shift in the flow of energy through the chakras. If not properly re-balanced following the opening of the third-eye, the healthy passage of energy through the body can become disrupted. Everything is interconnected, and when one part of the system isn't working properly, it can spread dysfunction to other parts of the system. Pharmaceutical drugs are meant to both heal you but at the same time, continue blocking the activation of your pineal gland. Natural remedies on the other hand help fight diseases and allow one to easier open their third-eye.

The human mind without the influence of an open third-eye grows accustomed to experiencing the world in certain ways. It creates a sense of being grounded in a common reality, and when the third-eye opens accidentally, that sense of grounding is heavily impacted as the awareness of other planes of reality interject on mundane awareness. A sense of detachment from the prior meaning of reality often occurs, imposing a feeling that nothing is real and that everything is presented in the form of deception. Without mindful understanding of the influence of the third-eye, it can become exceedingly difficult to regain a sense of understanding and clarity about the world and one's attachment to it. With the opening of the third-eye, comes a remarkable ability to identify the truth; as a result, the true nature of relationships may become known and previously strong relationships may suddenly seem superficial and meaningless. Dishonesty becomes more apparent, and the minor day-to-day deceptions may become intolerable. Consequently, interpersonal relationships may experience a tremendous upheaval with the accidental opening of the third-eye.

If a child is given a pencil and uses it to jab their eye, they are not using this tool properly, the pencil is not dangerous, it is the way the child thinks it is meant to be used, that makes it dangerous. In my opinion, a mental illness should be considered a mental advancement; it is the opening of one's third-eye. The activation of your pineal gland can create confusion, suddenly our brains aren't wired to understand how to cope with this ability and power, therefore our brain goes haywire, we end up mentally insane and locked away in a mental hospital. Had school taught us what should be learnt, perhaps children would grow up learning how to cope against what we consider an illness, which in actuality is a gift, we simply need to understand. Give a person a piano, let them play their song, it will sound terrible at first, let them practise, let them find their rhythm and they'll produce a beautiful harmony.

A 'psychedelic' substance is a psychoactive 'drug' whose primary action is to alter cognition and perception, typically by agonising serotonin receptors. Psychedelics are part of a wider class of psychoactive drugs known as hallucinogens, a class that also includes mechanistically unrelated substances such as dissociatives and deliriants. Psychedelic drugs make you hallucinate for the simple reason that they have helped unlock your subconscious mind, by allowing the activation of your pineal gland to commence. Your third-eye has opened but going from first gear into fifth is always very dangerous. An overdose of the mind, which unleashes signals to the body, that force it to collapse, can lead to death. One believes their mind is going crazy on them, when consumed on certain types of drugs or rather brain enhancers. When on psychedelic drugs, our mind goes crazy, it begins playing tricks on us by affecting certain areas of our brain. A person will see or hear stuff, which is not really there, yet to them it's all very real.

Unfortunately, as trippy and cool as this experience might seem, you are not in control and since most of us are obsessive by nature, it's advisable not to play around with psychedelics. Drugs in general are judged as deadly and rightly so, but it is because we don't use them for their rightful healing powers, we use them to party. If we stop the party and properly take the time to learn what different drugs are all about, I can assure you, drugs would not have the bad reputation they have today. Most drugs come from Mother Nature just like flowers, fruit, vegetables, water etc. Studying what drugs can do for good is just as important as the bad. Remember it becomes bad when you lose your self-control, when you allow the obsession to creep into your life, when you take a bite of the apple from the forbidden tree.

Calcification is the biggest problem for the pineal gland, fluoride accumulates in the pineal gland more than any other organ and leads to the formation of phosphate crystals. As your pineal gland hardens due to the crystal production, less melatonin is produced and regulation of your wake-sleep cycle gets disturbed. In addition to fluoride, halides like chlorine and bromine also accumulate and damage the pineal gland, which can be found in most of the food we eat and water we drink today. Eliminating fluoride may be the best first step for reducing health concerns and opening your third-eye. If you've been exposed to fluoride, your pineal gland has some degree of calcification preventing it from working well. Halides like fluoride, chlorine and bromine accumulate in your tissue, if you're iodine deficient, which is an increasing problem around the world. If you've cut back on salt and don't eat a lot of seafood, there's a good chance you may be deficient. The fruit from the African tamarind tree is extremely effective at removing fluoride from the body. Regular cleansing enables the body to naturally remove toxins and heavy metals from the body, including fluoride. What do you think are found in chemical trails sprayed through the sky?

The manifestation of the third-eye accounts for a seamless, gradual change in our ideas and perspectives in life. The change is not a forceful, ritualistic process but a continuous one. It is characterised by a gradual channelling of positive energy, which happens only when you want it to. It is truly a selfless quest, beat down the walls, believe, begin, be an up and comer, open your third-eye. I finally understood what had happened to me in the past, my brain was not malfunctioning, it was advancing, by the activation of my pineal gland. I was not going crazy, I was not imagining things,

I just didn't understand myself, I didn't know then, what we were all capable of being able to do. When I finished explaining what I meant about my third-eye opening, I realised Sam had been standing by the door that whole time, he thought I was a complete weirdo.

I was sure Dr Roseblack would find the insanity in what I said, had I just extended my stay at the mental hospital? Actually, to my surprise, I was informed I could go home, although Dr Roseblack warned me not to share my notes on social media, it would only complicate matters further for me. Once I left, I shared what needed to be shared, they had silenced me for six years, the seventh was going to be different, I was going to speak out every chance I got. Everyone including the staff, the patients and especially my family were as surprised as me, for someone had never been discharged so suddenly. Before leaving Dr Roseblack's office, I remember asking if I might be able to return to visit my new non-hallucinated friends, sadly that was not allowed. Luckily soon after, I began bumping into my mentally advanced friends as they too were eventually discharged and classified sane enough to return back to society.

That day, I packed up my belongings, said goodbye to all my friends, especially Floyd, who wished me nothing but luck with my future and reminded me to continue trying to reopen my third-eye once again. I couldn't believe I was going home, I had woken up that day with no hope, yet there I was walking out the door, into the sunlight, feeling the fresh air against my skin. I was happy to be alive, I valued the importance of life, I was not going to continue living a sad, pathetic life, I was going to completely change my mindset, I was aiming to be positive, no matter how negative life might seem around me. It was time for me to re-join society and to my lucky surprise, I was about to be granted legal assistance, perhaps my time at the mental hospital had been worth it.

Chapter Twenty-Five
Law and Chaos

After three weeks of rest, relaxation and sanity, I now found myself ready to face life again, I was no longer crazy, at least not on paper, although I was now officially not fit for work again. The first thing I did upon being discharged, was make my way to the theatre, I had a sequel to watch. After over two years of waiting, I finally saw the movie I most wanted to see, the one I had seen being filmed in London over a year ago. Inside my wallet, I kept the picture I had cut out of the character, which had been performed by my friend Steve, which gave me strength, during my time at the mental hospital. As I sat in the theatre, the lights were turned off, it was time to meet my friends again, on their latest movie tonight.

How could something so right, feel so wrong? After all I've been through, why did I feel like I didn't know myself? I had wanted to work alongside this franchise since I was three years old, if earlier, I cannot remember. Now I had actually become friends, with those who had helped keep this legacy alive over the years. I was friends with those who helped produce the content, which I always used to inspire me, to continue fighting in life, why did I feel so empty inside? I came to a realisation after watching their new movie that at one point in my life, working alongside my idols was always a childish possibility. Now although I was slowly making connections, without an ending to my original story, without closure, I had no money, no confidence and no hope to ever try and achieve this dream, ever again. I really needed to work on myself and a clear state of mind, if I hoped for a better future.

Once again, I found myself suddenly without my friends, my hallucinated friends, my real crazy friends, they'd all leave me at once. I missed all my illusions, it had been what I had learned through them, which had found me at that point in my life. I soon found myself locked inside my bedroom again, alone, still feeling left out of society. Gibraltarians now knew my story, although everyone now also thought I was crazy, all I wanted to do was explain myself, I might be crazy but I'm not mental hospital crazy. At that moment though, explaining my sanity was not a priority, or at least not something I could prove to myself, let alone anyone else. Upon my return to social media, I had nothing else to say, other than speak about my experience within the mental hospital. Once I returned back to my story, I realised, people thought I was insane, nobody was taking me seriously anymore, the best thing I could do at that moment was stop writing.

Everyone now knew I had been discharged from the mental hospital, I even wrote a musical about it, but it seemed to me, everything that had been brought up before, seemed to have been forgotten. I felt as though I were on my own again, keeping me away from my computer for so long, made me lose my momentum with readers. I had no credibility with them any longer; all they saw was a mentally-ill-political-window-smasher. As much as I hoped to be free, whilst locked inside the mental hospital, upon my return to society, I realised, I was too embarrassed to interact with others. I just wanted to keep to myself, and if lucky, my illusions might return, without me developing epilepsy, this time around.

A few days after being discharged from the mental hospital, it was my nephew Aiden's second birthday. Not only did I not have money to buy him a gift, it also reminded me, that since my nephew had been born, I had never had enough money to buy him anything. This made me feel terrible, the fact that I also knew everybody would be asking me how I felt, made me nervous, anxious and unable to step foot outside my house to attend his party. I stayed home that day, I couldn't find the courage to walk out my house and socialise with others at a party. A few days later, I also missed out attending my friend's wedding, most of my old friends would be there, I couldn't face them. Not when they were doing so well in life, compared to the mess that was mine, I didn't even have money to rent a tuxedo.

I had spent almost two years trying to take my government to court and months hoping to be granted legal assistance for it, now I found myself one step closer. I was granted legal assistance, under the condition that an expert in neurology examined my condition and confirm that my epilepsy did in fact stem as a result of bullying at work. I now also had a law firm backing me up, the first of three, Frank was my first lawyer, I began losing lawyers faster than I lost neurons. It was still a slow process; however, finally things were moving forward and eventually after searching the whole world, we found our expert neurologist specialist in Germany. Dr Von Neuter specialised in epilepsy, strokes, dementia, Parkinson's disease, movement disorders and neurophysiology. Had I not received legal assistance, I never would have been able to afford what was to come, the legal system was too expensive for me, I couldn't afford justice. Now that I had a lawyer, I didn't have to keep fighting by myself, I finally had someone helping me legally.

Dr Von Neuter was flown over to Gibraltar, I was examined thoroughly and a few weeks later, his legal examinational review finally arrived. I was excited for two reasons, if his letter agreed my epilepsy stemmed from a result of bullying at work, then I would be allowed full access towards my legal assistance. The second reason I was excited was for the first time, I'd officially know why I was ill, I knew why, but confirmation is always valued. Dr Von Neuter's letter confirmed everything I had been saying, he was very clear, that although as everyone is, I might be prone to being able to develop epilepsy, had it not been for the stress I endured at work, I probably would never have 'unleashed' my epileptic trigger and could have avoided seizures all together. "Nicholas does not have a family history of epilepsy; his anamnesis is free of epileptic like episodes in the perinatal phase or in younger age. There is nothing known regarding a perinatal brain complication or complication under his birth. No history of fever cramps, meningitis, encephalitis or brain traumatism as possible disposition to develop epilepsy later in life. No other neurological disease in his family."

Dr Von Neuter had been the first person in a long time, who provided me with a report that did not crush my spirits. "Temporal lobe seizures usually begin in the deeper portions of the temporal lobe, this area is part of the limbic system, which controls emotions and memory. This is why the seizures can include a feeling of déjà vu, fear or anxiety, and that is why some people with temporal lobe epilepsy may have problems with memory and depression. Mesial temporal sclerosis (scarring in the inner portions of the temporal lobe) may be caused by oxygen starvation to the brain, head trauma or brain infection but can also occur without an apparent cause. Over time, neurons die and scar tissue tends to form within the hippocampus and amygdala (areas in the temporal lobe responsible for emotions and short-term memory). Mesial temporal sclerosis (also known as hippocampal sclerosis) can cause a form of temporal lobe epilepsy with partial (focus) seizures that can spread or secondarily generalise and affect other areas of the brain. Treatments for temporal lobe epilepsy caused by mesial temporal sclerosis can include anticonvulsant medications and surgery. The described conditions to develop epilepsy do not implicate that the related epileptic seizures are not depending on external factors like stress, emotions, deprived sleep."

I was granted legal assistance to take my government to court, on both claims. Personal injury at work, relating to my brain injury (epilepsy), and unfair dismissal, relating to bullying and bad management, and this at the end, left me with no other option than to resign. This was very exciting but at the same time, I knew it was only the beginning of what I believed was going to be a very long journey. What I did not expect, was that as my journey continued, I would find myself with a new lawyer each time. Upon being granted full access to my legal assistance, Frank informed me, he could not continue with my case any further. Frank had too many cases to handle and could not continue forward with mine; sadly for me, no other lawyer in his firm was willing to take me on either. Frank did have a bit of good news for me, he had found another lawyer for me, my second lawyer. I honestly was not excited, this just meant I was now going to have to explain everything all over again to someone else, I was tired of telling my story. Best thing that ever happened to my case was meeting my second lawyer, he became a friend at the end, my legally intellectual friend Ian.

During this time, my parents finally managed to sell our house, it was time to start packing. I was getting ready to move, where? I had no idea. After a year being apart from each other, both my parents had found love again. My dad now had a girlfriend, whom he was living with and my mum had a boyfriend, who she wanted to move in with, where was I supposed to go? Both my parents had outgrown me, before I had them, I couldn't go with either of them, but had no money to go anywhere else. I was getting ready to set up camp and start living up the Rock, where I hoped the apes would share their bananas with me, so I could boil them at night, otherwise I had no idea, how I was meant to get to sleep out in the wild. Fortunately, my parents had a plan, they didn't want me living life as an ape, after selling their house, they had a gift for my sisters and me. As my parents handed me cash, I could not believe my eyes, for the last few years I had only ever had twenty-pounds at a time, now in my hand, I held five-thousand pounds, what was I going to buy first?

The first thing I did was pay Stacey back for the loan she had lent me, I might have been down over half my new income, but finally the stress of owing money was gone. Stacey had recently got out of a long-term relationship, just before moving into her own new home. Stacey had spent endless hours working towards a promotion and had achieved her goal, which helped her financially. I managed to pay Stacey back just in time, she still had to buy a tonne of furniture, paints, tiles and bean bag cushions. I was also able to finally buy Aiden a present, but when it came to my nephew, I realised money was not important; Aiden made me realise, one doesn't need money to feel appreciated. Meanwhile Kaylie's mood and behaviour had completely changed, due to an illness, we were unaware of at the time, this new Kaylie, was not the sister I had grown up with.

With the money I had left over, I began renting an apartment, happily alongside an ocean, sadly next to an airport. I really liked my new apartment, although much smaller than where I had grown up living, residing next to an ocean made me forget how small my new place was. I had just enough money left over for a two-month deposit, after that, if I didn't have more money, I'd be setting camp up the Rock. Ironically, Germaine had moved back to Gibraltar a few months earlier and was now my new neighbour. Every time I left my old house, either to visit London or move into my new apartment in Gibraltar, Germaine was always there, a familiar face is always welcomed. I'd join Germaine as she walked her dog, alongside the ocean, we'd sit on the stones above the water and stare over the airport strip and into Spain. I no longer lived next to the Nipperish, the happy place I once shared with all my friends, including Ashby, was now a memory of the past. I had a new happy place, one I discovered with Germaine, observing planes, listening to the ocean and watching the sunsets, along the stones.

Living on my own, forced me to find my confidence, and begin tackling life again, being granted legal assistance was a great confidence boost for me. As I began slowly rebuilding myself, I finally got around to accomplishing many things, I had been putting off from doing. I began working on my screenplays again, my passion had returned, I remembered I was a writer, I was going to keep on writing. I started going out again, granted I had no money to spend, but I started mingling with others again, though I still had a hard time keeping eye contact with others. I began shaving, I started putting on weight again, I started being a little more positive, how could I not, my case was finally moving forward. My legal proceedings against my government had finally commenced, and as excited as I was about all this, at the same time, I realised I couldn't keep my life on hold any longer. My case was probably going to take minimum of three years to sort out, I had to keep on living.

Now that I had legal assistance, I was not as worried as I once was about finding work, as long as I didn't exceed a certain number of hours, I should be safe. At this point, I had lived on twenty pounds a week for over two years, even an extra ten pounds a week would have made all the difference for me. As much as I wanted to work, I was still broken, I had recently been discharged from the mental hospital, I felt very pathetic, who would want to hire me? I had been putting off finding a job for three reasons, the first being I still associated bullying with work, I was terrified of having to interact with a new boss. Secondly, I hoped to receive legal assistance to take my government to court, and for the last two years, I had not been working, most of the time, I was out of my mind. I was going to keep on moving forward, I was determined to finally find a job.

I began applying at various offices, stores, construction sites but nothing to do with government, I never plan on working for them ever again, fuck a pension. Sadly, nobody was hiring me, I wasn't being the confident person I had been in my previous interviews before working for the Gibraltar Developing Company but at least this time I was there. I hoped someone believed enough in me, to give me a chance, even though my work record screamed 'don't hire him'. My Uncle Arthur called me one day, he needed someone to work part time in his pet shop, there were no tourists this time around but I was surrounded by animals again. I now had my own apartment, a job which paid me enough to continue living there, a court case developing against my bullies, one I was not paying for, life was good, all I had to do now was meet my new lawyer.

Ian read all my medical and work reports; in the course of a few days, I found myself with someone who knew about my past better than I did. This is a lawyer who is hard to come across, not only is he dedicated to helping his client legally, but emotionally he was also invested. Ian being familiar with law, could see the injustice I was facing, this was the first time a lawyer, made me feel like I had a case as opposed to not having one. Ian and I met once a week, we went over my evidence, we sorted out dates and money calculations, then we prepared a 24-foot-long timeline, detailing my whole experience. This was a big challenge, not only was it difficult stapling all those sheets of paper together, we then had to start adding information. The timeline we prepared, is something which has now become very important to me. Not only does it allow me to view my story clearly, it helped me realise many things, I had not realised before.

As our timeline of events took shape, I realised just how many weekends I had been forced to work, one after another. It also helped me realise just how much of my life I had wasted on these bullies. I knew it was seven years but when you see that in the form of a timeline, it makes you open your eyes, all three of them. Ian was very helpful and for the first time, things were not just moving forward, they were moving along at a steady pace. No more waiting weeks for appointments, no more waiting months for information, there was a nice flow. Not only was I happy that my case was moving forward, I was also glad that I now had meaning in my life again. I had something to wake up looking forward to each day, I had hope that I might get the justice I was fighting for.

As the year progressed, my court case slowly started getting momentum; finally, we were done with all our legal technicalities, now it was time to start dealing with my bullies and their lawyers. My testimony turned diary, which I had shared through Facebook, was turned back into my testimony and was sent to my bullies' lawyers. This was exciting for me, finally my bullies were going to have to sit down, either with their lawyers or superiors and figure out what to say. I hoped they would start going to work nervous of what was waiting for them, might they be suspended? Might they lose their job? Might they be caught out in their lies? Did they regret ever bullying me? I was very excited, unfortunately after almost a year, my time with my second lawyer was almost up, due to personal reasons, Ian had to leave his law firm.

Ian believed in me, in my case, but sadly I realised many lawyers didn't share our optimism, many had led me to believe this could not be won. This was something I always defended, the fact that I did have a case, unfortunately for Ian he too found himself, having to defend my case many a times, others didn't have the same faith as him. Sticking to his principles, Ian soon found himself having to resign for many reasons, one being not having the support he needed, to help me win my case. It was sad not having Ian to help me anymore, not only did I have to explain myself to someone new all over again, but Ian was my friend. I wanted to finish this with him, nobody had ever shown so much dedication to my problem. I hoped to continue fighting my case with Ian in the future but for now I couldn't wait around, I needed to find another lawyer, for the third time, luckily as they say, third times a charm.

Chapter Twenty-Six
Psychoanalysing Legality

Law protects a society from anarchism, it is a set of conducts that is established and enforced by a self-governing authority to ensure and maintain orderly coexistence in a society. Law refers to a command proceeding from the supreme political authority of a state and addressed to the persons who are subject to that authority. Law helps the society, citizens and civilisation to cohabit peacefully by providing them with a guideline on how to behave, act in social and business life and judge the conflicts between multiple parties. Rights and freedoms are best protected under the common law, irrespective of rank and status, all are equal under the law. Unfortunately for those of us who don't have much of it, money can buy justice. I came to realise if I had been granted legal assistance sooner or had money of my own for that matter, I wouldn't have wasted almost two years to start my legal proceedings, no thanks to the union and my government.

Equality before law means every citizen in a given area will be treated equally before the law and there will be no discrimination or privileges to any particular group or individual. From my point of view, this did not apply to me, I felt discriminated whilst my government, employers, bullies, all privileged. Without this fundamental characteristic, any law can lose its effectiveness drastically. If two different people are treated two different ways just because of their social background, that is a breach of equality before law and would propel instability and violence in the society. An authority or government must not use their power subjectively. Sometimes certain laws allow them to practice some degree of subjective power over citizens, but that power if used unwisely, then it might become contradictory with the higher laws and constitution, it will promote injustice in the civil society.

At that point in my life, I was still very unfamiliar with how the law worked within Gibraltar, even around our world. All I knew was I had a case against my government but no lawyer to help me continue fighting. First, I had lost Frank, then unfortunately I stayed without Ian, once again I found myself lost, except this time my legal proceedings were still proceeding along. I began approaching various law firms and was surprised, that even with legal assistance at my disposal, no lawyers seemed interested in taking me on as a client. I had two claims filed against my government, and as much as I wanted to take the union to court, since their main branch was located outside of Gibraltar, legal assistance would not cover these expenses for me. Luckily, I managed to stumble upon a particular law firm, Ellul and Co, where Eric worked, who would soon become my third lawyer. Eric was just as concerned about my health as Ian was, this is how I knew, I had picked the right person. I updated Eric on my case, we went over my evidence, thanks to Ian, I now had a timeline, which helped me present my case to others much easier and clearer.

Rule of law prevents government from using its power at will, and ensures that the convicts can defend themselves in front of law. The rights of individuals are determined by legal rules and not the arbitrary behaviour of authorities. There can be no punishment unless a court decides there has been a breach of law. Everyone, regardless of their position in society, is subject to the law, and held equally responsible, complete bullshit when it came to my case. Therefore, law is a formal and detailed code of conduct that shapes the economy, politics, culture and human rights in a country, if it is enforced by a knowledgeable higher authority. The basic function of law is to protect the society from crime alas crime is inevitable in any society, from both ends.

Not only was I facing a crime committed against me by my bullies, I soon had confirmation over something I had always questioned, the police could not be trusted either. A short while after being discharged from the mental hospital, I requested video of myself in the back of the police van, during my epileptic seizure, where my head banged from side to side on our way to the hospital. Even though I had looked at the camera just before falling over, I was told that this particular police van, was the only one without a camera installed, how convenient. First my file at work had been misplaced, and now the video of my detention did not exist, I hate people who abuse their power.

The possible reasons behind committing a crime are being a victim, eyeing an opportunity to gain something and absence of a proper supervisory authority. This is where law of the country comes to play its part by bringing the criminal under justice, convicting them under certain penal code depending on the nature of the crime and declare certain sentences for that particular offense. It is scientifically proven that the human mind always gets influenced by its surroundings, all mental factors and actions of a human being are dynamically interrelated with social, economic, biological and psychological events happening around. Hence, it is a tendency of human mind and civilisation to learn from past experience. Therefore, when in a society people observe a criminal being convicted and punished, they learn about the undesirable consequences of committing a crime, so that in future the rate of crime in that society decreases which is better for peace in the civilisation.

An important thing to notice is, good legal environment always allows the convicted person to get opportunity of self-defence, so that no innocent person is punished. In many cases, it is seen that a country does not always have appropriate laws against all types of crime. Therefore, those crimes happen with very much ease. Bullying is illegal when it violates federal or state laws prohibiting discrimination and harassment in the workplace. These laws protect employees from harassment based on protected characteristics, such as race, colour, national origin, religion, sex, age or disability. If a workplace bully is targeting an employee based on a protected characteristic, that could qualify as illegal harassment. The employee would have a hostile work environment claim, if the unwelcome conduct is severe or pervasive enough that a reasonable person would find it to be offensive, hostile or abusive.

In extreme cases, workplace bullying might violate other laws; if a workplace bully threatens to physically harm an employee, the employee might be able to sue for assault, if sexual, then it would be considered a sexual assault. Likewise, a workplace bully who menaces an employee on the way to and from work might be guilty of stalking. If you are being bullied at work, consider filing a complaint with your company's human resources department, although from my personal experience, it might be more effective complaining to someone on the outside. Even if the bully is not breaking the law, it is in your employer's best interests to put a stop to workplace bullying. Bullying drags down morale, performance and productivity, without any benefit to the company.

Keep notes of the mistreatment you have faced, including dates, times, what was said and who else was present, and never throw away any reports. Also keep records of the effects the bullying has had on you, including absences, stress and medical problems, best way to accomplish this is to create a timeline. These records will help your investigated claim and hopefully action taken to stop the problem. If you aren't satisfied with your company's response, your notes will also help you decide whether and how to take action against your company. If your company doesn't take your concerns seriously, talk to a lawyer right away, don't waste time as I did, go for it. If you are facing illegal harassment, you may have only a short time to file a complaint against a government agency. You must file such an administrative complaint before you can file a lawsuit, so missing this deadline will likely mean you have no legal recourse. As soon as your company, union, anyone trying to help, make you wait days on days for results, pester them, do not feel you are being a nuisance, don't remain waiting.

This had been my biggest fault throughout, I always believed everyone was trying to help, the first thing one must do is realise the big picture. Time is of most importance, not just in having your legal window open to file a claim but also for your health. I had spent five years dealing with bullies and two years trying to get my case to court, when I finally made things legal, everything finally began progressing. My life was finally exciting again, I'd wake up each morning eager to find an email or receive a call from Eric, every few days I had news regarding my case. This was the confidence boost I needed, my family and even a psychologist always suggested that talking about the problem would make me feel better, I believed otherwise, taking action against my bullies, that was my solution.

Rule of law has its own strength for protecting human rights, resolving dispute and establishing a peaceful society. It helps people to feel that there is always an invisible friendly hand who will act as a shield against the inequalities they face in their daily life. Although its establishment is very much dependant on the sovereign authority of the state. If they fail to make the law equal to everyone, deprived citizens will then feel that law of their state is a dictatorship for them. A government should enforce those laws which will go with the public interest, not for authorities' own illegal purpose, not against the public sentiment. They have to know that law has a wide array of implications in every layer of the society, law should govern us, not the other way around.

This is what an opposition is usually for, that is why I believed they might be able to help me or fight alongside me, and they didn't. The opposition is a form of political obstruction to a designated government, from allowing them to take full control, by going mad with power. In the past, I had approached my opposition hoping for their help, they didn't know how to handle my problem, instead I was ignored. By the time I developed epilepsy, I imagine they believed people would blame them for not acting sooner, as they would my current government, because of this I continued to be ignored. Near election year, I approached the opposition again; they seemed interested to help this time. I explained my case in full, they believed they would not look good and so nothing moved forward. Every other day I'd read in the papers about complaints the opposition had from our government, I came to realise, they only complained when it benefited them, not the citizens.

This is why rule of law is important, it will protect the society from any kind of crime, anarchy, inequality and it will defend everyone to get their proper judgment. The authority of the state has the power to create a new constitution, a new law but that doesn't mean that they can do as they wish. All are equal in law, everyone has to be stood in front of the law if any unlawful thing happens. So not only the public but also the government, the sovereign authority must have to obey the law and have to make the proper use of law to protect the civilisation from any hazards. Political leaders have too much power over us, the same person who rules over a society, should not be allowed to rule the law as well. Leadership is about doing the right thing, it is related to staying on the right path and not getting distracted by the desire to stay in power, by transient conditions, or by constraints of time or money. A great deal can be achieved in a short amount of time and on a restricted budget, strong people don't compete with each other, they help build each other up.

A manager does things right and a leader does the right thing, leadership is about doing the right thing and it should always be about that. There should never be any exceptions to that rule that is when a leader fails. When it comes to politics, an elected leader knows what the right thing to do is, but wavers from that path because taking the right course may alienate some voters and hurt the politician's chances for re-election. You can't lead effectively if your actions are motivated by staying in power, rather than taking the right actions. Since the recent financial meltdown, we are seeing many leaders failing to lead, rather than doing the right thing, they are doing the financially practical thing, putting costs ahead of strategic leadership. Although finances need to be taken into account, to completely change the focus of the leadership, to make it all about the money, is a path to failure.

When you are in a leadership position, vision, integrity and compassion are infinitely more important than the words you say.

These three traits are as important to your survival as air, food and water.

A critical necessity for these competencies is the tone at the top, what is the character of the leadership team? Once this is determined, expect the country to follow suit. Often leaders don't realise how closely they are being watched by their staff, citizens and supporters. The leader's job is to set the organisation's vision, once it is established, others must be brought into the execution and implementation of that vision. Personal leadership and motivational leadership are the same, to lead others successfully, you must first become a role model, how many do not respect their leaders? Be they bosses, police officers, political parties or even presidents? How can someone lead effectively, if they are not believed in?

Leadership is about doing what's right, leadership is not about doing what's popular, leadership is not about tweets, television cameos and golf. Results will be based on a leader's ability to be authentic and have integrity. As a leader, their vision paints the target, it sparks and fuels the fire within the organisation and draws everyone forward, and it illuminates the way others are to follow. I've never been a follower, I hate to be led, we are all smart enough to rule over ourselves. A leader to enforce the rules might be beneficial for a society but a leader to rule over citizens is no more than an egoistic person in power. It is time for each person to be their own leader; at this point in time, if only few people step forward, they will not succeed, when many begin choosing to lead themselves, that is when our leaders will disappear. It might be a long process, but at some point, humanity needs to start standing up for themselves. If not for our present lives, for our rebirth in the future, I for one do not want to come to this current world on my return and neither should you. Life is a gift, without a receipt, why not try to aim for the most perfect one available?

My leaders were failing me, not only did I not feel they were advancing our society, I felt like they were holding us back. I had been trying to follow the rules for seven years, I never shouted or attacked my bullies. When I developed epilepsy, and was forced to resign, I continued to try and deal with my situation the legal way, but as the years continued, I realised the justice system is a mess. I was forced to follow a system that did not work and if I broke it by attacking my bullies, I would be the guilty party. This is why many people feel forced to break the law, it just doesn't work or apply the same way for everybody, so why follow a broken system? This applies in school, if a child is being bullied, picked on or even find

215

themselves in a physical alteration, if they fight back, they find themselves too suspended from school. What is the child supposed to do? If the school does not act, if the school does not put a stop to the bullying, if the child is attacked, why must they suffer the consequences of defending themselves?

Parents get arrested worldwide for providing children with medical marijuana to cure their illnesses when nothing else works. Who the fuck decided this was illegal? A broken system, one that thinks it knows best but in reality, is either created by ignorant people or those too smart for us to even comprehend. If I followed the legal system rule by rule, I think I probably wouldn't be here writing this story today, I was able to continue life because I started thinking for myself and because of that I succeeded. Dr Roseblack was very persistent that I stop taking marijuana to stabilise my epilepsy, if I had listened to him, chances are I'd be hooked on pills, which didn't cure my epilepsy but rather simply controlled them. I am tired of having to follow a system, laws that do not work and should not exist in the first place, and if broken definitely not punished for it. In my case, the law my bullies had broken, was one that worked, all I had to do now, was make that law apply to me.

Together me and Eric prepared my claim, consisting of my testimony and a set of carefully selected questions. I had two claims directed at two separate defendants, the first being the Gibraltar Developing Company and the second Her Majesty's Attorney General for Gibraltar. Both claims were based on both defendants regarding unfair dismissal from work and the other personal injury, regarding my epilepsy. We considered each set of questions carefully, I didn't only want answers that would help me win my case, I also wanted answers to help me continue living my life. We asked my bullies questions such as: Were you aware Nicholas was being bullied? Did Nicholas ever bring his bullying to your attention? Were you aware Nicholas began suffering from epilepsy as a result of stress at work? Had Nicholas informed you beforehand that he was stressed? Had Nicholas provided you with medical certificates proving he was anxious and depressed whilst working for the Gibraltar Developing Company?

As I waited for their response, the wait had never felt so long, I was used to waiting but this was driving me insane. Not only would it give me an idea towards how my bullies were going to approach these accusations but for the first time in seven years, my questions were finally going to be answered, on a legal document. Nothing could be lost, shredded or misplaced now, finally my bullies were not able to hide their actions anymore, they were going to have to confront them. Finally knowing my bullies were having to go to interviews regarding what had happened between us, made me happy. They were now experiencing the same stress, they had made me feel for five years whilst under their employment. Year 2015 was turning out to be a good year, life was moving forward and best of all whilst I waited for my bullies' defence, every night I got to bring home puppies to play with, I loved my new job.

Chapter Twenty-Seven
Pet Shop Boy

I still hadn't accomplished what needed to be done, my bullies were still at large and finding new victims to destroy but at least, finally after seven years, I was starting to recover. Working at the pet shop was one of the best things that had ever happened to me, and I had my Uncle Arthur to thank for that. When nobody was willing to hire me, when nobody trusted my work record, my uncle was able to overlook all that, he knew the person I truly was. I was very grateful for this opportunity, I believed I was unemployable at the time, this was once again bringing down my moral, it quickly skyrocketed upon my employment. Uncle Arthur had opened up his pet shop over twenty-five years ago, unfortunately with so many supermarkets now carrying pet products, at cheaper prices, the pet shop was unfortunately struggling financially. Uncle Arthur wished to retire soon but having the pet shop doing so poorly, did not make retirement seem like an option for him, he was afraid he would have to continue working his entire life. Uncle Arthur would spend the whole week driving up through Spain, buying products and animals and then bringing them back to Gibraltar, before making the same trip again the next day. I hoped that I could somehow find a way to boost profits at the pet shop now that I was working there, I hoped to return the favour.

After over two years of being unemployed, this was a difficult adjustment at first; luckily, I only worked in the afternoons, this meant I could still live life without an alarm clock. Ever since I was young, I've always hated being forced out of bed in the morning, apparently many believe this is a way of life, it's not, it only is if you allow it to be. I'm more of a night person, I prefer staying up late, writing at night rather than during the day, I'm inspired by moonlight. Thanks to my working hours, I could still stay up late writing and have a nice rest, wake up without an alarm, before going to work, fuck that nine to five bullshit nonsense. During the day, I had time to search for my third lawyer; once found, Eric and I had to spend a lot of time together, before preparing my claim for my bullies, I did all this in the mornings.

I would now wake up early in the morning excited, not only did I have somewhere to be later on in the day, a reason to get dressed, I also had hobbies again. The first thing I bought for myself with my new salary was a canoe, which I'd use in the ocean right next to my apartment. I would ride my canoe to the other side of the airport, at times planes would fly over me, on the other side, I'd observe the people in Spain. This was my new Nipperish, I was no longer hiding at the top of the Rock, I was exploring the ocean; at times, all I wanted to do was continue canoeing towards Africa. I was enjoying life, I had money again, I was able to pay my own bills, buy my own food, take care of myself, and on the bonus side, I was able to start collecting memorabilia again. Slowly, I was becoming part of society again, my confidence was returning, but it still wasn't completely all back, I still needed a little push.

Every five minutes, I'd be forced to start a conversation with someone new I had never met before; finally as I spoke to others, I had the ability to make them laugh again, intentionally this time around. I was starting to make eye contact whilst speaking again and most importantly, I didn't seizure out midway through our conversation. This was what had me most nervous before I started working at the pet shop, not the fact that I had no idea what I was selling but the fact, that I would have to mingle and interact with people on a daily basis. Apart from dealing with customers again, mostly locals as opposed to tourists this time around, I had a new boss who did not frighten me and brand-new co-workers. My new work colleagues were the best, no drama just the occasional poop or two to clean up after, I worked alongside dogs, cats, rabbits, hedgehogs, squirrels, hamsters, mice, chameleons, snakes, bearded dragons, turtles and fish. The best part of all this was I got to take the dogs' home with me most nights, animal rehabilitation is the best way to combat stress and loneliness. Walking home every day with between four to eight puppies, always had people stopping me in the street, I got many dates because of my new four-legged friends.

Playing with or petting an animal can increase levels of the stress-reducing hormone oxytocin and decrease production of the stress hormone cortisol. These hormonal changes can help a nervous person feel more relaxed. Pet owning patients with high blood pressure can keep their blood pressure lower during times of mental stress than patients without pets. You can always talk to a pet, without the fear of being judged, unless you have a cat, they can be very judgmental of who you bring home. There's a reason dogs are referred to as 'man's best friend', we can learn so many things from a dog's behaviour, personality, manner, resiliency, and most importantly, their willingness to provide their owners with unconditional love, loyalty and companionship down to their very last breath. Dogs are faithful companions, loyal, affectionate, easy and quickly become part of the family. They ask very little in return other than good-tasting food, water and a comfortable place to sleep. There are many different species of dogs, we mostly dealt with Chihuahuas, Dachshunds, Maltese, Yorkshire Terriers and my favourite Pomeranians.

Apart from working alongside a bunch of animals, I also had a human co-worker, without her the animals would have taken the pet shop over from me. Nicola had been working at the pet shop for the last two years, dating my cousin Steven for the past eight years and I still had never met her properly. Although we had known each other for years, this was the first time I ever socialised with Nicola. Together we had attended family dinners, birthday parties and funerals but somehow, we never introduced ourselves to each other properly. Nicola's main ambition in life is to become a dancer and because of this she had many dancer friends, who always joined us at the pet shop. If I ever had to work with animals again, I would want to do it alongside no one else but her, I'm scared of cats biting me, whilst I give them their tablets. Animals, dancing, music, a good boss, a fun co-worker, customers becoming friends, money in my pocket, was this real life or was this fantasy?

On my first day at the pet shop, Nicola asked me if I could wash one of the cats in the back room, I had never washed anyone apart from myself but how hard could it be to wash a cat? As soon as the cat touched the water, it jumped out and ran into the shop, I tried to catch it, in doing so the cat ran up the wall, behind a display unit. We couldn't reach the cat, I was supposed to be there to make things easier for Nicola, instead she was having to tell customers to wait, whilst we tried to retrieve the cat. Eventually, I had to take apart the whole unit in order to get to the cat, who was now ten times dirtier than when Nicola had first handed him to me. The next day, a new parrot was brought to the store, I accidentally left the cage open, we had to close the shop and windows, hoping the parrot did not fly out, our customers were forced to wait outside. So far, I wasn't making the shop more money, I was losing money instead, I needed to step up my game; the next day, I accidently lost a snake in the shop, nobody wanted to come in.

I've never been a fan of pet stores and zoos, keeping animals locked up is immoral, what a pet store does have going for it, as opposed to a zoo, is that a pet store's goal is to find an animal the right home, not using them for show. I always felt bad for the smaller animals, birds, hamsters, snakes, chameleons, if they got sold, they were simply being transported from one cage to another. When selling an animal, it always made me happy knowing the owner had a garden, and especially so if they had another of the same pet at home to keep their new one company. I would take the dogs home with me at night, in the morning Uncle Arthur would come and collect them, he would take them to the shop, Nicola would open and later on that day I would be reunited with the dogs. I had to stop naming the animals, especially the dogs, I would get very emotional when I sold one of them. They would usually spend no more than three weeks with us waiting to be sold, but if that time exceeded, I would become very attached, as would Nicola, who also took the dogs with her home at times.

I only worked a few hours in the afternoon, when I'd arrive at the shop, Nicola who had been there all day would leave and I would continue the shift. At the end of the day, I would clean up the shop, throw away the rubbish, collect all the dogs and lock up the shop behind us. Hours flew by like minutes to me, as opposed to my previous employment, where I would look at the clock thinking it was lunchtime, only to realise it was only 10:30 am. Throughout the day, I was busy cleaning and taking care of the animals, it's a never-ending process and along the way I'd stop to deal with customers. The customers were loyal and mostly regulars, some even had expensive hobbies, such as my friend Jackson, who would spend hundreds of pounds on fish throughout the month. One of the best parts about working at the pet shop was all the new friends I was making, and catching up with many old friends who had animals themselves and would visit the pet shop. Unfortunately, sometimes people came into the shop, which I hoped to feed to the snakes.

One day all the dogs began barking, snakes hissing and cats growling, the shop suddenly became cold, the fish went into hiding and the rabbits screaming in fear. Beverly had walked into the shop, she went straight towards the aquariums and hadn't realised I was standing behind the counter. I was so tempted to throw her out, I was even considering blaming her for having stolen something from the shop but at the same time, I wanted to be better than my bullies.

When Beverly turned around and saw me looking back at her, without a single word, she turned around and walked out of the shop. This made me feel so good, for the first time since I had seen her, she had nothing to say, no bullying to share with me, she felt as I had, back in the day. Our shop also had a window, which looked out over the square and right at what once used to be my office whilst working at the tourist branch, which had now been turned into a police station. Every time I looked at what was once my office through the window of my new employment I wondered, why did I not quit sooner? I never felt lonely whilst at work thanks to the animals, the customers and that window, and now at home I had puppies to keep me company.

Aiden loved visiting me at the pet shop; every time he came, his favourite thing to do was feed the fish, all kids enjoyed doing this, we had some pretty fat fish. As much as Aiden enjoyed visiting me at work, Mama June enjoyed it more than him. Mama June would visit me most days, she enjoyed sitting behind the counter, watching me interact with customers, and informing them I was her grandson; on occasions, she even managed to sell a dog for me. Since I no longer lived with my family, most of our interactions now took place at the shop, when they'd finish work, I would begin mine. My parents were especially happy to see me working, sadly they were no longer on speaking terms, parents can be so childish at times, because of this, when they bumped into each other in the shop, it was very awkward. I felt I had wasted the last few years of my life, now that I was feeling better, the family I once had, were now divided, I had missed out on so many family memories, which I could not make up for anymore.

As my time at the pet shop progressed, I realised we weren't doing any better than before I had started working there, we weren't selling many animals except for fish and anything you could put inside an aquarium. I asked my uncle to bring frogs and shrimps, people wanted anything they could put inside their fish tanks. We didn't carry frogs or shrimps at the time, I knew this would be a good investment and it was. The frogs sold well but the shrimps sold like crazy and they were really expensive to buy, so we had to sell each shrimp at four pounds and surprisingly, they all sold out. I brought home some shrimps and a small aquarium and started breeding them. It took a few months but once they started it was crazy; every week, I found myself with over fifty new baby shrimps. When they were older, I would sell each one at the pet shop at a profit, I was financially helping myself and my uncle too, sadly this didn't boost our sales enough for Uncle Arthur to retire.

A shrimp is a small free-swimming crustacean with an elongated body, male shrimps prefer to be called king prawns. The names 'shrimp' and 'prawn' are often used interchangeably and understandably so. Shrimps and prawns have tonnes in common, they are both crustaceans, they both have ten legs, they both are found in salt and fresh water, and they both live near the floor of whatever body of water they inhabit. Despite their similarities, biologically speaking, they are different animals, things labelled prawns are often larger but aren't necessarily true prawns and plenty of shrimp aren't tiny in size at all. Shrimp have branching gills, a side plate that overlays segments in front and behind, and carry their eggs outside of their bodies beneath their tails. Prawns have lamellar gills, side plates that overlap tile-like from front to back, and carry their eggs inside their bodies near their tails. Have you ever wondered the difference between a shrimp and a scampi? I had, one's cooked and the other isn't.

For the longest time, my friends consisted of hallucinations, crazies, frogs, shrimps, dogs, rodents, rabbits, fish, birds, a bear, the occasional pig or two and a bunch of weirdos. Now after a few months working at the pet shop, having just found my third lawyer, I was ready to start making friends. Many of the customers who entered the pet shop became my friends, I joined many of them outside work for drinks but whilst making new friends I also began interacting with old ones. Isven was a close neighbour of mine; when I lived in my old house, we'd go for spins in his car up the Rock and on occasions even visit the beach. I hadn't seen Isven in a while but now every now and again I'd join him for a spin in his car, this time he had upgraded to a Mercedes. Davey was one of my friends from my old group of friends, the ones who would join me to smoke at the Nipperish. I hadn't seen Davey since I had missed his wedding after being discharged from the mental hospital, it was nice catching up with him again, accompanied by his new wife. Liam and I used to be friends when we were very young, I knew he was an artist but I had no idea he liked drawing comics; I liked writing, together we created a few comics and even wrote a pilot episode for a show based on potheads. I hadn't had friends in so long, I hadn't realised how important it was to interact socially with others, it was nice meeting new people and then I re-met Jensen.

Walking home one day, as I carried a few puppies, I came across Jensen, he stopped to play with the puppies, as everybody did, soon after we were sat on the stones, next to the ocean, sharing a joint. I had known Jensen most of my life but we never spent much time together, although growing up, he was always there. Jensen's grandparents were neighbours to mine; every time I went to visit Mama June and Grandpa Alberto, I'd come across Jensen playing outside in the patio. In school, Jensen and I didn't share any classes but we had played basketball together before in the playground and in the past, joined by other friends, we had found ourselves in the same places, once even inside my house. Once before she left to live in England, Germaine and I joined a few friends for a BBQ at the beach, Jensen was also there with us, making pinchitos. I always knew who Jensen was, but it wasn't until I began working at the pet shop that I came to realise, Jensen is one of the smartest people I've ever met; he's a walking, talking Wikipedia.

Jensen has a good energy, it was not only positive, it was strong too, I knew Jensen had experienced many rebirths, this time around he brought a companion with him, seeing as Jensen's a twin. I was fascinated by twins at the time, spiritual connections, telepathy, dream sharing, I believed this was easier to study between twins rather than individuals. Usually when I spoke about the dreaming world, many people didn't pay much attention to me or had nothing to provide to the conversation; with Jensen, I actually started learning more about the subject. When I spoke to Jensen about this, not only was he intrigued, he had his own ideas and thoughts on the matter. At times, Jensen had experienced lucid dreams and was very knowledgeable when it came to dream telepathy. Twins are sometimes able to communicate with each other through their dreams, they can each recall the same dream, they both shared together the night before.

This sort of psychological connection isn't necessarily mysterious, any two people who know each other very well and who have shared many common experiences, including non-twin siblings, old married couples, and even best friends may complete each other's sentences and have a pretty good idea about what the other person is thinking. However, the idea of twin telepathy is very intriguing, no matter how far apart they are, they still have one and the same body. Therefore, whatever impression, physical or mental, one of them perceives, has its after-effects on the other. In some cases, one twin will know about something that happened to the other twin when such knowledge was clearly impossible. I was glad my new friend was knowledgeable when it came to dreaming, I hoped he could help me understand how people can share dreams with others who are also alive, as opposed to just dreaming with the dead.

Together Jensen and I renovated the entire pet shop, we removed all the display units, we cleaned the shop thoroughly, we then gave the entire shop a complete paint over. Jensen suggested we go with white, it would make the shop look cleaner, I wanted to go for green but in the end, I'm glad we went with white. The pet shop now looked completely new; we then reorganised the entire shop, moved the counter, fixed the displays, changed the cages around and even caught the white lizard that had escaped inside the pet shop many years earlier. As the weeks past, Jensen would continue helping me at the pet shop in the afternoons when needed; at the end of the day, we would clean up after the animals and close the shop together. As much as I now enjoyed having real mentally stable friends, I still missed my friends back at the mental hospital, and most importantly, I missed my illusions, I considered them my friends too. Now that I was somewhat settled in life, relaxed and stress free, perhaps it was time, I attempted making contact again, and that is exactly what I did.

Chapter Twenty-Eight
Don't Medicate, Just Meditate

When I first began developing stress, anxiety, depression and a fear for the world around me, the only alternative I was given by others, which did not include relying on pharmaceutical drugs was meditation. Meditation reduces bad feelings such as stress, depression and anxiety, a bit of stress can be good for you, it keeps us alert but many people carry too much stress, which in turn affects their health. Everything in moderation is good for you, too much is bad, we must learn self-control before becoming self-aware, all part of reaching the goal of meditation. Meditation has been practised for thousands of years, originally it was meant to help deepen an understanding of the sacred and mystical forces of life. These days, meditation is commonly used for relaxation and stress reduction, this means, those people are only reaching the halfway point through their meditation process.

In order for us to grow, we need necessary energies such as calories from food, minerals from water, oxygen and sunlight drawn from our surroundings. Conversely, plants need sunlight, food and water as well, along with carbon dioxide. Humans can absorb and heal through other humans, animals and any part of nature. That's why being around nature is often uplifting and energising for so many people. Humans are made of energy too, meditation allows us to communicate with this energy that can travel via dark matter and return back to our brains, with the information requested from us. There is a feedback loop between human beings and earth's energetic-magnetic systems. The earth has several sources of magnetic fields that affect us all. Two of them are the geomagnetic field, that emanates from the core of the earth and the fields that exist between earth and the ionosphere. These fields surround the entire planet and act as protective shields blocking out the harmful effects of solar radiation, cosmic rays, sand and other forms of space weather. Without these fields, ice as we know it could not exist on earth. They are part of the dynamic ecosystem of our planet, these energetic fields are a function of solar activity. The rhythms taking place on earth's magnetic fields have an impact on our health and behaviour.

A person must be fully relaxed and self-aware if they wish to communicate with the energy flowing throughout our universe. Energy which can reach the mind, even from as far away as another galaxy. Energy can be a form of other souls, currently continuing their test of life solely as energy, without the protection or constraints of a human shell. Meditation is a form of soul retrieval, reconnecting with the missing pieces of your soul. Meditation allows you to reach the spiritual world, this world consists within our dreams. Dreams are more than real, why does dreaming keep revealing what our minds conceal?

Dreams do not only have to take place whilst you're asleep, unable to control them and enjoy its experiences or remember its knowledge. You can experience the power of a dream during the day, daydreaming is only the first step towards achieving this goal. Long ago, I realised that meditation is a form of lucid dreaming, only when you let go of your conscious thoughts, can you unlock your subconscious mind, open your third-eye, activate your pineal gland, discover the dreaming connection.

Meditation is considered a type of mind-body complementary medicine, which can produce a deep state of relaxation and a tranquil mind. When I was younger, I could start writing the moment I sat at my computer, as I've grown older and life has become tougher, my creativity, my thought process, does not come as easy. I cannot begin writing unless I meditate before, it increases my ability to study and focus; what exercise is for the body, meditation is to the mind. Meditation is very important, it is in a way the opposite of medication, don't medicate yourself to sleep, meditate yourself to a greater awakening. Since as far back as 2010, I had always tried meditating in the hopes of reducing my stress and anxiety but sadly I could never seem to achieve strong results. As the years progressed and I became more familiar with the concept of meditation, I aimed to achieve a reunion. Without an epileptic short cut, meant I would have to travel the long journey of finding inner-peace before I could return back there someday.

During a mindfulness meditation, you broaden your conscious awareness, you focus on what you're experiencing during meditation. You can observe your thoughts, feel your emotions, hear your messages, sense your mind and get a taste of just how powerful you can be. The best way to meditate generally requires focusing your attention, one of the most important elements of meditation. Focusing your attention is what helps free your mind from the many distractions that cause stress and worry. You can focus your attention on such things as a specific object, an image or even your breathing. Relaxed breathing is a technique involving deep, even-paced breathing using the diaphragm muscle to expand your lungs. The purpose is to slow your breathing, take in more oxygen, so that you can breathe more efficiently. I've been using this technique on a daily and hourly basis, not just during meditation.

A quiet setting is always most effective during meditation, unless you have the great ability to ignore the world around you. As you get more skilled at meditation, you can practise it anywhere, especially in high-stress situations where you benefit the most from meditation. You can practise meditation whether you're sitting, lying down, walking, or in other positions or activities. Just try to be comfortable so that you can get the most out of your meditation. Lastly and most importantly, have an open attitude, let thoughts pass through your mind without judgment. During meditation, you focus your attention and eliminate the stream of jumbled thoughts that may be crowding your mind and causing stress, this process may result in enhanced physical and emotional well-being. Spending even a few minutes meditating, can restore your calm and inner-peace but in my case, back then I found this impossible to achieve.

Whilst meditating I always had my bullies, epilepsy, financial worries and all kinds of thoughts running through my head. Like a circle in a spiral, like a wheel within a wheel, never ending or beginning on an ever-spinning reel. As the images unwind, like the circles that you find, in the windmills of your mind. In order for meditation to work, one must first let go of all their problems, not forever, but at least during meditation, to achieve this, a person needs to stop concentrating. Meditation and concentration isn't so much trying to stop your brain from thinking what's on your mind but rather letting it think for itself, similar to a dream. Sometimes we must stop controlling our brain, so it can communicate its message to us. If we are forever on concentration mode, how is our subconscious supposed to activate, therefore opening our third-eye, allowing ourselves to reach a state of self-awakening.

First you must free yourself from a negative mindset, most of us are switched on negative mode, we must learn to switch off our negativity and switch on our positivity. It goes without saying that certain people, places and things are loaded with negative energies that bring you down. If at all possible steer clear of such energies, if you can't, try to unwind by grounding or cleansing afterward. If you were to grab a pen and paper and spend one minutes writing down the first thoughts that come to mind, most of them will be negative and loaded with self-criticism. This is what is going on in our heads most of the time, our thoughts are full of negativity. One must feel positive through meditation, since negativity surrounds our world, to reach inner-peace, one must stop thinking. When the mind is in a negative state, it can launch an endless response of insults and animosity at us, all in vicious defence of our supposed worthlessness. Negative self-talk is an epidemic, and one that needs to heal, for if we can learn to be kind to ourselves, we will find it easier to be kind to each other.

Keep in mind, for instance, that it's common for your mind to wander during meditation, no matter how long you've been practising meditation. If you're meditating to calm your mind and your attention wanders, slowly return to the object, sensation or movement you're focusing on. Experiment, and you'll likely find out what types of meditation work best for you and which ones you enjoy doing most. Adapt meditation to your needs at the moment, remember, there's no right way or wrong way to meditate. What matters is that meditation helps you reduce your stress and feel better overall. There are many types of meditation and relaxation techniques that have meditation components; my personal favourite included passing out after a seizure. Other more sensible methods include guided meditation accomplished through imagery or visualisation, with this method of meditation you form mental images of places or situations you find relaxing.

Mantra meditation is where one silently repeats a calming word, thought or phrase to prevent distracting thoughts. Mindfulness meditation is based on being mindful or having an increased awareness and acceptance of living in the present moment. *Qi Gong* combines meditation, relaxation, physical movement and breathing exercises to restore and maintain balance. *Tai Chi* is a form of gentle Chinese martial arts, where you perform a self-paced series of postures or movements in a slow, graceful manner while practising deep breathing. During yoga you perform a series of postures and controlled breathing exercises to promote a more flexible body and a calm mind. As you move through poses that require balance and concentration, you're encouraged to focus less on your busy day and more on the moment. Smoking cannabis, when not abused therefore not completely stoned can help us relax, reaching meditation much quicker. For you have stopped using your brain, it is then that your mind can control your thoughts. The method most of the world relies upon when aiming to achieve the goal of meditation is through sleep.

I for one used to get so caught up trying not to think, picturing relaxing sceneries, counting sheep etc...that I did not allow my brain to speak to me, run wild, do what it needed to do. When you sleep, your dreams are basically thoughts which you are not controlling. Ironically, dreams have more meaning, importance and value than those of our daily thoughts, processed only by our conscious mind. Your body is relaxed, your concentration is shut down, your brain is allowing all areas of your mind to guide your thoughts. Another interesting and safe way to achieve a higher understanding of yourself through meditation is simply by going to sleep. Whilst we are sleeping, we allow our mind to reach a meditated state, which increases our brainpower, highlights both visuals and sounds so strong, that we dream our thoughts into fruition. If you can manage to reach this state of meditation and become good at it, you can even perform this meditation whilst you sleep. The process of meditation takes place when a person reaches a state of REM sleep. To gain the full experience, a person's body and mind must reach a deep state of sleep without actually falling asleep in the process.

When you reach this point, you're able to concentrate in your own dreams and when you're able to do that, you finally realise that dreaming is actually more advanced, more complicated, more technical than any computer. At the time when I didn't have real friends or a job for that matter, I would sometime spend almost an hour trying to meditate. Only to be interrupted by voices, hallucinations and my subconscious thoughts but perhaps is that meditation itself? Meditation can give you a sense of calmness, peacefulness and balance that can benefit both your emotional well-being and your overall health. These benefits don't end when your meditation session ends, meditation can help carry you more calmly through your day. The emotional benefits of meditation can include gaining a new perspective on stressful situations, increasing self-awareness and increasing imagination and creativity. The results of meditation are always confusing but I had come to realise, once my seizures ended, that the dream world I was interacting in, might be what meditators hope to achieve. Only when the mind illuminates, we are introduced to a world the eyes cannot see.

Within my lucid dreams, I would gain a new perspective on stressful situations, build skills to manage my stress, and most importantly, I had an increase in self-awareness. Whilst focused on my dream, it helped me reduce negative emotions, whilst increasing my patience, tolerance, imagination, creativity and having a much better understanding of myself. We all want to go places, ask important questions, meet specific people and understand ourselves, thanks to the lives we lead, our reality can't accomplish that; luckily, within our minds, humans can accomplish anything. My biggest inspiration in life, Jim Henson, once said, "The only way the magic works is by hard work, but hard work can be fun."

I believe him, if I wanted to get back there someday, back to the dreaming connection, I had to work hard at it without forgetting, it's all part of a fun journey. The results of meditation are always confusing, but when you begin to feel better for it, that's when you know it is working for you.

By 2016, a few months after having started working at the pet shop and making friends again, I thought my mind might finally be able to properly concentrate on meditation. My goal was not solely to find inner-peace, it was to do so, in an attempt to re-open my third-eye. Once again activate my pineal gland, I was hoping my subconscious and conscious mind could interact together again. Anyone can practise meditation, it's simple, no matter how hard we've been programmed to believe it is, we can all control our thoughts. Meditation is also inexpensive, meaning it is not a privilege only bestowed upon the rich, it is a gift every human being can participate in. Long-term meditation can decrease your blood pressure, strengthen your immune system, kill diseases because meditation concentrates on the mind. Pharmaceutical drugs aim to control your illness, whilst blocking your mind from healing it itself. Our mind can do many things, it can heal our body, change our DNA structure and even slow down our aging process.

Meditating correctly only for a matter of weeks, increases your brain size in three crucial areas; the left hippocampus, which is responsible for your ability to learn and retain information; the Posterior Cingulate Cortex, which control the ability of where your mind wonders; and the Temporoparietal Junction, responsible for empathy and compassion. Meditation doesn't only grow the good parts of your brain, it decreases the cell volume in the Amygdala, the part of the brain responsible for fear, stress and anxiety. Most interestingly of all, meditation is the most effective way to control the length of your telomeres. Short telomeres are a marker for accelerated aging, through meditation you can control the length of your telomere, grow them, therefore physically aging at a slower pace, in energy, health and youthful looks. Meditation is the key to a longer, healthier more fulfilling life, turn off the television for a while, live a longer life because of it.

Meditation allows you to consider death a thing of the past, for energy from every soul can communicate with each other, either whilst here on earth or roaming other realms. Telepathy is the ability to perceive the thoughts of others directly, on a mind-to-mind basis, without using speech or body language to communicate. Most people will never come close to unlocking the full potential of their own minds. This doesn't mean that the potential isn't there, just that it remains inactive in most. The fact is that many people have developed their psychic abilities, including mind-reading telepathic powers in a deliberate way. Following various training methods that are designed to awaken and strengthen these hidden abilities, one such method is through meditation. Meditation is useful for developing psychic abilities such as telepathy, because it helps you to quieten your mind, and to alter your state of consciousness. In order to begin tapping into your latent psychic powers, it's very helpful to slow the mind down and quiet the chatter of everyday thoughts. In practical terms, this involves slowing your brainwave activity from the rapid beta state (13 Hz+) that is associated with normal active consciousness, down into the alpha (8-12 Hz) and theta (4-7 Hz) states. We all enter the alpha state naturally when daydreaming or in other states of light relaxation, and the theta state is experienced during creative work or while drifting off to sleep.

When you meditate on a daily basis, and your mind becomes used to relaxing deeply, you're setting the stage for your telepathic abilities to flower. However, many people find it difficult to maintain these more relaxed brain states for any significant length of time, as it can be very difficult to really slow down thought and quiet the mind. This is unsurprising, as most people don't have any experience with thought control techniques. Fortunately, learning to meditate is much easier if you use a brainwave entrainment recording and tapping into the right state of mind required for the development of telepathic powers is made easier still if you use a recording that is especially designed for this purpose. Brainwave entrainment basically involves listening to a recording that features repetitive sounds of certain frequencies. Thanks to a natural phenomenon called the frequency following response; the brain has a tendency to match its own brainwave outputs of the frequency of the sound it's hearing. This makes it much easier to enter different states of consciousness that will, as your brain is basically getting a helping hand so to speak from the recording. If you can learn to deeply relax your mind, tapping into your latent powers will become easier.

Meditation can be practised wherever you are, whether it's at the top of the mountains, inside a warm bath, gazing at the stars or even during your lunch break. All you need is the head on your shoulders, granted most of us usually leave home without it. When I was at my worse, I tried meditating in my bedroom, during the day it was useless for me, at night I was sometimes able to switch off my mind and meditate for approximately seven seconds. My favourite place to meditate was at the Nipperish, as the sun set down over Spain, I would look across the ocean, at the mountains which made up Africa, I heard the birds singing above me, this is where I most gained from meditating. Now however my new favourite place to meditate was on my canoe, far from the Rock, lost in the ocean, between Gibraltar, Spain and Africa. However, a dolphin once scared me half to death during meditation, I now prefer meditating on land. At the end of the day, once it was dark, closing up the pet shop, before turning off the aquariums, I would remain standing motionless in a trance observing the fish. The pet shop was dark, the florescent lighting which illuminated each individual fish aquarium, was always a very relaxing sight for me. Each night, when I closed the pet shop, if I were alone, I would sit and meditate, a few months later, I woke up in a dream without having fallen asleep.

Chapter Twenty-Nine
Pull Your Own Strings

Does following the rules give you an advantage or disadvantage in life? Rules must be obeyed for legal purposes and accountability, obeying rules in a faculty setting also promotes trust and fairness, if you worked for my bullies, following the rules meant you ended up with epilepsy. Consistency is another important trait, because it means fewer scattered and impromptu decisions, rules are tools to get things accomplished, or so they appear. When I removed myself from society, when I stopped being a puppet to it, I was able to gain a better understanding of life, and I was much happier for it. It wasn't until I learned through my bullies that loopholes are the way to move forward, that I too begun to succeed in life. I had played by the rules, I had followed our justice system; sadly being part of the system, simply means your puppeteers have control over you.

Are people puppets of society? Do we control the social system or does it control us? Society is said to mould individuals, but to what extent? The truth is we are puppets to society but only because we allow ourselves to be, nobody is truly moving our strings for us or speaking on our behalf. We all have free will; sadly, we are influenced by society yet our fate is not determined by it. Many might have been turned off by my story at the very beginning, when I began discussing cannabis. Nobody has forced those individuals to stop reading but perhaps having cannabis attached to this story, has turned them away. Our society is manipulated into believing cannabis is something to frown upon, like everything too much of it is indeed not a good idea. However, when I didn't allow society to rule my judgement, I was able to learn that cannabis is in fact, one of our most important resources from nature to combat illnesses and diseases.

If we were to follow the rules, those experimenting with cannabis, will never stumble upon the cures humanity valuably needs. Those brave enough to go against the rules, end up in prison for it; having been in prison, society then looks down upon you. A young mother, jailed for three years, simply for feeding her child cannabis oil, in the hopes of curing her from an illness, where is the justice? This mother decided to stop being a puppet, she decided to go against the rules, and when she did, the law stepped in, and put her back in her place within society. As much as we try to break free from the system, through loopholes, they are able to keep us in check, reform us back into being an obedient member of society. Prisons are intended to be used to indicate that certain forms of behaviour will not be tolerated and to protect ourselves against people who refuse to play by the rules.

Prisons are simply another form of schooling, educating us back into the system, keeping us locked down, trapped and fear of going against the rules. Granted if you murder someone, this is a good rule to have, but when you decide to grow a marijuana plant in your house and are imprisoned for it, that's just ridiculous. We've got to find a way, our minds need to be set free, there's just one way, we've got to meditate our way to freedom.

My great-grandfather committed no crime, other than sharing his negative opinions on a once Spanish leader. He was sentenced to death for this crime, since he was now a British national, he managed to escape this fate. Sadly, my great-grandfather spent a lifetime in prison for simply sharing his opinion. What law had he broken? None, his opinion was just different from those in charge of him, through loopholes, he managed to survive yet locked away for life.

The law is a very valuable tool for our evolution, but only when the justice system works for everybody, not just those who control others. Years ago, a father was attacked in the street alongside his two sons at knifepoint. The mugger stole the father's wallet, watch and mobile, and then attempted to steal one of the son's chains. When the father began to tackle the mugger, in an attempt to remove the knife from his hand, the father accidentally stabbed the mugger before making a run for it with his children. Who was to blame? As I see it, the father was simply acting within self-defence yet in the society we find ourselves today, we only have one set of rules to follow. If you stab a person, you are considered guilty of intending to wound another human being. The father was sentenced to a few years in prison, whilst the mugger began receiving medical benefits from his government. Had the father been a puppet to society, one of his son's might have ended up getting stabbed instead, sometimes the rules must be broken, sometimes we must play the system, simply in defence of our human rights.

The Gibraltar Developing Company have a rule, that anyone convicted of a crime regarding marijuana is not to be employed. I don't really feel this is a logical rule, but to each their own, they have every right to enforce that rule. However, when I applied to work for them, as an information officer, at the Gibraltar Tourist Branch, I followed their rules, and I answered honestly. They on the other hand, did not follow the rules set upon them, and hired me anyway, only to realise, it was a far more serious rule that needed to be followed than they first believed. Instead of accepting responsibility, they broke the rules, in order to pretend to be following them accordingly with the Gibraltar Developing Company. Had I played them at the start, I could have simply not have mentioned my convictions, and for all I know, none of them would have ever found out. However, I didn't play them, I was honest with them and in return they played me, they treated me like a puppet. The truth is that if you follow the rules literally then you will always be held down in society, you will always be a victim to puppetry.

Society had me believe, that a young boy from a small Rock, could never make the big time in Hollywood. In my mind all I knew, was that one day I hoped to have the chance to make millions of people happy. In order to do that, I had to stop thinking like a puppet, and think as my own person, and so far, life seems to be working in my favour. My school had taught me to think one way, my idols helped me to think a different way, the way I preferred to think. When I stopped listening to what I was being forced to learn, and learned what I believed was valuable, was when I truly began to realise who I wanted to be in life. We might have multiple lives waiting for us in our futures that does not mean, that right now, this life is not the one of most importance, it's the one you share with family and friends on a human level. Believing in spirituality, that is one rule we should not let society decide for us, for if we conform to the rules of reality, we'll never truly understand ourselves.

When I began falling into a depression, living with stress and developing epilepsy, life didn't make sense anymore. I had followed the system, I was an obedient citizen, I did as I was told, why had my life broken before me? I started to realise that when I played the system, when I went against the rules, in every sense of the form, I would feel better for it. If I were to go by society then as soon as I began hearing voices and hallucinating about the dead, I should have immediately admitted myself into a mental hospital. Instead, I began to break down the rules of reality and began to see life through a different eye, my third-eye. One must not only break the rules of law, one must break the rules of life, one must play the entire system, if one hopes to break free from being a puppet to life in general. Life is far easier when you're different, it's not that easy being normal, one becomes like so many ordinary things. When normal is all there is to be, it could make you question what's the point. Be different, you'll be fine, it's unique, it's how everyone should be.

When my problems at work began to get out of hand, I hoped my union would act on my behalf as advertised. This was the normal procedure, when working within a society, one which stopped me from accidentally running over my bullies with my car. I followed the rules, the union in return played me, the rules did not apply to them. When the union misguided me, I continued to follow the rules and set out to find a lawyer, I had no money for justice, the legal system had already failed me. When I decided to play the system, I soon found myself with legal assistance, three different lawyers, legal proceedings against my bullies, a salary and free puppies to play with. Only when I too started to play the system, did my life get better for it, our justice system relies on having money. This is why the rich can get away with anything, whilst innocent people sometimes have to face an unfair jail sentence as they cannot afford to defend themselves properly.

Before sharing my story on social media, I was told that by doing so I'd be jeopardising my chances in court. Had I not shared my story online, having made the noise I made, I probably wouldn't have been granted legal assistance. Had I not started thinking outside the box, being labelled unfit for society and locked inside a mental hospital, my life would still be on pause, waiting for the system to do its job. Hoping for legal assistance means one must have no income, though as I witnessed if you have connections, you can receive legal assistance, even if you're guilty or have the money to afford the legal fees yourself. I had remained unemployed in order to receive this assistance, once I had, I began working on an 'as and when required' basis. This meant my income was not officially labelled, and as long as I didn't exceed a certain number of hours, I felt safe that my legal assistance was in no jeopardy. Follow the rules yet find loopholes along the way, rules do not always apply the same to everybody, one must be fully aware of that fact.

After nine years waiting on the housing list, I had been offered a house; sadly unlike Stacey, I had to turn it down, I had no finances at the time. As the years past and I began working at the pet shop, I began requesting a house, having been offered one recently, I should still be at the top of the list, or so one would think. Since I have no partner, since I'm not married, since I have no children, since I don't follow the norm in society, I end up going down on the housing list, instead of remaining at the same spot. Families are a priority, but simply because I'm not a newlywed, I don't have the same right to own a house. Society leads you to feel that living life a certain way is the correct way, they do so by giving privileges to those who conform to work, marriage and raising children. In the eyes of society, there is a right way and a wrong way to live one's life.

After I lived in my childhood house, when I moved into my rented apartment, I informed housing, since I had moved into a new address, I immediately lost many points. The way the system works in this case, makes one consider the fact that lying or omitting information, might be more beneficial. Had I not informed them that I had moved house, I wouldn't have lost my points. Those clever enough to state they're homeless, which in reality is the case, even if you are living under someone else's roof. Those who have done so already own a house, not because they played the system, they simply didn't follow the rules. They made their own decision, on what was best for them, that is admirable and worthwhile, and shows how one can work around a broken system. Everyone deserves a house, the system should not decide who is more deserving of one over another, this is one example of why people might rebel in a society. If we were to look at it from the eyes of our ancestors, we are being denied from creating our own shelter. The homeless are considered a nuisance by society, sleeping in the alleys, under bridges, inside abandoned buildings. Yet society bans them from sleeping in public places, does not offer them a home, luckily good-hearted individuals organise homeless shelters, a priority that should be our governments.

Work, religion, law, media, education and family determine our behaviour in life, which in turn causes us to behave a certain way amongst others. If we wish to continue being part of the system, we must learn to obey its rules, but if you do not follow the system, what other alternatives do you have? When I found myself almost homeless, I considered pitching up a tent somewhere along the Rock, as soon as they'd find me, I'd be fined. I considered buying a caravan, parking near the beach, if they'd find me, I'd be fined. If I didn't have to worry about being fined, I might have just built a house for myself, and be done with it, but I could only assume, if I started to build a house, I'd be fined. If I started growing my own fruit and vegetables, I'd be fined, if I started collecting healthy, clean rain water, I'd be fined, if one doesn't send their children to school, they'd be fined, that's just not fine. Most of the time, the law doesn't even know what it's doing, and those who follow it blindly, end up doing a worse job because of it.

According to society, a person with a brain malfunction, is immediately considered crazy, out of touch with reality. If you stop and think, might one consider, that those who are labelled mentally disabled, might actually be mentally enabled. Puppets are all controlled the same way, puppets believe the way our brains are wired is the correct way, are you a puppet? Who says being the black sheep of your family, friends or even society is a bad thing? Sometimes thinking differently from the rest gives you a different life than they lead, is that something that makes you happy or sad? Don't be a follower, be your own leader. We are all ruled over, some might prefer the stability, others might realise we are simply being stabilised into conformity for the greater good of certain individuals. Humans shouldn't be pets, we shouldn't have leaders, we shouldn't have any bosses and we certainly shouldn't have any bullies. We should all lead ourselves, and we should all lead each other.

We live in a world overloaded with rules and information on how to follow them and live accordingly both in morals and spirituality. There is information everywhere about any and everything one can imagine, from the origins of dragons to the time of travel from earth to mars. Having so much information available to us, makes it easier for us, to stop thinking and simply obey. It's wonderful having so much information at the click of our fingers, but it is important to not just believe whatever is being fed to you. In these times of fast media and ever-growing Internet, we are under so many external influences that it can be difficult to know when we are thinking for ourselves. Unless you are a discerning, very aware person, you most likely don't even know when your thinking is not your own. Not that all outside influence is bad or detrimental to forming your own views, but being unable to think for yourself can make you miserable at best, or a puppet of someone else's programming, at worst.

Media manipulation is a series of related techniques in which society is controlled by an image or argument that favours the particular interests of those in control. Such tactics may include the use of logical misconceptions, psychological manipulations, outright deception, rhetorical and propaganda techniques. Media manipulation often involves the suppression of information or points of view by crowding them out. Inducing other people or groups of people to stop listening to certain arguments, or by simply diverting attention elsewhere, away from the actual problem. We are all led to believe one way, we are all informed through the same outlets, this moulds us into the society we belong to. Hoping to stay within that society, we adapt to it, thinking we are doing so by choice, that cannot be furthest from the truth. From what we choose to wear, to our religious beliefs, our political views, our taste in music and all the other stuff. It is important to examine what you believe in and the values you choose to stand by for yourself, do not let anyone manipulate you, don't be a puppet to anybody or anything.

There are many benefits when it comes to thinking for yourself, first of all you develop self-confidence and trust in your abilities, you begin to believe in who you are, not who you think you need to be. You attain a greater sense of accomplishment, that feeling of self-worth that many carry with them daily, will be gone, knowing who you are, gives you a sense of worthiness. You expand your mind and boost your brainpower, allowing areas of your brain, you were unaware of, to activate and experience a greater understanding of why you're here. You gain respect from others by standing up for what you believe in and by being original, this in turn gives you a positive vibe, rather than a negative one. You are more aware and alert to what the media is trying to sell you, nobody can con you, nobody can pull a fast one over you, you're more aware of who you surround yourself with.

You are more open to self-improvement and alternative viewpoints, this is not just an individual bonus, this allows the world to grow together. You are more interesting to others by expanding their thinking and options, and in turn will find yourself in the presence of people who mentally challenge you to always keep improving. You've got to stand up for what you believe, you should always believe in yourself, if you're passionate, use that passion. Don't look the other way, don't wait another day, let your passion flow. In my case, it was when I stopped following the rules and started thinking for myself that helped me find an ending to this story.

Chapter Thirty
The Test of Life

Life isn't just that awkward moment between rebirth and death, when one's soul takes human form and flesh surrounds our energy. You never reach an ending in life, never think the next step will be easier, never think you've made it, if you are truly living, you are forever trying. Nobody knows where they're going, nobody knows where they've been, but once you know who you are, the path will become clear again. I've always been fascinated by strange, difficult to understand, sometimes unbelievable tales of assumedly past events in the history of our world. These wonderful, secretively and creatively worded messages used to make sense many years ago to those who were around, when these tales were first shared. Sadly, yet luckily and fortunately throughout the many years, we as human beings have grown, progressed, evolved and developed. Sadly, our knowledge has not become greater, yet our technology sophistically advanced. Perhaps it is time we read those stories, interpreted in a way that human civilisation can relate to today.

Life is all about connections, past, present and future, share your energy, keep it positive, a good soul gets you far. After the last few years of my life, all my beliefs are different now, nothing is right, nothing is wrong, it's just all misinterpreted along the way. When I think of what life is all about, the true meaning of our existence, I personally come to the conclusion that life is simply one big test and the world is a school for all. In order to graduate and move on to a higher learning, one needs to pass a few different tests, which at the end, when put together, determine if you're ready to be part of the universe. Unfortunately, schools are also filled with bullies, who don't give a fuck, about graduating and just make it harder for those actually interested in studying for their tests.

We have our tools provided for us in order to take our tests, such as pencils, sharpeners, rubbers and rulers, to make life much simpler for us. At a young age, we learn that if we stab ourselves in the eye with a pencil, the sharper it is, the further it hurts and the more likely you are to lose an eye. We learn not to stick the sharpeners up our nose, we learn that if the pencil tip breaks, you insert it into the sharpener and it can become sharp again. You don't swallow your rubber, you use it to correct your mistakes and rulers are not used for scratching one's back in pleasure, it is used to allow your pencil to draw a straight line. We learn this at a young age, so we stop using our tools incorrectly and use them for what they are worth. These tools help us collect, correct, erase, replace and organise the knowledge within our heads. Make sure your information is recorded because perhaps in a couple of years, you might completely forget, all that you've learned throughout your life.

Tests don't necessarily have to be boring, and in this case, nobody ever gets a perfect score, but remember, every storm we ride, is its own reward. It's a complicated test, there are no shortcuts, there is no cheating, there is no copying or even stealing other people's tests. This is your test and you have to pass it on your own, no matter how difficult, complicated or unanswerable the questions might seem, at least you've got to try. If you don't pass your test, then you'll never graduate, to the place you truly want to be in life. Don't take my word on any of this, without proof you really shouldn't believe anything anyone tells you. That is why it is always important to study what has been provided, do your own research, come to your own conclusions and don't let anybody tell you how to think, be your own boss. You do for yourself, whatever it is you believe needs to be done, in the hopes of passing your own test and not the same as everyone else.

Share your experience with as many people as possible, you can always and forever remain connected to everyone around you. Energy is strong, it is powerful, in each and every one, even a tiny stone found across the vastness of the universe can still become a mighty Rock. Family come with you from the past, friends are made in the present, the future holds your test, be ready for what awaits. The world has got a smile today, the world has got a glow, there's no such thing as strangers, when a stranger says hello then everyone is family, we should all be having so much fun. Our world should remember, it is far more valuable to make love, not war, use protection, not weapons, connect with other souls, not just physically but mentally too.

Friendship is one of the strongest medication to cure loneliness, how do some of us not realise this sooner? Being amongst others, sharing our experiences, that is when our energy thrives, it is a human experience in the hopes of developing our energy in various forms. Since as far back as 2008, I slowly started to lose friends, I found myself alone, sometimes in the company of hallucinations or animals. New Year 2016, after many years uncelebrated, I was ready or rather I was forced by Jensen, to celebrate the start of the year. I was now working, I had a bit of money, my bullies were squirming, my legal proceedings furthering, life was good, yet after so many years, not celebrating the new year, had become my new tradition. That year, thanks to a friend, that tradition was about to change, it was time to celebrate the New Year, amongst real people! As I walked around Gibraltar accompanied by Jensen, I found myself wishing everyone, a happy new year. Fireworks in the sky, people talking to people, drinks and music, I felt normal, being part of a celebration with everyone.

Being in the presence of so many people at once, is sometimes overwhelming for me, too much energy from so many people can be exhausting to both the body and mind. Energy exists all around us, every aspect of our world in varied degrees of vibrational density. From the divine energy that created your soul, to the negative energy created through the judgement of a damaged person. The energy that surrounds us, is constantly moving and changing, redefining us and everything around us. Positive energy vibrates at a higher frequency, whilst negative energy vibrates at a lower frequency. The happier the energy, the higher the frequency, the easier it becomes to communicate with other people's energy fields. If you want to live, give freely, and you will find that what you get in trade, my friend, is piece of mind. A better understanding of who you are, allows others to know you better, we have so much, that we can share, with those in need we see around us everywhere. Energy flows through each and every one, perhaps it's time, we all join as one, our universe works on that plan, and forever keeps expanding.

Quantum physics states that energy and matter are interchangeable and the String Theory suggests that differences in physical matter are simply variations in energy vibrations. In a similar fashion, each human is composed from the divine energy of the soul in the form of body, thought and spirit. Energy does not derive or reflect from a person, the energy is the person, the core. This understanding is fundamental to maintaining your energy field and body in harmony. Since the body is a manifestation of human energy, unbalances in the energy field will cause disease in the body. If the human energy field is out of balance, the body will also be out of balance. Just as there are three aspects of the incarnated soul, the mind, body and spirit, there are three ways that humans exchange energy through thought (mind), physical contact (body) and spiritual centres known as our chakras (spirit).

Energy does not dissolve or fade, it combines and redefines itself, while influencing you as you move through life. The truth is that your core energy, is imposed upon countless times on a daily basis, because the most common method of energy exchange between humans is core-to-core transfer. The most common method of core-to-core transfer is through thoughts and words. Thoughts generate words and words create energy, so when someone speaks to you, their energy is attempting to alter your energy. In order for someone to alter your energy with their words, you have to believe what they are saying, otherwise their words will have no impact on you. This is why it is important not to let the world around you affect your judgement, whilst at the same time hoping to help others, find their own way. It is vital to your spiritual growth and your ability to achieve your life mission, to understand who you are and where you come from, don't let anyone try to answer that for you. Your life is a test, one you need to pass on your own, allow outside influences to guide you but not influence you, for every person's test, have a different answer.

Human energies form from our personalities, composed of self-concept, consciousness and higher self. The self-concept is part of the subconscious that controls the memory and body functions. The body has its own natural intelligence, but we can put other information into that intelligence. This is the most basic part of the self-scheme, the sense of being separate and distinct from others and the awareness of the constancy of the self. Self-concept is the image that we have of ourselves, how exactly does this self-image form and change over time? This image develops in a number of ways but is particularly influenced by our society. Self-concept is generally thought of as our individual perceptions of our behaviour, abilities and unique characteristics. It is essentially a mental picture of who you are as a person. In other words, the self-concept has adapted the beliefs developed through our life span and believes we will die if we change them.

A soul must stay focused and follow the teachings of its mentors, prior to your incarnation, those who continue to guide you through your dreams. The more you forget what it is that you are meant to be doing with life, you will struggle in all aspects of your test and achievement of anything you try will be a struggle. Do not let bullies redefine how your soul views its spiritual self, never allow anyone to change the belief in the divine beauty that lives from you forever. There is a grand design in the universe, we are all part of it, our brain cells and DNA are structured very similar to that of the way of our universe. All systems seem to be self-organised, from the complex way that replicate RNA organises a new strand of DNA to the way the brain produces a single picture of reality that organises the firing of billions of neurons. The constants that rule the evolution of the universe are so precise that stars are organised to live through definite, orderly stages, and the formation of galaxies from interstellar dust follows its own life cycle.

Consciousness is our waking life and creates new awareness, it is creative and innocent until a choice is placed into action. Its function is to be the frontline of new experiences, where we make choices and gain skills. As we grow in awareness and spiritual illumination, we extend our consciousness and become increasingly able to live in the awareness of a high self and be conscious of the dynamics of our self-concept. Higher self is a term associated with multiple belief systems, but its basic premise describes an eternal, omnipotent, conscious and intelligent being, who is one's real self. The higher self exists as a spiritual form in our personal consciousness, which is always in contact with the soul. Since the higher self exists in a spiritual dimension, it cannot violate anyone or anything. To reach this self-awareness, one must first avoid all temptations, alcohol, drugs and forbidden apples aren't the most dangerous temptations. Suicide, murder, bullying, abuse, obsession, cheating, war and stabbing yourself in the eye with a pencil are some of the most dangerous temptations of them all. Even if the higher self has better wisdom and knowledge for you to live by, it will not displace our conscious choice unless we ask it to.

Physical touch is a very powerful way to share energy, thoughts and words can only combine with our core energy if we invite it in, the energy exchange that occurs through physical contact is instantaneous. There is no contemplation involved because touch is reality where thought and words are open to interpretation. To touch another person in any way that is not beneficial to their spiritual growth is wrong, to touch another person to only feed your needs is also wrong. Use your energy to lift up the broken, protect the frightened, heal the injured or steady the unsure, create positive energy that can be shared between everyone involved. Another way for energy to redefine us is through our spiritual channels, known as our chakra system or seven spiritual centres. All energy can be defined by type, and energy is drawn to the spiritual centre associated with its energy. While positive energy can serve to rejuvenate a chakra, negative energy can clog or even close down a chakra; in the process, one might develop a mental illness, in my case, epilepsy.

The larger a gathering, the more powerful our energy becomes as it seeks out similar energy and attaches itself, combining and redefining its vibrational aspect. A good example is a New Year's Eve party. After a certain age, most of us stop dancing our cares away, and eventually start working them away. Fortunately, the rare occasions when we're part of a large positive social gathering, alcohol and music aside, the urge to dance begins to emerge. Togetherness is a powerful energy because you are giving or sharing the best part of yourself, your joy and love with the people around you. Sadly, the effects of human energy can also work in reverse, this is how riots get started, the more people who engage in the negative or destructive energy, the more powerful and overwhelming it becomes. Problems shouldn't worry us when half the fun is guessing, our world is always changing, every day's a surprise. Live a lifetime of surprises, dreams can open your mind, never forget to see the wonder in your eyes.

Protect your chakra system and your core, achieve this by maintaining a positive energy field, remember the energy you omit does not only affect you, it affects others around you too. Whilst I was instituted inside the mental hospital, apart from people who were 'crazy', I was also surrounded by many others who were simply depressed. The energy I found myself sharing with my mentally advanced friends at the mental hospital, soon began bringing me down along with everybody else. We must own our energy, if we hope for a better world, we need to consider the energy that we put out into our shared home. The best way is through meditation because negative energy needs to be reconditioned before you release it to the world. Energy is all around us and it is constantly in motion, defining and redefining itself. The energy that we allow into our lives, the energy that we allow to define us, is completely under our control. All we need to do is take ownership of our energy, the energy we allow into our core as well as the energy that we release to the world. Always remember to protect your core with the diligence it deserves, for this is where the soul gains its new energy.

The soul is your essential divine nature plus experience, the soul is a coherent, intentional system, fulfilling its nature. This divine energy is formless, timeless and eternal, no place on earth, compares with home and every path will bring us back from where we roam. The soul is what connects you not only to your own value and essence, but to the value and essence of every other living being. Most of us do not know that we have disconnected from our soul and have come to accept as normal a numbness and lack of meaning in our lives. The shamanic practice known as soul retrieval is perhaps the most important level of healing in spirit medicine. Once the spiritual-energetic nature of an illness-causing intrusion has been addressed, the cause is still unresolved. As long as these empty spaces remain unfilled, there is no guarantee that the intrusions will not reinvade given an opportunity to do so because those holes are like open invitations. When a cold wind blows, it chills you, chills you to the bone, but there's nothing in nature that freezes your soul, like years of being alone. Always remember to keep your soul warm, for only when we're amongst family and friends, does it truly feel like home.

There is a profound shift in consciousness occurring, this shift is part of the intentional evolution of human consciousness wide across our planet. By being mindful of our thoughts, we are able to shape our reality in a number of different ways, assisting in the overall evolution of the transpersonal consciousness of humanity. The earth is a living system of which we are all an aspect, human beings are fundamentally interconnected with the earth and with all its life forms. The boundaries we have set up between nature and the human soul are illusory at best and self-destructive at worst. Neither the earth's environmental problems nor humanity's unsustainability problems can be resolved without first taking full account of the interconnection between human nature and Mother Nature. If we can become more attuned to the subtle forces of the ecosystems we inhabit, and more responsible with the not so subtle forces that we contribute to, then we can rediscover innate aptitudes that will help us to mend ourselves, our communities and the planet.

By experiencing more of the higher states of consciousness with more frequency and with more profoundness, we are able to make personal progress in our shifting of consciousness, which in turn helps in the shifting of the global consciousness. This shift is part of the evolutionary process of consciousness transformation, a test we're all currently taking together. At this point, I realised standing up against my bullies, was not all I needed to be happy with life, although granted, I wanted some form of ending to the situation, preferably a happy one. Life is about finding your way alongside the non-bullies, sharing your energy with the right people, increasing your energy, as it evolves through various lives. My life was ready to start the next chapter of my story, but before that happened, I had to finish this test first.

Chapter Thirty-One
Loopholes and Assholes

It had now been over eight years since I had first started working for my bullies, eight years of dealing with assholes, eight years into realising that life is made up of loopholes. A loophole is an uncertainty in a system, such as a law, security and even life, which can be used to avoid the purpose, explicitly stated, of the system. My bullies were good at being excellent assholes and experts in loopholes. If they gave a prize for being mean, the winners would be them, they love their jobs because they think it gives them power, if they became a flavour, you can bet they would be sour. Our world is full of assholes, you gain power through loopholes, the important thing to always remember, is just because you use a loophole, doesn't mean you need to be an asshole when doing so.

The very first time I witnessed an asshole using a loophole, was back in 2008, when Beverly altered my application form. Beverly had found a way to play the system, she was going to avoid fault, by attempting to blame another person for her mistake, that person being me. Had Beverly's plan gone through, I would have lost my job; they would have got rid of the problem and could have 'proven' it had not been their fault by showing I had been terminated from my position. Beverly had found a loophole in life, to continue progressing forward within her role at the Gibraltar Developing Company. After that incident, the assholes only got bigger and the loopholes even more complicated; Shale was an expert in both these areas. Shale was always careful, if she planned on making me work more than three weeks straight, she knew how to layout the roster, as to avoid unfairness on her behalf. Getting me angry, getting me to shout, getting me to act out, this in return would have cost me my job. Shale hoped to find a loophole in her life, to get rid of someone she did not want in it.

Ricky used the smartest loophole of all, he moved away from the problem, as the bullying progressed. Ricky moved position and as my government had been doing throughout, he hoped someone else would take the blame, for the problem created under his supervision. Darcello claimed he would not accept my medical certificates as he did not believe they were real; he knew they were real, believing they weren't, allowed him to ignore the situation. Darcello found a loophole to ignore the problem, the more you use loopholes the wrong way, the bigger an asshole you become. Hector was the biggest asshole of them all, he put himself in a position that allowed him to help others and gain knowledge and trust because of this. Instead of using his position to help, he uses the information received to put a stop to the individual asking for help. Hector's biggest loophole in life is working for one team but pretending to be on another one.

Work is all too often like school, there are cliques, everyone's usually a lot more interested in the gossip than the work. There's typically always somebody who likes to throw their weight around, intimidating others and taking credit for work that isn't theirs. Unlike the stereotypical social misfit who ends up the school bully, workplace bullies are often charming and socially skilled. At one time or another, we've all wished the line between what some people call bullying and what others call strong leadership wasn't so fuzzy. All too often, people widely seen as domineering and intimidating by their colleagues are viewed as simply being assertive by their bosses. This logic follows that those in power are generally assholes, because to reach such a position, one first needs to know all the loopholes, there is to know in life, no matter who you fuck over along the way.

I've had a couple of accomplishments that I wanted to achieve in life, truth be told, most of them I've accomplished through loopholes. The biggest difference between me and my bullies is that when I use a loophole, I'm not necessarily being an asshole to anyone who doesn't deserve it. A medical loophole helped me find my way from being charged at the police station to being admitted into a mental hospital. Changing my testimony into my diary entry, allowed me to share my problem without affecting my chances of using my evidence in court, a legal loophole. The greatest loophole of my life, was reaching the dream world, achieving the goal of meditation, through the use of seizures. A loophole many use to accomplish something similar, is by taking psychedelic drugs, a shortcut into activating your pineal gland momentarily therefore allowing you to open your third-eye, whilst under the effects. Assholes kept me from meditating to where I wanted to get, but loopholes had brought me back there once, and I hoped to return again someday. Always judge an asshole but never a loophole, for sometimes a loophole is exactly what one needs to progress in life.

It had been a long journey filled with both assholes and loopholes but finally at the start of 2016, thanks to my lucky third law firm, I was exactly where I wanted to be. Eric and I had finally sent my testimony alongside Dr Von Neuter's medical report and numerous questions we wanted to be answered by my bullies. Weeks past and we had received no reply, granted they had three months to answer, but were they really going to make us wait that long? They did. The waiting was always unbearable; luckily this time around, I had somewhere to be during the day and friends to meet up with after, this time around waiting didn't seem that long. Recently, I had started to realise that my life had reached a point, I always hoped to reach but feared I might never. I had confidence again, I had a job, I had social skills, I had friends, I had turned the tables on my bullies, this is what excited me the most. Remembering back to only a few years earlier, I could not believe my days were filled with crying, depression, stress, anxiety, seizures and loneliness. Now not only had I battled all those emotions but I had also done so without having beaten my bullies, this was something I thought I'd never achieve unless I proved my bullies wrong.

Life had changed so much throughout the years, it had been a rapid down fall but a steady rising, one I was confident in, enough to keep me going, despite what my bullies defence might state. My mum was just as excited as me; if anyone had been by my side constantly throughout this whole ordeal, it was certainly my mum. Everyday my mum would call me and ask, had my bullies' defence arrived? Alongside me, she was the person who most wanted this to be over and done with. My mum was happy I was continuing with my life again, but as she would point out, she knew I couldn't fully move on without closure. Mothers are always right, she knew me better than I knew myself, I was happy with life but something was still holding me back. As happy as I was, I still didn't want to invest in a long-term relationship, marriage was nowhere near the horizon, and my dream of travelling to Hollywood was still paused indefinitely in my mind.

Growing up I had all these hopes and dreams, I had accomplished some already but that didn't mean there was not more to accomplish from these experiences yet. For the first time in my adult life, I was actually closer than I had ever been to living out my childhood dream to its fullest; yet at the same time, I found myself for the first time, unexcited about my dream. As you grow older, life changes you; luckily those still young at heart, can sometimes get you back on the right direction. I could always make Aiden laugh, no money was needed, just attention and positive energy. I no longer dreamed of reaching Hollywood and becoming a screenwriter, I was happy working at a pet shop, I welcomed the stability. Aiden on the other hand was now getting ready himself to journey to Hollywood and every time we were together, he would remind me, that we had to go there. I had excited Aiden about Hollywood, the same way I had excited myself as a kid, by believing all my favourite television and movie characters lived there. Aiden's enthusiasm for me to get to Hollywood, always kept reminding me, this was what I've always wanted to do, I had to keep writing.

At one point when we were younger, it was my sisters, Stacey and Kaylie, who would get excited alongside me about travelling to Hollywood. In fact, when we were kids and our parents announced we were going to America, the first thing they asked was if we were going to Hollywood. Nowadays, they are so tired of me claiming I will one day go to Hollywood that they both look at me, wondering if I should have ever been discharged from the mental hospital. Stacey continued to get promoted at work; sadly, the cost of living nowadays is so high, that being a single female in her twenties was proving to be financially very stressful. Kaylie on the other hand had slowly started falling into a greater depression; she was having problems with her intestine, which in turn affected her fallopian tubes. This was not allowing her to get pregnant again and Aiden desperately wanted a little brother or sister. Sadly, the only way for her to be cured of this illness was by having her fallopian tubes removed, which would make her unable to have another baby. Kaylie already had her perfect family, but if she wished to continue growing it, she was going to have to find a loophole of her own.

One afternoon whilst having lunch with my dad, Stacey and Kaylie I received a phone call from Eric's law firm; my bullies defence had finally arrived. I was so excited, I excused myself and made my way to meet Eric at his law firm. I had to get my hands on my bullies' defence, I had never been so eager to read anything this badly in my entire life. As I read their defence, I could not believe what I was reading, they had mostly claimed that they could not admit or deny any of the accusations, what had been the whole point of all this? I knew they were going to lie but they were denying responsibility of having had any knowledge of anything that had happened. They knew I knew I was right, but at the same time, I knew they weren't going to go down without a fight but I did think they would be cleverer about it. If I'm honest, this didn't catch me by surprise, I was expecting them to answer just as they had, although I didn't expect the giant smile on my face. I quickly came to realise that one thing both defendants shared in common, was they were both trying to blame each other, if any wrong doing had in fact taken place. These two defendants once worked very close together, and now they were throwing each other under the bus as things started becoming too legal for them to handle.

That night whilst in my underwear, eating a bowl of cornflakes and smoking a joint, I began to argue each defence in my mind. I went over all the questions, I looked through all ten of their pages, and I came to realise, I could finally expose my bullies for who they truly were…liars! The only thing they admitted was that I was once an employee of theirs, other than that, I was going to have to prove them wrong. Years ago, I toyed with the idea of getting rid of all the reports Shale had handed me throughout the years, hoping to crush my spirits. I was so obsessed with these reports, that even though I was suffering from short-term memory a few years earlier, I had still managed to memorise most of them. I had almost one hundred pages of bad reports, based on almost every encounter I considered bullying. What I considered to be an act of bullying, Shale considered it an act of betrayal by me, and so each report was somehow related to each of the problems I wanted addressed.

My bullies knew exactly what had happened, I knew they had lied on an official government document, how had they felt so confident to do such a thing? They believed I did not have any past reports based on my time working for the Gibraltar Developing Company. The day I resigned, my file had unexpectedly got lost or rather misplaced as they claimed. My bullies believed I had no evidence to back up my claims, little did they know Shale had not only started this for me, she had also been the one who was going to help me end it. I brought out all my reports, notes, evidence, everything I had and using that, I was able to prove that they had lied on every question. This was an official legal document which members of my government had lied on, if they were lying now, what kind of lies would they come up with once in court. After I had proved on paper how my bullies had lied throughout their defence, I contacted Eric, who in turn emailed my bullies' lawyers with proof that their defendants were lying.

At this point, it wasn't only that my bullies didn't want to take responsibility for their actions, they also didn't want this to become any more public than it had already become, and our next step was soon receiving a court date. When things first got exposed by myself through social media, I was locked away for three weeks, inside a mental hospital, it could have been worse, it could have been a prison. However, the fact was that wherever I was, I could not continue speaking, which was what worried my bullies the most. After sharing my story, I did make some noise, but not enough to scare my bullies into taking action, either positive or negative. However, when you make legal noise, everyone becomes either interested or worried. My bullies knew I was getting ready to make noise, as soon as it became official, as soon as it was released in the chronicle, as soon as our court date was issued, they would no longer be able to keep the situation hidden from the public.

Hoping to put a stop to my noise, my bullies' lawyers did not send a reply to our email, instead they had found a loophole that was convenient for my bullies. Dr Von Neuter had forgotten to sign his name on one of the pages of his medical reports based on my examination. This had not been a problem until we were close to an actual court date. Instead of simply asking us to contact Dr Von Neuter and have him sign the missing paper, they wanted a new doctor to examine me, they wanted Dr Roseblack. My first lawyer and I had spent weeks searching, contacting and arranging travel plans for the world's top neurologist specialist to be flown in from Germany to examine me. However, this was not the right doctor for the job when my bullies were concerned, the best doctor in their mind, was one who worked locally at a mental hospital, one who was willing to blame all my problems on cannabis. I knew they wouldn't succeed in this, however this now meant, there would probably be another three-month delay whilst this all got sorted. These assholes had found a loophole, they had nothing to defend themselves with, instead they tried to find loopholes, hoping to escape this legal disaster they were facing.

I was always used to waiting but after so many years, although things were moving forward, instead of seeing a finish line, all I could see was the race being prolonged even further. There were so many legal technicalities and loopholes, which my bullies' lawyers used, hoping to stop me from receiving my court date. If this was being prolonged, I could only imagine, how much more of my life, I would have to give up, in order to continue fighting my bullies. For the longest time, my fear was not getting to the legal point I had arrived at, now my greatest fear was that I would miss out on my thirties, as I had my twenties, trying to defeat my bullies. I was twenty-nine years old at the time, my thirtieth birthday was just a few weeks away, I was questioning my whole life, what had I truly accomplished in the last eight years? I needed this over with, I needed my bullies to realise I was never going to stop fighting, and if I continued for another five years, they would have to do so too.

On the bright side, something that did put a smile on my face, was knowing how the tables had turned in the last eight years. I was always the one who went to work, bombarded by accusations, which if not answered or handled correctly, would have cost me my job. My bullies now found themselves in that position too, they were now facing stress at work. I could only imagine Shale sitting at her desk, receiving a call from human resources, informing her she had to speak to their lawyers. To make matters worse, she would be speaking to their lawyers, based on accusations regarding her work ethic by no other than myself, she must have hated that. These assholes could no longer affect me, I had found a loophole that made sure of that, no matter what negativity came towards me from them, be it personally or through their lawyers, I was now always able to find the positive. In this case, the sillier their defence, the more they denied, the more it proved to me, that I had a very strong case, that I might in fact finally be able to prove. I was now very much into meditation, and for the first time after years of trying, I learned how to shut down my brain. My new loophole in life, when dealing with bullies, was to stay positive and keep on meditating.

As I sat inside the pet shop, watching the various kinds of fish swimming from side to side, I finally realised, I was happy enough with my life, that meditation now seemed possible. I wouldn't become angry at my bullies, I wouldn't stress over their actions, I did not think about them, instead I enjoyed the very fishy scenery. I had discovered loopholes, I finally began using them; in doing so, the only people who could consider me an asshole, were those forcing me to find a loophole, and so I couldn't care less what they thought of me. All I knew was that every night, I was in the company of friends, puppies and positive vibes, all that was missing now were the return of my illusions. Life was good, the excitement that one of these days, I was about to receive my court date, kept my energy positive, my chakras flowing and my meditation levels increasing.

Chapter Thirty-Two
Make Your Dreams Come True

When your world seems insanely unfair and you wish that you weren't there, just meditate, illuminate and you can go anywhere. I missed my garden of dreams, everyone was there, every person was aware and everybody knew my name. Was I dumb, or was I blind? Or did my soul just lose its mind? Why'd I go and throw my perfect dreams away? Looking back, I'll never know, how I ever let them go, but hopefully destiny, could see we deserved, to have another day. Epilepsy once led me there, right back, to where I belonged. I followed the dream and there I was, and heaven seemed so near, epilepsy had once led me there. It is important to follow your dreams whilst sleeping, but lead them when awake; in my case, I wanted to find my way back to becoming a lucid dreamer once again. There's magic in the air this evening, in the form of dreams from everyone, the world is at her best you know, when people love and care. Every time we dream, all sorts of funny thoughts run around our heads, it isn't really anywhere, it's somewhere else instead. Bring back the wonder, that used to be ours, we lived in a glow, bring back the wonder, we knew long ago. Life was so new, it would last on and on, dreams are forever, reality will fade.

Dreaming is something we all do, scary dreams, sad dreams, wet dreams, we all have them, we all visualise something as clear as a television screen playing within our minds. Even though everybody dreams, even though our brain is showing us what we can do; eventually, we just wake up, get out of bed, go to work, and forget the magic we had just experienced the night before. When I was younger, when I was a proper stoner, I'd spend weeks at a time without dreaming, or at least not even remembering a single moment about them. Drugs have many beneficial uses, but one of the negative effects is that too much of it will cause you to stop dreaming. Not dreaming is a very big deal, it means your mind is not working to its full potential, if you're not dreaming, you're not progressing, you're just stuck, welcome to the world of pharmaceutical drugs. The same way one would worry if they lost their television signal, is how one should also feel, when dreams aren't part of your life anymore.

Most nights after closing up the pet shop, I would remain there meditating alongside discus, neons, red tail sharks, loaches, guppies, goldfish and all other kinds of swimmers. What I enjoyed most about meditating at the pet shop was that it would force me to keep myself awake whilst doing so; when I meditated at home, I would always end up falling asleep. Many people get bored of meditating very quickly, for about five years, I was one of those people. However, just as it takes a person almost ninety minutes to reach a state of REM sleep, it takes just as long, if not more, to attempt this through meditation. Usually after ten minutes, I would get bored; my mind was forever wondering and was normally always thinking instead of relaxing. Meditating with fish kept me focused on them, which in turn allowed me not to think or bore myself along the way. Although I had spent years meditating, it wasn't until I started doing so at the pet shop, that I first began to notice its effects. One day during the summer, after spending over an hour, sitting on a dog bed, looking at the fish, whilst meditating, I realised I had fallen asleep.

I was having a dream, this meant I was asleep, then I realised, I was aware that this was a dream, I was finally having another lucid dream. Suddenly it all clicked, as I looked around me, tears began to flow from my eyes, within my dream, I couldn't believe it, I was back in my garden. The sky was still orangish, the water a bright purple, blue giant flowers, grass as green as could be, it was the exact same place I had longed to get back to someday. Emotions were running wild through me, and I could not have been happier, this was the exact feeling, I craved for each day. To know that you're in a world, where anything can happen, anybody can show up yet you're aware of it all, feeling the same sensations, you'd feel in reality. I could not believe I was here again, I hoped I could return, but honestly, I didn't think I'd be able to do so as soon. It had been over three years since my last lucid dreams, three years since I had said goodbye to my hallucinations and three years to long. I looked around me, hoping to find some familiar faces, unfortunately nobody was around to greet me. As I walked through the garden, it seemed like it had grown, since the last time I was there. This time I had an understanding of what was happening to me, something I did not have in the past. The fact that I had also got back to my garden, on my own merits, with no epileptic shortcut, made it feel extra special for me.

As I walked around, I did something I had never done before, something I had always wondered about. I climbed a fruit tree and picked out an apple, I was nervous a loud voice would banish me; luckily, it didn't and as I bit the apple I realised, my taste buds were working alongside my dream. I could taste the apple, I want to say it was delicious, but when it comes to apples, I'm not a fan. I wanted to toss the apple away but felt embarrassed to do so, I laughed thinking to myself that I was alone in my own dreamt up garden yet could not find the courage to toss away the apple. I was looking for a dustbin, there wasn't one, maybe I could imagine one? Nope that doesn't necessarily work, I ended up placing the bitten apple, nicely displayed on a large shiny stone alongside the river. Apart from my few seconds of apple anxiety, I realised how peaceful I felt again, this was an emotion, I had only ever felt within my dreams. I loved being aware inside my dreams, not only could anything happen, the sensation of relaxation you experience is not an emotion I've ever felt, whilst I was awake. Certain emotions are even locked away from us inside our minds, we are our own computers, many just forget to update their systems.

It felt a little strange walking around my garden alone, I was honestly very used to being in the presence of others whilst I was there. If it wasn't a relative from my past or a friend I had never met, at least a stranger would approach me. As I continued walking through my garden, I heard the voice, I most hoped to hear, whilst in this dream. Mama Angela was calling out to me, I turned around and there she was, with the biggest smile I had ever seen on her. Having already dealt with my grandfathers in my dreams, I did not expect the overwhelming emotions that took over within me. This confirmed in my mind that Mama Angela was okay, she had reached the place I had hoped, she continued to be part of the universe. My grandfathers had evolved years before I met them again inside my dreams, and until that point I never thought I would see them again. Mama Angela on the other hand had only evolved almost three years earlier but since she had gone, I had been hoping to see her again.

The best part, which came as a huge surprise to me, was how well we were communicating with each other, we were able to have a proper conversation. In the past, when communicating with others in my dreams, most of the time, it seemed more like a one-way conversation; on this occasion, questions were answered and jokes even exchanged. Mama Angela was so happy with her new life, apparently, she had also been there before, in her own garden, whilst she was still alive, we had never talked about that. Mama Angela informed me that my one-way conversations in the past were due to me not being fully present to communicate with others. Apparently now that I had reached my garden through meditation and not a coma like seizure, I was somehow able to take full control of my dreams. As I continued speaking to Mama Angela, I suddenly began to hear Nicola calling out my name in the distance; was she there too, I wondered. Mama Angela told me I would be leaving soon but in case we didn't see each other again, she promised me, I would regain my life again, what did that mean? Before I could ask Mama Angela my last question, I found myself face to face with Nicola inside the pet shop.

"Are you okay?" Nicola asked me, I wasn't sure what to say, I wanted to share this with someone, but for the first time in a long time people didn't think I was crazy. Instead, I pretended I had fallen asleep, which might actually have been the case. Nicola had come to collect her wages, after that she left and I remained looking at the fish in amazement, I couldn't believe I had just returned from my garden. Although my body might have been sleeping, my mind was more alert than it had been in a very long time. I was so happy over what had just happened, even though the dream began with me knowing I had been meditating in the pet shop, as it went along, I completely forgot that in reality I was not in my garden, it feels like such a real experience. Meditation is supposed to help you gain a clearer understanding of who you are, it is the dream of the heart, a special time of growing, the way of life made clear. I came back from my garden, pumped and ready to continue tackling anything life had to throw at me. I had to keep fighting for justice, keep writing for achievement, keep believing for wisdom and always remain dreaming for a better understanding of who I am.

The next day, Jensen had joined me on my canoe as we made our way travelling the sea, from one side of the Gibraltar Airport to the other side at least. Jensen and I had spoken about the power of dreams before, our conversations were usually more focused on telepathy rather than spiritualism. Apparently, all twins have a connection with their twin sibling, this connection could simply be blood, the connection that all siblings have, but there can be a greater connection, known as twin telepathy. Twin telepathy is when one twin can assess the thoughts or feelings of another twin without the other twin giving them any signs. Through telepathy, a twin can sense what the other twin is thinking or feeling, even if they are not in the same place, it acts as a sixth sense between the twins.

To fully understand twin telepathy, it is pertinent to know the biological background of twins. Twins can be either monozygotic or dizygotic. Monozygotic, or identical twins, are formed when a single fertilised egg divides, causing there to be two eggs with the same genes and almost identical DNA. This makes the twins look very similar and have similar mannerisms since they were created from the same egg. Dizygotic, or fraternal twins, are conceived and delivered together but are formed from two separate eggs. This makes fraternal twins the same as any other brother or sister, except that they have the same birthday as each other and that they were raised together. Telepathy tends to occur more in pairs of identical twins, yet it is noted in fraternal as well. The closeness between identical twins genetically plays a large part in why they experience telepathy so often. The genes of identical twins are the same, and the DNA has minor differences. This is why identical twins look and act so similarly, and therefore, is an important element in twin telepathy.

I was always interested when Jensen and I had these conversations, but I always wondered why I only dreamt about people who were dead, I wanted to dream with a real person.

I told Jensen what had happened to me in the pet shop the day before during my meditation, Jensen asked me to bring him back an apple next time. I told Jensen he should come and join me in the garden and taste the apple for himself, we both laughed but I was being completely serious. If Jensen too was a lucid dreamer, could I perhaps experiment with him, in the hopes of sharing my dreams with someone I knew in reality? At this point in life, I had returned to the place I most wished to be, this now allowed me to ask myself further questions, I hoped to find answers too. I asked Jensen to think about me every night before he went to sleep, he thought I was being weird, I was actually trying to be scientifically spiritual, could we make our dreams work through teamwork?

Later on that same day, I met with my mum, I just couldn't help but share my dream with her, I truly hoped I would not open the gates for people to once again question my mentality. I told my mum how I had returned to my garden and Mama Angela had visited me there, how this confirmed, at least in my mind, that I was actually dreaming with the evolved. The best part about this conversation was, that my mum believed me, she didn't fully understand what was happening, but I could sense she didn't think I was crazy. I had returned to the world I had hoped; yet this time, I was not suffering seizures over it or making myself appear crazy in front of others. I had best of both worlds and now all I hoped was that my last visit was not simply a fluke, I hoped I could go back there someday again, and hopefully, eventually, whenever I wished. A few days later, after another meditation session, this time in my living room, I returned to my garden. Living is a game, now I seem to play in dreams, reality will never be the same, when it feels really good, like a feeling should, when it's understood, you've got to pass it on.

As I walked around my garden, I eagerly anticipated who would eventually show up, this time I was not there by myself alone. Soon Mama Angela joined hand by hand with Grandpa Arturo were standing before me. Later on, I was also accompanied by Grandpa Alberto, Ashby and everyone else joined me at some point throughout my dreams. The thrill of seeing Mama Angela and Grandpa Arturo together again made my dream all the more special. These were two people I had not seen side by side together in over ten years, this felt magical, they were both together again and all the happier for it. Grandpa Alberto is eager to interact with Mama June again one day but that doesn't mean he necessarily misses her, for he looks over her every single day. When a person evolves we might not get to see them but that doesn't mean they don't get to see us, they are always watching over us, unless they get tired of waiting and decide it is time for another rebirth of the soul. Ashby was very happy, for one very important reason, something he had wanted to happen, ever since the day he left his mother behind, was for his mum to get herself a dog. Finally, Mati and Angel the Dog had found their way to each other. Mati now had a reason to leave her house every day, she had an Angel to walk alongside.

The best part about this dream, was not the fact that I was aware, it was not the fact that everyone was there, it was that we were able to properly communicate with one another. For so long, I felt frustrated in my dreams, with my hallucination whilst awake, for they were there, but most of the time, it felt like we weren't communicating properly amongst each other. I always believed that made my experiences a lost opportunity, one I wasn't experiencing to its fullest. However, this time around it felt like a giant family Christmas gathering, one where everybody had a story to share and everyone was interested. I felt like I was right where I belonged, I could see those illusions looking back at me, like old familiar friends, what better place could anyone be, when my hallucinations are real for me.

It's all I've been looking for and so much more, and now I'm here, now they're here, nothing can go wrong because I was right where I belonged. Before I returned to my living room, I asked Mama Angela what she meant last time, when she told me I would regain my life again. Mama Angela informed me, I was soon going to return to a point in life, I very much missed.

A few days later, I made my way to work, life was good. I finally knew how to return to my garden without all the problems I carried with me in the past in doing so. Jensen had joined me in the pet shop that day, whilst we were performing a water change on the aquariums, the pet shop phone began to ring. "Hello pet shop," I answered as I always did, it was my mum; apparently, my lawyer had been trying to call my mobile but couldn't contact me. I wondered where my mobile was; as I looked around, I couldn't find it, maybe I had left it at home? "They've offered you a settlement!" I heard my mum exclaim over the phone...what? This wasn't happening, I was certain I was in another coma again, you wait so long for something, not sure if you'll ever receive it and then in a blink of an eye it's there. "Mum" was all I said, I couldn't speak, I had no idea what to say, I wasn't expecting this at all, if I knew how to do a backflip, that would have been the perfect moment. Instead, I told my mum I'd visit her later, I knew she was just as excited as me but at that moment, all I wanted to do was bring out the animals and dance. I didn't even have to explain myself to Jensen, seeing me dancing around the pet shop, unembarrassed by the customers in the shop, he knew exactly what that call had been about.

Chapter Thirty-Three
It's Time to Get Things Started

In April 2008, the movie I had hoped to live out had been paused, my bullies had forced me to shoot additional scenes, I was unaware were also part of my movie. In September 2016, I found myself with the option to continue living my movie, right where I had left off eight years ago. The next day after having been informed that my bullies were willing to offer me a settlement, I had a meeting with Eric early in the morning. My mum had joined me that morning, when most thought I was being naïve trying to take my government to court; my mum was one of the few who didn't discourage me. As we ate breakfast in town that morning, before our meeting with Eric we began discussing a topic, I had never really put much consideration into...money. I was entitled to well over £100,000, but obviously in a settlement negotiation, it won't be nearly as much. A few weeks earlier, Eric had actually helped me calculate how much I was actually entitled to, and when someone scars your brain, that's a lot of money.

All this time, I had been so concentrated on justice that I never really considered the payout I'd get if I did in fact prove my case. I had spent over two years unemployed with no income other than social assistance in the form of twenty pounds a week. Since then I had been working part time at a pet shop, money had become a thing of the past for me. Granted I wanted money to pay back my family, give back to others instead of being a charity myself, buy a house, travel to Hollywood but at the end of the day, buying a car, a jet ski or even new socks, that had never crossed my mind. During breakfast, my mum and I had been contemplating with the idea, that in a settlement offer it's never wise to accept the first settlement you are given, if they offer it once, they'll offer it twice. Part of me wanted to follow everything I had learned from the movies and decline their first offer yet another part of myself kept reminding me that this was never about the money. This was always about finding justice, so that I could live on with my life and that day I finally had the chance to move on.

A few years earlier, I had visited a psychologist by the name of Gustavo, on a few occasions, even though I knew psychology was not the answer. This was nothing against Gustavo, he is a great psychologist but the way I saw the situation, talking about my problems were not the same as solving them. I should have been using my time back then to speak with a lawyer, who could act on my behalf, not with a psychologist, who was basically telling me what I already knew. Gustavo always asked me why I felt I could not move on, my reply was always the same, I couldn't live with myself, knowing I had allowed my bullies to win. Everything I ever hoped to achieve in my life at that moment was put on pause, no thanks to my bullies, my illness and at one point the state of my mentality. It is always very easy for a person to say that they don't care about money but when the chances of you having a lot of it arises, a person learns if they truly meant what they had said.

Finally, it was almost time for our meeting with Eric, we both finished our breakfast and made our way upstairs to Eric's law firm. Eric had been so kind to me throughout, not only is he a terrific lawyer, he's a genuinely nice person, who was always just as concerned with my health as he was with my legal case. As the three of us sat down in his office, I looked at my mum, I couldn't believe we had actually reached this point. I hoped someday I'd reach it but now that I had, it just didn't feel real, reality seemed like an illusion this time around. I had spent years broken, my mum always helped me find the strength I needed to continue and worried I might die if alone during a seizure, she had gone through all that with me. Now together we were going to decide if this journey we had taken together should come to an end that very day; finally, I had control of my life again, if I wished.

The number my bullies' lawyers had presented me with was much higher than I expected it to be the first time around. It was still nowhere near what I deserved but enough that I did not feel ridiculed, they were taking this seriously. I looked at my mum, we both couldn't wipe the smile off our faces, we both assumed they would start out very low, in the back of our minds we didn't believe it could all actually end at that moment. They had offered me enough to accomplish everything I hoped to achieve in life, what was most important was the document that rested in front of me on the table. When a defendant offers the claimant a settlement, it can only mean one thing, they don't want this to get to court, because they know you're right; they're wrong and you will ultimately win at the end. This document that rested in front of me, legally proved I was right and they were wrong, and most importantly, my bad work record would no longer follow me for the rest of my life. As I sat in Eric's office, accompanied by himself and my mum as they waited for me to decide if I should sign the document in front of me or not, took me back to 2008.

I remember when Shale, Beverly and Ricky hoped I would sign my resignation letter, one they had prepared for me, that is when all my problems first began. Now to end my eight-year struggle, on the happy note I had hoped for, found me in the exact same position, last time I was clever enough not to sign their document, would not signing it be a mistake this time around? Since the day I first began suffering grand mal seizures, I knew I wanted to achieve two things. The first was not to let my illness define me and certainly not associate it with my bullies, if I was going to live with this illness forever, I was not going to do so remembering how I had arrived here, every time I had a seizure. The second thing I knew I wanted to do, was write a book. I not only wanted to share my experience with others, I wanted to help people who felt bullied. At that moment, the only way I could think to reach such a wide audience, was by attempting to write a hopefully inspirational book, which might help others find strength within their own movies. As I looked at the document, I thought to myself what did I want to do now? Did I want to be greedy and continue fighting for a larger settlement or should I accept it and finally move on with my life, having had my bullies provide me with the ending I always wanted for my story?

This time around, I had no voices in my head suggesting what I should do, no illusions commenting and hovering around me, this decision was all on me, what direction did I want my life to go in next? I signed my name and accepted their settlement, not for the money but rather the ending, this was exactly the way to end my story, the victim conquered his bullies. Now I could do what I always wanted to do, live the life I wanted, knowing that when life gets hard, all I need to do is find a loophole. After thanking Eric for all his dedicated work, I walked out of his law firm, accompanied by my mum and found ourselves outside, where we both realised what had just happened. It was all too much to take in, not only was that part of my story finally over, it had ended exactly as I hoped it would, I was no longer a victim to my bullies. My life was back on track, I could now attempt to do the things I've always wanted to do, and not the thing I felt I was forced to do by life itself, but those are the true tests we each take every day. As an added bonus, I now had more money than I ever expected I would have by the age of thirty, it might not be enough to live on forever, but it is enough to allow me to do the things I've always wanted to do, it was time to get ready for Hollywood.

Hopefully having proven my bullies were in fact also liars, I hoped this would now force them to stop bullying all together, and perhaps others would benefit in this process. Since the first time I decided I would one day share this story, I knew that for my intentions of it to be an inspirational story, I could have no other ending than the one I've ended with. Sharing this story with you and everyone else who has kindly taken the time to read it, this is the true ending to my story, it wasn't when I accepted their settlement, it was when I finally shared my experience with others. As I signed my name accepting their offer, this story was the only thing I had in mind, I was only signing, so I could move on to writing about this experience. As you can see you're only a few pages from reaching the end of this book, when you reach the end, that to me is when I've officially accomplished what I had set out to do. I was not going to let the last eight years of my life be taken for granted, I want to look back at my time and know that every second of it was worthwhile. The settlement was not worth eight years of bullying and suffering, but if I can help just one person not waste as much of their life as I did with mine, thanks to politics, bullies and insecurities, then that would have been worth my journey. When life gives you lemons, don't throw them at your bullies, you'll get in trouble and that's exactly what they want, instead make lemonade and serve it whilst starting a conversation regarding your situation, you'll find many people have the same problem. Together raise your voices high; alone it is difficult to get heard, when all join as one, our voices get heard by those who choose not to listen.

A few days later my cheque arrived, I was able to pay back my parents, help make life easier for as many people as I could, most importantly for Stacey, Kaylie and Aiden. My life had completely changed overnight, I had to open a savings account, I couldn't believe I had not only opened a bank account but a savings account too. As soon as my cheque had cleared, the first thing I actually did was return to social media. I addressed all my bullies in two new separate messages, both of which I posted on various Facebook groups as well as my Facebook page. Gibraltarians are lovely people and they were all very supportive and this time not a single hater commented on any of my posts. What I was achieving here was not so much praise, support or to ridicule anyone, I wanted to see if my bullies would try to silence me and again as I expected, nobody said a word. They were no longer my bullies, if they were I'd still be intimidated by them, since that day I've never felt intimidated by them ever again.

New Year 2017 was going to be very different from those of the past, this time I was willing, ready and excited to celebrate the year to come. The year before, Jensen had to convince me to leave my house and celebrate the New Year with him; this time around, I was the one to make a plan. Jensen and I spent the New Year 2017 hallucinating through Amsterdam. Mushrooms cause people to hallucinate, I had spent almost three years of my life hallucinating, what could possibly go wrong? A giant shoe chased me all the way up until the bells ringed in the New Year; at one point, I think it actually ate me but I managed to crawl back out. Afterwards I turned really small or everything grew much bigger, but I was walking around feeling no larger than an ant and then my ears began shouting at each other. This just proved to me, that when a person tries to reach fifth gear, when only on first, then crazy shit begins to happen. The power was still there, the power of hallucinating thoughts is within all of us, but to truly experience them, one has to get there changing gears correctly, not through shortcuts.

As weird as my Amsterdam hallucinations had been, I was still eager to continue getting there through meditation. Although my hallucinations have never returned, at least not yet, they are still with me in my dreams, and you can bet we've celebrated my victory in our garden on a few separate occasions since. Am I crazy? Might I just be losing my mind? Maybe so but if I didn't listen to what my mind has been telling me, I would have given up a long time ago. I could now return to my happy place hidden within my dreams but at the same time, there was a happy place in my reality, I had not visited in a long time. The Nipperish had always been a part of my life for so long, especially towards the end, when I was most broken, before I moved house and no longer lived near the area, but now I felt the urge to return. Ashby's memorial picture was still standing, no matter how nasty the weather, how heavy the showers, his picture did not fade. I sat down and looked across the ocean, towards Africa and Spain. The last few times I had sat up there, I only felt sadness, now there was nothing but joy, I also realised the apartment I was now living in could be viewed from the Nipperish.

Now that my bad work record had been proven to be lies, I had the opportunity to apply for whichever job I hoped, without fear of being held back through lies on behalf of my former employers. At the same time, I had already come to realise that working with animals is a far more rewarding job than working inside an office. I had already decided long ago that whatever I did with my future, one thing was for sure, I would never work for a government department ever again, at least not unless I was in charge of it. Although the doors were now open for me to start a new career, I couldn't find it within myself to leave the pet shop. The pet shop was struggling financially and Uncle Arthur needed all the help he could get, I was not about to abandon him in his time of need. Although we were now able to afford stock that had been missing from the shop, it still didn't solve the fact that the products were just not moving anymore. As the months went past, I continued working at the pet shop, whilst carefully considering what my next step would be. So far, my plan included writing a book, attempting to make a go at a life in Hollywood and regain keeping my confidence, which had taken me years to find again.

Believe it or not, that shift in happiness I was expecting to take over suddenly didn't come, it took a while, it wasn't until the beginning of 2017 that I finally felt reborn. After six months of not waiting by the phone, being able to apply for any job I wished with a clean record, not stressing on a daily basis, sleeping well, eating healthy, I was finally me again. I always had hope that things would turn out right in the end for me otherwise without hope I would not be here now but the reality of it is so much more rewarding, never in a million years did I ever think I'd feel the way I feel now, I've never been happier with life. The last few months of my life have been the best, not because I won but because I found peace. I've written this story and not once have I cried or become angry, nothing that I've written affects me anymore, this story is not to shame any bullies, it's in a hope to get victims to open their eyes, much sooner than I did. Remember that life can take you by surprise, and sweep you off your feet, will this happen to you, or will you just be dreaming?

When I first began attempting to write this book, it was proving to be far more difficult than I first anticipated, as much as I had to say, my focus was not all there, I could not concentrate on telling a good story. Was I being bullied again? Was I beginning to suffer from epilepsy again? No, it was none of that, life was simply not allowing me to focus on what I felt I needed to do. I always enjoyed bringing dogs home from work with me, but when you're trying to write and have eight puppies running up and down your living room, barking every time you type, it's hard to concentrate. For me to properly lose myself in one of my stories, I need no time restrictions, I need to meditate beforehand, I need to be relaxed, I need to be out of civilisation. I really needed to find a way to get over this writer's wall I had created for myself. My government only settled because as much as they tried, as much as they lied, as many loopholes they tried to use, our next step was receiving an actual court date and they didn't want that. They knew they would lose, but most importantly, they didn't want me sharing my story and making it public, that's exactly what they paid me to afford to be able to do, write with no financial restrictions.

Eventually after countless hours of barking puppies, I was able to finish my twenty-page proposal based on my life story. I emailed a number of publishers, hoping at least one would respond and was I in for a pleasant surprise. All my life I had written screenplays and at times other book proposals, I had sent hundreds of emails and never received a single reply for my work. However, this time around I had interest, and this came from a story I never would have had become part of my life, had it not been for my bullies. This was the first time I felt my journey had been worthwhile, had I not suffered eight long years because of it, I might have never received the replies I hoped to receive. Always try to find the positive in life, this is a very dark and depressing story but I've made sure to take the lemons life has thrown at me, and I've made sure to turn them into lemonade. You can't control the test your life forces you to take but you can practise throughout and hopefully still receive the high score we all deserve.

Once I realised, how much interest I had in this story, I was determined to write something worthy of being read, I truly hope you have enjoyed the time you've dedicated to this story. Nicola and I both wanted to leave the pet shop, our lives there weren't progressing exactly how we'd wish but we could not leave Uncle Arthur to deal with this problem alone. Together Nicola and I, helped Uncle Arthur find a partner, who has not only invested in his pet shop but has also taken control of the day-to-day duties, he now runs the shop as Nicola and I once did. Now that the pet shop had new life, someone hopefully as dedicated to it as Uncle Arthur was, both Nicola and I began to consider what the next step in our lives would be. Nicola still aimed to become a professional dancer, but through her journey, she still needed to apply for another job, she became a dance teacher. I, on the other hand, had no idea what to do, should I just get on a plane and move to Hollywood, there was nothing stopping me from doing this any longer, why had I not gone yet?

Without spoiling the financial plan I have set up for myself, I could only use my winnings to attempt a life in America only once, after that, when it came to travelling to Hollywood, I was back at square one. Something I had learned during my eight-year journey is you can't rush things, you can find loopholes, but to accomplish great things it takes time, I did not want to rush into this without a plan. The first thing I felt I needed to accomplish was write this book, not only would it finally free me from this section of my life, it would then allow me to move on properly, and in the next three chapters, I will finally reach that fulfilment. As a child growing up watching television, a storyline amongst writers within movies or television shows always involved those around them getting angry for not having a real job. When a writer truly dedicates themselves to their project, in the eyes of those around them, they are not working a real job, not one that helps pay the bills along the way.

I never truly understood why they didn't just work during the day and write at night, that is how I wrote my screenplays after school. As I grew up, I learned life isn't as easy as it once was during our school years, life clogs up the mind, and to do what you love, a mind must be opened, not locked. If you have a family to maintain, this isn't really fair to them, you've committed to giving them life, give them the best one you can; sadly in today's society, you need to be able to afford a good life. I still don't have a family to support and now find myself with extra money that could actually support me for a while without the need to be part of a working society. I was going to leave civilisation again and keep on writing, this is what I've always wanted to do in life, and now for a short while at least, I have the chance to do so. This doesn't mean it's an easy-going life from here on out, not at all, life always has a different test for one to take, as soon as you've finished the first one, granted maybe not as complicated. Life continued to throw lemons at me as I wrote my book, but these days, I find it much easier to handle situations, most notably in my mind because I have a better understanding of who I am. I am a person who wants to share his story with the world, find justice for as many people as I can, encourage victims, discourage bullies and travel to Hollywood.

Chapter Thirty-Four
Hollywood Exposed

There's no business, like show business, like no business I know, everything about it is appealing, we're all hopeful for that magic feeling, we wish to feel. It makes us all want to travel to Hollywood, riding flashy cars and dancing with famous stars, some of us wish to get there, but is it what we expect? Hollywood is the place of movie studios and fame, the ultimate district of American cinema. It is the district in Los Angeles California that attracts millions of tourists every year alongside many aspiring stars. Since I was a child, travelling to Hollywood, in the hopes of writing movies and making millions of people happy, had always been my dream. Growing up my inspiration continued as I followed the franchise that started it all for me, when I was only three years old. Back in 2012 when I was at my lowest, what kept me motivated, was the fact that I came in contact with my childhood idols. This experience gave me the strength to realise, I needed to fix my life, to get back to the movie I hoped to continue, and if I put my mind and heart into it, I could achieve this.

There was only one problem, one month after I received my settlement, one month after I was ready to join my friends in Hollywood, one of them got fired. I've grown up with Steve's characters since I was three years old, most of my inspiration comes from words spoken by him. Many YouTube videos I watched during my time with epilepsy, hoping to find inspiration, were mainly centred around his characters, his performance, his dedication. Steve's performances continue to influence and inspire an army of fans around the world after over thirty-nine years. Steve spoke out for integrity, for creativity, for fans and in turn many stood behind him in support; sadly our voices were not loud enough, and Steve was not allowed to return to his life's dedication. I could sympathise very much with Steve, I had been in his shoes for the last eight years, I felt I was being treated unfairly at work, I was forced to fight to return to my job, I could imagine how he felt.

This happens worldwide to everybody, not just people in Hollywood; however, since Steve's performance was the inspiration that helped me get to the point I am in my life, it affects me very much. A good example to use as a comparison with Steve's situation, has actually presented itself, at the time of writing this particular chapter. I've never actually watched *Star Wars* but I know exactly who Luke Skywalker is, and as popular as he is in pop culture, also makes me aware of the man behind this character, Mark Hamill. For the past few weeks leading up to the release of *Star Wars: Episode VIII*, Mark Hamill was voicing his displeasure with the direction his character of Luke Skywalker had been taken in the film. Mark Hamill stood up for what he believed, for integrity, for the art, for fans; sadly, his voice went unheard and his character was not portrayed how he believed. Since I've never seen *Star Wars* I'm not exactly sure how Luke Skywalker should behave but I'm sure the man who gave this character life, must know better than anyone else, no matter if that's director, writer or even producer.

After the release of the movie, *Star Wars* fans were furious at the portrayal of his character, a backlash began against the movie. Mark Hamill did know best, as his concerns were the main reason behind the backlash, once fans had seen the movie. Although people have united over a movie, it still goes to prove we have strength in numbers, their voices are being heard. This was a similar situation regarding Steve and his main character; sadly his fan base is not as big, loud and protective as that of *Star Wars*, I don't think any other fandom is. After following this story and realising how hard Mark Hamill tried to protect a legacy so important to many, I have the utmost respect for him. I will now be watching the first three original *Star Wars* movies ever made, purely from my admiration of Mark Hamill. I always hoped to reach Hollywood and work alongside the whole team, even that weirdo I respect so much, who once told me to shut up. I wanted to work alongside all of them, frankly now I don't give a damn anymore. I just don't feel the desire to try and work alongside a company, a franchise, who have closed their doors on one of the people, I believe helped get me to where I am in life now, being alive is one of those reasons.

Fans to a franchise, are as important as citizens are to a country, without them, there is no point of ruling or entertaining, as that is how money is made. In Hollywood sadly these days, the art behind the filmmaking is not important, a film does not need to be good, it just needs to make money. If fans keep supporting bad films, that is what we will continue to get, when we vote with our wallets, that is when we will begin receiving theatrical masterpieces once again. The same dedication and passion we show for our entertainment, should also be shown for our rights, our humanity, our freedom. Give us good movies and at the same time allow us to live our lives as we so choose. When the world unites, we can be very powerful against those who choose to rule over us; speak out together, that is how we will get things accomplished.

Life is full of surprises and at times very ironic, I had spent my whole life hoping to work alongside Steve, and when my movie was back on track, when I had the opportunity to at least try, Steve was no longer there. Without him, I don't desire on trying to attempt this once childhood dream of mine. I cannot turn my back on one of my heroes, and so now, I found myself with no direction in life again. I was no longer sure what to do, my aim was to work alongside a franchise I admired, with one of the people responsible for my obsessive fandom. Now I had no idea what to do, and so I meditated, and immediately came to the realisation, I still wanted to travel to Hollywood. What did I want to do once I'm there? I have no idea, but I'm through planning, life never goes as planned, some of the best moments in life come by surprise and that's how I'm going to tackle Hollywood. As upset as I was in this new change of mindset, which I never expected, at least I was still being positive, I was ready for Hollywood.

After twenty-seven years of wishing to travel to Hollywood, I now had the perfect opportunity, I had no job to worry about yet money to spare, it was finally my time. Year 2018 was the year of Hollywood for me, all I had to do was finish writing my story, get this out of my system and concentrate on the next scene in my movie. Unfortunately, after eight years of wanting to escape my problems in Gibraltar and wishing I could runaway to Hollywood, I was about to realise, bullies are found everywhere. At the same time that I was planning my trip, searching for hotels, looking over flights, Hollywood was exposed, all the nasty stuff about Hollywood that nobody ever talks about, finally took centre stage. Sexual harassment became the talk of Hollywood with many brave women and on occasion men too, standing up to their abusers, many powerful and influential men who once run Hollywood.

The first man exposed in Hollywood was apparently one of the most influential people in the business. These accusations had been held against him for years, but with power and money it's easy to find loopholes. A few brave women with the support of a very dedicated magazine finally exposed the truth to the world and since news broke more women have come forward. Many women accusing the same person, as well as many others, this was a problem many faced and by the same individuals. Women started to realise they were not alone, this experience they had gone through by themselves, they could share with others who could understand exactly where they were coming from. As the months progressed, more women and men came forward naming their abusers, taking legal action and in turn, Hollywood started to clean up its act.

This has been seen time and again in Hollywood, the casting couch culture is unfortunately very real. The casting couch refers to the malicious practice of powerful Hollywood executives, sexually exploiting actors, primarily women, who are trying to land a role. The casting couch mentality is the trading of sexual favours by an aspirant, apprentice employee or subordinate to a superior for entry into an occupation, or for other career advancement within an organisation. It was, and still is, a toxic culture among film producers, directors and other power players in the industry. The allegations of assault surfacing have echoes of the many sexual harassment and casting couch horror stories that have emerged through Hollywood's chequered history. In part, the victims feel trapped into silence, they feel powerless against the abuser who could end their career or smear their name and makes open threats to do so. The 'you'll never work in this town again' cliché became a cliché for a reason, it's all too real.

Hollywood has prolonged a loose sexual culture that encourages frivolous sexual relationships, as well as mentality to do anything you need to do to land a role. It is this culture that has allowed perverted harassers to flourish. Men in roles of power are not being held accountable, possibly making them think it is acceptable to treat women this way. There needs to be many fundamental changes in order to cleanse the entertainment industry of wicked sexual deviants and it has started, with power in numbers. Everywhere you go around the world, you will face problems but since Hollywood always knows how to grab attention, this story began encouraging men and women around the world to stand up to their sexual bullies. Sexual harassment is bullying or force of a sexual nature, or the unwelcome or inappropriate promise of rewards in exchange for sexual favours. You may be concerned about retaliation if you talk to someone, particularly if the person causing the harassment is of high power.

Sexual harassment plays a bigger part in power than lust, when it comes to the harasser. Sexual harassment is, above all, a manifestation of power relations; women are much more likely to be victims of sexual harassment precisely because they are more often less powerful than men, are in more vulnerable and insecure positions, lack self-confidence, or have been socialised to suffer in silence. In order to understand why women endure the vast majority of sexual harassment, it is important to look at some of the underlying causes of this problem. Sexual harassment is a form of subtle rape, and rape is usually more about fear than sex, harassment is a way for a man to make a woman vulnerable. While sexual harassment may on first glance be taken as simple social ineptness or as an awkward expression of romantic attraction, this view is wrong and malicious because it can lead women who suffer harassment to blame themselves, believing that something in their fashion choice or behaviour might have brought the unwanted attention.

The use of harassment as a tactic to control or frighten women, which is most frequent in occupations and work places, where women are new and are in the minority. No matter how many men they encounter in the course of their work, women who hold jobs traditionally held by men are far more likely to be harassed than women who do what is wrongly considered women's work. Seen in this context, male workers who harass a woman on the job are doing more than annoying her. They are reminding her of her vulnerability, creating tensions that make her job more difficult and making her hesitant to seek higher paying jobs where she may perceive the tension as even greater. In short, sexual harassment creates a climate of intimidation and repression. A woman who is the target of sexual harassment often goes through the same process of victimisation as one who has suffered rape, battering or other gender-related crimes, frequently blaming herself and doubting her own self-worth.

As more victims come together, more sexual harassers are exposed, many removed from their positions of power. This is not only karma but also a way to protect other women from suffering the same abuse at the hands of these specific powerful sexual harassers. When you're a sexual harasser, at the end you'll live your life alone. When you're alone, you'll never feel like you're home; nobody can help you scratch that itch, nobody can help you make the bed, nobody can help lick your head. When you live alone, nobody is there to laugh alongside you, nobody is there in case you hear a noise outside. On the plus side, when you live alone, nobody is there to bother your art, nobody is there to hear you fart, nobody is there to eat your food but nobody is there to grab you when you fall. When a victim stands up to their bully, it is the greatest feeling in the world to them, I applaud all of the brave people, who have shared their stories and put a stop to these sexual bullies for others.

Throughout 2017 all I was learning from Hollywood simply made me want to stay away from it, this was not the place I had always envisioned as a child. Now that I was more aware of the world around me, I felt foolish, for not having realised this earlier, my passion for Hollywood had blinded me to the reality behind it. All I knew was I wanted to stand next to the Hollywood sign and begin the movie I hoped to film ever since I first learnt of Hollywood. It's fitting that the Hollywood sign, the worldwide symbol of the entertainment industry, was conceived as an outdoor ad campaign for a suburban housing development called 'Hollywoodland'. After all, despite the high profile of the film biz, real estate has always been Hollywood's primary economic driver. Although the sign's appearance and purpose have evolved over the years, its basic aspirational message remains the same, this is a place where magic is possible, where dreams can come true. Back then, the dream was a beautiful home and lifestyle. Today, the sign's promise is subtler and can only be described as a symbol of fame.

I soon began to admire Hollywood, for yes it was full of problems, as is the rest of the world but the fact that so many accusations were coming to light, meant people were standing up for themselves. People were joining forces to put a stop to these bullies, although I might not be too keen on the industry anymore, these are the kind of people I want to be around, those who join together to help right wrongs. I had made up my mind, this was always where I wanted to go, and I still do, I don't exactly know what I want to do anymore, but I do know I want to be part of a place of change. Right now, I see Hollywood going through a massive change, which I hope to be a part of as I attempt my journey at becoming a screenwriter. Screenwriting, like any other form of professional writing, is a specific, learnable craft that requires study, talent, training, practice and an immense level of commitment. It is at various times frustrating, exciting, fulfilling, exhausting, lucrative, unfair, depressing, gratifying and fun.

Becoming a big shot Hollywood screenwriter is the dream of hundreds of thousands of people, most will never take the necessary steps to become successful at it. They simply don't see the profession as a craft, they see it as a way to get rich. Granted, there are many screenwriters who have made millions of dollars over the course of their careers. For the most part, becoming a successful screenwriter is just like anything else of value, hard work. The first step into becoming a screenwriter is to first start writing. Too many people get caught up in the mechanics of screenwriting, they spend months, if not years in classes and reading books on how to write a screenplay, and never actually write anything. After you get the basics down, just start writing, don't overthink this process, sit down, relax and start writing. Once you start writing, remember to keep writing, that is just as important. This is where many people get hung up. Once they start writing, they can rarely get themselves past a certain point and they simply stop trying, and as in life, in order to succeed, you can't stop trying.

I've always considered myself a storyteller, ever since the age of three, when I would use my toys to play out stories. As I grew older, I realised if I wrote my stories, I could keep them forever and share them with others if they chose to read them. I've always been so fascinated about the idea that you can create a scenario in your head, which can then be produced and projected onto the big screen, for viewers to experience, the story that first started in one's mind. Growing up I've always tried to share stories; unfortunately, I've never had much of an audience to share them with. This is why Hollywood has always meant so much to me; as a kid, this was the place where I had to go, to share my stories with the world. No matter how many powerful players might be controlling Hollywood, I'm not going to let their ignorance, get in the way of my dream. This is why, a few months after winning my settlement, I realised, it was finally time, I bought my plane ticket for Hollywood and I am now ready to find out, what my next book in life will be about.

Chapter Thirty-Five
Everybody Has a Story

Everyone matters, everyone has a story to tell, each one special and unique, each story stands on its own. What makes it so important for you to write your life story? If you don't, who else really can, with any accuracy and detail? No one, it's all uniquely yours, no one else has been through precisely what you have been through. No one else knows exactly what you know, you have life lessons to share, you have much wisdom to impart. People are unique primarily because of differences in personality and beliefs. Every person has a different way of perceiving the world around them and attaching meaning to different situations. There were various ways I could have interpreted my mental hallucinations, I could have just considered myself crazy, I could have explored the science, I could have accepted it as a spiritual journey, or many other scenarios. Everyone has their own opinion on how the world around us works, having different opinions shared by many having experienced the same experiences, will always further our evolution.

Each and every one of us, can write our own unique stories, for the authors of our lives, are only us, nobody can describe your world but you. Most importantly never believe your story is not interesting to others, for it is when we share, that we realise how similar we all are. The best way to take your test in life, is not by having others answering your questions, but by using all information, to find your own answers. This has been my story, which I hope might help you, on directing your movie towards what I consider might be helpful for a better self-future. Had this been your story, which I had read, I am sure, the unique life you've lived, would help me gain a better understanding of mine. I've always enjoyed writing, as a means to escape reality, I never expected, I would ever write a story based on my life. Before I conquered my bullies, I had already experimented on writing about my own personal experiences, and as I've mentioned before, it is very therapeutic.

If like me, you tend to be more of a private person, and don't enjoy sharing your business with others, at least write about it, this helps you share your thoughts with yourself. If I could offer advice to anyone, on how a broken person can find their strength, I would recommend writing about yourself. It is when you put your life into perspective, when you view it as an ongoing story, which you get a better understanding of who you are, where you've come from and where you hope to go. It is always much easier to get invested in a movie, you've watched from start to end, rather than one you only recall by certain key scenes. Treat your life like the spectacular movie that it is, write your story, choose your ending and make it happen. Having a direction in life, not only makes the journey far more rewarding, it helps encourage you to keep on going. In my case, to keep writing, something I never aim to stop pursuing, what's your story?

Sharing stories brings people closer together, when you tell a story to a friend, you can transfer experiences directly to their brain. They feel what you feel, they empathise; they can understand your experience and most times even relate to them, this in turn brings people closer together. What's more, when communicating most effectively, you can get a group of people's brains to synchronise their activity. As you relate someone's desires through a story, they become the desires of the audience. When trouble develops, they gasp in unison, and when desires are fulfilled, they smile together. For as long as you've got your audience's attention, they are in your mind, when you hear a good story, you develop empathy with the teller because you experience the events for yourself.

When a person enters your life, you immediately become part of their story, and they become part of yours. In my case, as you will have realised throughout this book, those who entered my life, be they good or bad, became part of my story. Throughout my personal movie, I've had a cast of characters accompany me along the way, and their stories although not mine to tell, are just as important. I am so thankful to everybody who I've mentioned in this book, be they family, friends, animals, illusions or even my bullies, they've all helped make this story, what it turned out to be in the end. People come into your life for many reasons, the most important ones are usually the most unexpected, but everyone you allow into your life, becomes a character in your movie, so be very careful who you let in.

Shale became a main character in my story, this was something I did not expect or desire but in the end, as you have read, had it not been for Shale, I probably never would have discovered who I really am. Shale opened my eyes to the epidemic that is bullying, how people with power will abuse it for their own benefit. I'm sure the same thing applies to Shale, she must hate the fact that I'm a character in her story but without me, she wouldn't have learnt, that if she continued to bully those around her, she would end up losing it all. Shale, to my understanding, no longer works as manager of the Gibraltar Tourist Branch, I have no idea what she's doing now, all I know is after allowing the government to be ridiculed, she does not hold the same position of power she once did. Shale lied to everybody for eight years, including her superiors and in the end, it cost them a big payout, that is the best way to deal with a bully.

Beverly retired from the Gibraltar Developing Company just a short while before I received my settlement, damn it! On the bright side, if we come across each other now, she is the one who turns her face away in disgrace, not me and at one point in my life, that was all I truly ever wanted. Now I couldn't care less, all I know is that the woman who set out to destroy my reputation over a mistake she had made, has greatly regretted her decision. As for Ricky, I have no idea and honestly, I don't care, he was clever, he managed to move away from the problem before it got out of hand, that was a clever move on his part. Darcello's incompetence to manage accordingly found him no longer in charge of the Gibraltar Tourist Branch. As far as I'm aware, management have no idea what to do with him, because of this he continues to be moved from department to department. Hector continues to manipulate, cheat and ruin, what many consider to be a union, set up to protect them instead. As time passes, others reveal their dealings with Hector and soon many will realise the pattern forming before them and with luck, action will be taken.

After I was able to legally prove who were the bullies and who was the victim, many other Gibraltarians began to speak out. Many had also had bad experiences working alongside Shale, Beverly, Darcello and especially Hector and Unite. Gibraltarians began standing up to their bullies on social media, many began to realise, they shared the same bullies and although a slow process, bullying is finally beginning to be dealt with in Gibraltar. As for my government, they're still in power, they still continue to act on their best interest, as opposed to those of their citizens. I've come to realise that with my current government, change will never happen and that is exactly what is needed, hopefully that change will eventually come. Dr Roseblack as far as I know, continues to be a doctor, one I believe is worthless but that's his story to tell, not mine.

All three of my past lawyers continue fighting for justice; Frank continues at his same law firm; Ian moved to a new one, a firm that knows how to support him; and Eric continues to run his own law firm. Ironically enough, as my story continues, a fourth lawyer gets introduced into my life, William joined the list, soon I'll probably be able to publish a twelve-month legal calendar. As much as I knew about my own case, I did not know the legalities, terms or loopholes that could be used to further it along. I am so grateful to all of them, they prove the justice system can work properly, when the right people are involved. So now I've got some new legal partners, who can help me think things through if this world gets too legal, I'll know exactly what to do. I wish them all the best of luck with their careers, for if you come across a bully, finding a lawyer is not as important, as finding the right one.

Bullies, lawyers and hallucinations, they're all important, my illusions no longer manifest themselves before my eyes; perhaps with extra meditation, I might get there again someday. For now, I enjoy visiting them instead within my dreams, if not in my garden then at other locations, the important part is I still get to interact with them. I would have never imagined, ever in my life, that one of my happy places, would be right inside my mind, it's much closer than going to the Nipperish. The garden within my dreams continues to grow, that is what I now find most baffling, every time I return, it only strengthens my motivation, to keep on meditating and never medicating. The best part about being able to return to this happy place, is knowing I'll never have to say goodbye to anyone ever again. Life is a continues journey, when not in body, then in soul, and the more you remember what you've studied, the easier it will be for you to handle. My illusions and I kept interacting in my dreams but soon enough someone in my actual life, would be joining me too.

All my friends at the mental hospital continue living their own unique movies and best part of all, most of them have since then been discharged and labelled sane enough to walk amongst society again. Fortunately, like me, they know never to go completely back to being sane, for that is when life becomes boring. Floyd and I meet up occasionally in town and enjoy eating waffles at a specific restaurant, this is something we both craved whilst our time inside the mental hospital. Rowlf returned back to his family and alongside his son now creates new music, which they post on YouTube, and I must say, sometimes being a little crazy makes for a wonderful melody. Walter and I met again, this time not in a mental hospital but during a dinner with all our old friends, who we both hanged out with back in the day. As for Madam Janice, she continues to be a mystery, one I find very intriguing; on occasions when our paths cross, we try to help each other understand.

As for my Hollywood friends, they continue producing my favourite kind of content, in many forms, ones that can be enjoyed by the whole family. Bill was someone I always hoped to meet and when I did, I realised if you put your mind to it, you can achieve what at times you might consider impossible. This is the person I most trust in Hollywood, he is not only an inspiration, and friend but has also been a mentor, I am truly honoured to share his energy and I'm a big fan of his accomplishments. Bill recently starred as a lead in a new movie, I can't wait to see him on the big screen, I wish him all the best in life. Cristina continues helping everyone she can and making the world better for it; hopefully one day, she will appear on the big screen too. I cannot wait to reunite with her soon, she is now one of the main reasons, I still want to travel to Hollywood, I want to see my friend again. As for Steve I am not sure, all I wish is that his story has not ended yet, and I hope to work one day alongside him. Heidi continues her practise at Upper Cervical Care, I will soon be visiting her again, I'm long overdue for a follow up appointment, I must make sure my epilepsy doesn't creep its way back into my life.

After retirement, Uncle Arthur was able to relax, meditate and enjoy life to its fullest, having always been around animals, he ended up adopting five Chihuahuas and also has two parakeets. I hope he is now able to find time to continue writing the book he first began, over twenty years ago, I for one cannot wait to read his story. Nicola opened up her own dance studio and now wakes up every morning, not dreading her job, but excited to begin dancing her day away and getting paid for doing what she loves doing. Germaine and I continue sharing our walks together alongside the stones near the ocean. We are now accompanied by Samira, Germaine's four-year-old cousin, who she now cares for and does a great job at it, a single female, with her own career, raising a child in need of a home, I am very proud of her. Germaine and Samira join Mati, Angel and at times myself included, for picnics at the Nipperish alongside Ashby's memorial picture, created years ago by all his friends.

Mama June and I meet up at least once a week in town, and we make sure we're keeping a balanced diet by eating fish, fruits, vegetables and anything we think might be lacking in our diets. A few months ago, Mama June and her church group won the lottery and have now gone on a trip, travelling across Europe. Mama June is one of the people in my life, most excited to read this book, I truly hope she enjoys it and doesn't consider me any weirder than I already am for it. It's true what they say, when you have children, you realise how quickly time goes by, as you're watching them grow. I'm not a father yet, hopefully I will be one day, but I do have a nephew, one who makes me realise, that every moment in life matters. Remember right now you're the eldest you've ever been and the youngest you will ever be again. Aiden has since taken over my memorabilia collection and is becoming as big of a fan as I am of the franchise which has inspired me since childhood, I hope it can now do the same for him too.

Kaylie underwent an operation, luckily, it all went as planned and, slowly, the sister I had grown up with returned back to me. After her recovery Kaylie went back to work, continues trying to get her business started and always remains a wonderful mother to Aiden. Kaylie although the youngest of the three of us, has been the first to begin her family, and I see Stacey being next; I the eldest, will probably be last to start my own family but for now I am very grateful for the one I have. Stacey continues rising in her career, building up her new home, playing old classic Nintendo games and being Aiden's favourite aunty. Stacey is a good example of how today's generation are choosing to live their life. Making sure they're successful, whilst at the same time not forgetting to enjoy life. Taking advantage of their youth, finding their house and then settling down, starting a family and making it a home.

Eileen and Stanley were the first people I ever met in life, the only people I can call Mum and Dad and for the longest time, whilst we were still a family, I was completely broken towards the end. Life separated them and they rebuild their lives, they found love again, and in doing so, they began living again. My dad and his girlfriend have gone on many holidays together, they're making sure to travel the world; recently, they just returned from Las Vegas, next time they go to America, hopefully I'll already be there. My mum and her boyfriend bought a boat together, they spend their days travelling through Spain and Africa; if they make the trip towards America, in the hopes of a better life, I will certainly be joining them. My parents however had stopped speaking to each other, a short while after their separation. I imagine it was easier for them to handle it that way but for the rest of us, it only made things harder. Having them at odds with each other made family gatherings very awkward, this was stopping me from truly enjoying my achievement, as I could not share it with both of them, at the same time.

You don't get to choose your family but you do get to choose your friends, that might be the reason I don't have many. I choose my friends very carefully and one who has truly been there when I needed a friend has been Jensen. We've worked together, we've travelled together, we've analysed the human brain together and we've also got arrested together. One day as I was writing chapter twenty of this book, there was a knock at my door, who could it be? I had an idea. It was the police, they asked if they could come in; in reality, I wanted to shut the door in their faces but one must follow the rules and so legality crept back into my life. I allowed the police officers to enter and once inside they asked me, if I knew Jensen, I did. Then they asked me if I knew what had happened the night before, I did. They asked if I'd mind coming down to the police station to give them a witness statement. I honestly wanted to continue writing my book but if it will help my friend, of course I will. There was nothing to hide, this was nothing more than a simple misunderstanding, one I hoped I could help them clear up. As it turns out, I became a suspect in a crime that did not exist…my life is so ridiculous. I'm starting to think Gibraltar isn't the place for me, am I supposed to leave my Rock or am I supposed to fix it?

Once we arrived at the police station, before my interview began I was asked if I wanted a lawyer to represent me. I had done nothing wrong, and neither had Jensen for that matter, I needed no lawyer, I just had to share the truth. As it turns out even when you are innocent, it is always wise to have a lawyer present alongside you, if nothing else, to control the bullying tactics one might face. A camera began recording my interview, how handy this time they had a camera present, I quickly realised this interview had become more of an interrogation than anything else. I was in the presence of a good cop and a bad cop, it was exactly as depicted in the movies, one was trying to frighten me, whilst the other pretended he was eager to join me for a best friend sleepover party. As I gave my statement I realised, they were not interested in the truth, they were simply interested in the version they had already released to the public, in no less than twenty-four hours. I spent years trying to name and shame my bullies, those within government, with no luck at every turn I took. Now in less than twenty-four hours, a citizen had been accused of a crime with no evidence yet details immediately released to the public. Gibraltar is a small community, news spreads very quickly, that is why my government never wanted me to speak out.

At the end of my witness interrogation, they accused me of lying and used that reason to detain me in their custody. Life was getting difficult again, tests always keep arising, once you've answered one question, always expect the next to appear soon enough. It seemed like an eternity, time moves slow in the cooler, I was getting familiar to the lingo used in the joint; luckily before I got myself a tattoo, my fourth lawyer showed up. William had apparently been hired by my dad to get me out of this mess, one a simple vacuum cleaner could not help handle. At first, I wasn't sure I needed William, if I were going to use a lawyer, I always imagined I'd contact either Ian or Eric but honestly, I wanted out, I had a chapter to continue writing. After twenty-four hours detained in police custody, knowing my friend was on the other side of the concrete wall, I was brought in for a follow up interview; this time, they had video evidence to show me. The first time around I had told them exactly what had happened, neither I nor Jensen were to blame for what had happened; after looking over the evidence, they realised I was telling the truth and was released without charge. As I walked out of the police station, my eyes began to fill with tears, both my mum and my dad stood outside together waiting for me. Upon our reunion, I realised they had begun talking again and all it took was the fear of me being locked away for a couple of years, it was a Christmas miracle.

I was glad this was over, now to keep on writing but I couldn't, there was one problem, Jensen was not released behind me. Jensen was kept in police custody and charged unfairly for the crime, that they had first announced to the public. This didn't make sense, from the evidence available they should have at least asked a judge to grant them a proper extension to properly analyse their evidence. Instead since they either had to charge him or release him, not wanting to go back on their initial claim, they continued to prosecute Jensen for a crime he had clearly not committed. I now felt lost again, I knew in my heart my friend was innocent, although I was not fighting for my own justice, his is just as important, and that is exactly what I began to do. The next day was Jensen's court date, since his lawyer was not available, it was adjourned until the next available court date. This meant my friend was going to be detained for four weeks in the big house, with Christmas only five weeks away.

A fifth lawyer soon came into my life, Jensen's lawyer, who I'm certain will be able to prove his innocence. As the days went past, I could not visit Jensen immediately, he has a very big family and understandably I had to wait my turn. A week later, I visited my friend; he looked broken, being locked away is one thing, but knowing you are there for a crime you haven't committed is another thing altogether. I assured my friend that he would be getting out very soon, I would have not been allowed to walk had I not been telling the truth, and the truth was, Jensen was not to blame. As the days past, I found myself unable to write, instead studying the law, revising facts, trying to prove my friend's innocence. At first, I never thought it would be difficult but as the days went by and the police continued contacting me for more information, I realised they were not interested in the evidence they had, they were interested in the story they first shared publicly, before gathering any evidence whatsoever.

A few days later, the police arrived at my house; they wanted to ask me more questions, I was done with them. They weren't listening, if they wanted to ask me any further questions, they could do so in court, I had nothing left to say to them. I informed William, who called them on my behalf, he arranged a meeting at his own office alongside myself and two police officers. In this meeting, they informed us that they believed they might have come at me a little strong during my interview and believe they might have scared me from telling them the truth. No, they simply did not like the truth and wanted another version and if they have admitted to being strong against their witness, does that not show how biased they are truly being? I could not believe how people in power abuse it so easily, this is my friend's life they are trying to destroy, I thought the police were meant to find the truth no matter what?

Writing, meditating, nothing was working anymore, I was worried about my friend, stress was starting to kick in again, I needed to find a way to relax, and so I went to sleep. That night I had another lucid dream, this time I wasn't in a garden, I was in a jail cell. Accompanying me, for the first time ever, was a face that was still part of my life. I was locked away with Jensen, lucid dreams are wonderful, I missed my friend so much, and although this was only happening in my head, the emotions still felt as real. The first thing we began discussing was how funny it was, that I was having a lucid dream with him, what Jensen found even funnier, was that he was currently sleeping in his cell, this meant he was also dreaming. When I woke up, I wondered if this lucid dream had been nothing more than a dream I was aware in or if it had a stronger meaning. In all my lucid dreams throughout the years, I had never dreamt about anyone currently alive in my reality, this was the first time, I had many questions, but no way to answer them.

I hoped I would get to visit Jensen again soon, but before I did I had another lucid dream, another one accompanied by Jensen and so I asked him within my dream, if he knew what all this meant. Jensen and I were having the same conversation we would have had in our real lives, and according to him, he was freaking out as well. Was I creating this story of us being able to communicate through dream telepathy simply as a way for my brain to handle the stress or was it all very real? After around four weeks, Jensen was allowed bail and released back into society, his family, I and especially Jensen could not have been happier. Jensen was finally reunited with his family, just in time for Christmas, and I got the present I wanted the most, my friend's freedom. There is still a long road ahead of him, this is his story to tell, and I hope he shares it one day but for now we must hope the justice system does not fail him, as it had with me in the past. It truly feels like Christmas when you're amongst friends, family and illusions, and I was the luckiest of them all, I had all of them. Jensen and I were finally able to discuss our dreams, had he had them too or was it all one sided on my part?

Chapter Thirty-Six
Someday We'll Find It

My life begun for me, as soon as I left school, before that it was simply child's play, if only we were all able to continue living as children. As you continue to evolve in life, remember one very important aspect about yourself that none of us should ever lose, our inner child. The body might age, but the soul remains forever young and since our soul lives within us, most of us find ourselves fighting the desire to let it free. Remember you can never fail at being yourself but when you try to be someone you're not, you have already failed, even before you get started. As a great inspiration of mine, Jim Henson once said, "The most sophisticated people I know, inside they are all children."

Growing is learning and adapting but does not consist of changing who you are; for the person we believe we are when we were young, is actually the person we're meant to become. We're all part of the system, we must learn to break free, the first step in doing so, is finding freedom within yourself. If just one person believes in you, strong enough and long enough believes in you, before you know it, other people will believe in you too. The trick is to always have someone believing in you, and that can be very easily accomplished, believe in yourself.

As soon as I started working after leaving school, life became real and since then, it only keeps on getting further complicated yet far more rewarding. Every test in life is temporary, so when your test is easy, make sure you enjoy it, and when your test becomes harder, remember that it will not last forever, easier questions will then follow. Looking back now, working at the Gibraltar Tourist Branch is something I would still go back and do all over again; it was a difficult journey, but I value where I have ended up because of it. This is how I've always wanted to look back on my life, with no regrets, and now I have none. When life finds you in a bad situation, don't just try to fix it, try to understand it, when you do, you'll realise why life gave you that specific test in the first place.

Suffering through pain sucks, but it always brings a message along with it. We must stop and listen to what our pain is telling us, every time life gets hard, there is a lesson to be learned. It is human nature to make mistakes, it is when we keep repeating them that causes us to fail in life. We must all overcome fear in order to become who we were meant to be. Fear is nothing but our mind telling us we cannot, when we can do anything we desire to accomplish, do not let your mind hold down your soul.

It has been a long journey, one I could have never have accomplished had it not been for my family. They stood behind me when I was ill, when I appeared crazy and even when I was determined to take my government to court, they supported me every step of the way. Always cherish your family, for when things get tough, friends might disappear but family will always be there, even if at times you wished they weren't. Friends are the thing I most regret having ignored for years. I lost myself with my illusions and I pushed those in reality away from me. Having people who care about you and who you can share your experiences with, is one of the best cures for stress, depression and anxiety, at least I know now. When I celebrate the New Year, no longer must I find myself alone, an army of friends can be found everywhere, for if you stop and say hello to a stranger, they will then become a friend. At the same time, it is not important how many friends you have, be they in real life, social media or even your own mind. At the end of the day, it is the ones who are there for you, that truly matter, it is not uncommon to be able to count true friends, with one hand.

As important as friendships can be, keeping in touch with your spiritual side is just as important; in my case, my illusions keep me focused. Even as I write this story, I sometimes feel foolish, for even I would have a hard time believing such dreams but my intention has not been to try and provide answers but rather questions. I hope you find these subjects interesting enough to try and answer them for yourself. I've learnt a lot through others, but many times I have also learned backwards because of them; don't believe everything you hear, research it and deliver your own answers. There is still so much to learn, power to discover, there are more secrets hidden in our pasts than many of us are aware, it's time to start listening to yourself. When you listen to yourself, you can be sure of one thing, nobody is talking shit, when you listen to yourself, you will realise that most of your life, you've spent listening to someone else.

There are still so many problems throughout our world that needs our attention, so many things that could easily be fixed. The only problem is that to do so, we must all be on the same page, and right now, we're not all there. There are many problems humanity will be facing in the future; one of the biggest being that most people aren't even sure what the problem is. Over half of the world's wildlife has been killed in the last fifty years, trees are being cut down, none are being planted to replace them; at the moment, humanity is earth's biggest enemy. Nuclear weaponry, armed conflicts, spread of infectious disease, energy not being created efficiently, terrorism, poverty, hunger, politics, bullies, we need to open our eyes, before it's too late. As bad as our world is, compassion is evolving amongst many victims, and soon, we shall realise that together our voices are louder than those who hope to keep us quiet. Compassion brings us all together and helps light the path to a new world. The world is so bright, so perfectly unfair, bullies hurt, victims cry, for a minute we've got a chance, why couldn't we live? I know we'd get by, just a non-political push and we're on our way, a better future, one everyone can enjoy.

There's a rising, there's a timing, one within our dreams, meant to wake us up instead of morning, and a reason that the universe will never break its promise. We are all one when it comes to the grand design behind the universal plan, it is on our planet that we divide ourselves amongst each other. You are not part of this earth, you are part of our shared universe, a universe who thought we were worthy enough to exist as we are and does not charge us a single penny for it, yet we still live our lives, working to maintain our existence. I don't want to be a puppet in life, I want to be my own puppeteer; we all should and in order to do that, we must first stop allowing others to control us. Someday we'll all find, everything that makes life good; freedom of the body, mind and soul, that is the key to a happy, healthy and fulfilling existence. There's a rising slowly occurring throughout humanity, one we are all part of, from him to her, from you to me and everyone around us, it's time to join as one.

Smart people underestimate themselves and don't believe in power, whilst ignorant people believe they are brilliant and all they want is power. Those who are highly skilled believe that things that come easy to them come just as easy to others, and because of this, they do not realise just how powerful they can actually be, if they so choose. However, the unskilled are so incompetent that they can't recognise their own stupidity, that is why our world is ruled by idiots. Those who understand know better than to bully and overpower, and those who don't, do exactly just that. Remember most of us are crazy because we live in an insane world, an upside-down world, on every aspect. It's time to think outside the box, time to get things done, time to put on a show, it's time to realise, it's time to unite instead of divide. The world needs to begin growing together, learning from each other, not discriminating against other people's beliefs. Soon we shall live in a world with glow in the dark trees, robotic drivers, three-eyed fish, talking monkeys, flying motorcycles but is that truly evolution?

Our world, our home, our freedom, life is only as clear as your mindset, say no to politics, put a stop to bullying and think for yourself, this is how we grow together. We reflect on our reflections, and we ask ourselves the question, what's the right direction to go, we believe, we don't know. We look out through our eyes, and we don't recognise, the ones we see inside, it's time for us to decide, are we humans or are we illusions? We're both, we're all in touch with our human side, but our illusions, you must get in touch with your spiritual side, together is when they are both valuable. Close your eyes and dream, a reality that you can feel, taste and explore, to all your questions, answers can all be found, when the mind is relaxed, and not the other way around.

My test in life is still far from over but my most difficult questions, those I think I have already answered. I find myself living now, the exact life I always hoped to have, ever since my alarm clock would sound since as far back as my school days. I've wanted to write without boundaries, ignore the clock, work another day and make my way to Hollywood. For the longest time, I was not living, I was not growing, I was stuck and that is the worse feeling, and sadly a problem we all share at one time or another. I will never stay stuck again, especially for so long, because I will always remain positive, being positive in negative situations, is the best way to overcome any situation and move away from them quickly. Falling into a depression, although hard to battle, is just another test life throws at you, and medicating is not necessarily the answer. If you can't be positive, at least don't spread your negativity, by not doing so you will not repel others, you will attract them instead and they in turn will help change your energy.

I will continue my hardest to keep my energy positive, I will always find answers whilst dealing with questions and I will make sure to live and let live forever. Thank you for reading my story, at one time I did not have the confidence to share it, when I finally did, I never expected the chance, to share it with you. This has been about my life, I wish you all the best with yours and remember, your life is about you, it's not about them. You have a unique story to tell, what you've learned in life is your own unique encounter, share your dreams with the world and that is when they'll begin to come true. The world is not as big as we think it is and together, someday we'll find it, the dreaming connection, the believers, the dreamers and you.

The Beginning